“How Tall *Are* You

Also by Don Doxsie and from McFarland

Iowa Baseball Greats: Sixteen Major Leaguers Who Were in the Game for Life (2015)

Iron Man McGinnity: A Baseball Biography (2009)

“How Tall *Are* You?”

The Pros and Cons of Exceptional Height

Don Doxsie

Jefferson, North Carolina

ISBN (print) 978-1-4766-9204-3
ISBN (ebook) 978-1-4766-4950-4

LIBRARY OF CONGRESS AND BRITISH LIBRARY
CATALOGUING DATA ARE AVAILABLE

Library of Congress Control Number 2023007916

Printed in the United States of America

Toplight is an imprint of McFarland & Company, Inc., Publishers

Box 611, Jefferson, North Carolina 28640
www.toplightbooks.com

To Emily and Ryne,
who inherited their height from Dad

Table of Contents

Preface

I have been studying the plight of being tall very nearly as long as I have been tall, dating all the way back to my great growth spurt of 1970, 1971 and 1972. As far back as 1978, I was penning letters to various people asking their opinions about different aspects of extreme height and reading every book and magazine article I could find on the topic.

Through the decades, there were many times when I set aside my research for a long time (sometimes years) only to come back to it again at some point. Fortunately, I'm a highly accomplished pack rat. I kept everything.

Upon retiring late in 2021 after nearly a half century in the newspaper business, I found the time to pull together all those collected pieces with a great deal of new research and formulate it into something that hopefully is coherent, insightful and perhaps even profound.

I'm not alone in my fascination with this subject. Many others have been scrutinizing the plight of the tall for a very long time and this book would not be what it is without the trails that they blazed.

Thomas T. Samaras, an engineer who is the founder and director of Reventropy Associates in San Diego, has written a few books and numerous articles and research papers on the impact of growth and body size. He is a brilliant and extremely gracious man who has devoted his life to this topic and who even now, in his 90s, continues to dabble in it. The fact that I sometimes disagree with him in these pages and am occasionally critical of some of his assumptions and generalities does not detract from the fact that he is a relentless and remarkable student of human growth, arguably the foremost expert ever in this area.

Several other authors who have written on this subject inspired and informed my research, including Ralph Keyes, Arianne Cohen, Stephen Hall and the late Gwen Davenport.

Thousands of scientists and researchers—including Thomas Samaras—have done hundreds of studies through the years to analyze various aspects of height and wellness, and their work is reflected in this book.

My research also was impacted by the many fellow tall people who have chronicled their observations through the years, including incredibly articulate *New York Times* columnist Russell Baker, persistently profane Australian comedian Lewis Spears, basketball superhero Wilt Chamberlain, and Alfred Payson Terhune, an early twentieth-century essayist who wasn't really that tall but who suffered some of the indignities of height nonetheless.

Men such as Rued Riis and Tom McMillen, who have expertise in specific aspects of being tall, offered significant insights. I also need to thank the many members of Tall Clubs International who have lent their support and input, including Sue Morrison, Nancy Jacoby, Mark Piotrowski, Rick LaRose, Julie Whitman Jones and many others.

I also want to express my gratitude to members of my family. I've occasionally mentioned the height-related experiences of my children, Ryne and Emily, in these pages, and my wife Gale (who is not tall) was very patient as I labored over this project and allowed a plastic storage bin full of files, books and papers to decorate a corner of our family room for many months.

1

You're Not Here for the Convention, Are You?

As far as I can remember, the first time I ever encountered it was on a spring break trip to Florida with my family back around 1972.

We were walking through one of those orange grove establishments that were popping up as tourism magnets all over the state in that era. It basically was a giant gift shop built around a juice bar and we were only there for a few minutes when I sensed I was being watched. There was a cluster of people sitting on stools at the juice bar, sneaking glances at me and whispering to one another between sips of vitamin C. I couldn't tell what they were saying, but I seemed to be the focus of their attention.

Finally, one of them came over and posed the question. I've heard the same question thousands of times since then. Maybe millions. Or maybe it only seems like millions. At this point in time, it was something new.

"How tall are you?"

I quickly surmised that these folks had been placing wagers on my height. I don't think I had quite reached my full height of 6'6¾" then and I think I told them I was *only* 6'5". They all seemed disappointed by the response. Most of them thought sure I was a 7-footer.

It's been the same way almost every time since then. People are always certain I must be taller than I really am.

"Really? That's all you are? Are you sure?"

Sometimes the question takes a different form: "Did you play basketball?"

Sometimes people will just come up and say, "You're really tall."

Like I didn't already know this. Someone get Lester Holt on the phone. We have breaking news here.

Sometimes it's phrased less respectfully: "How's the weather up there?"

I've always resisted the temptation to do what some have suggested, to spit in the air and say, "It's dry up here but I hear it's raining down there." I've also resisted the temptation to lie although I know if I had told the juice bar crowd that I was 6'10", they would have nodded and said, "Yeah, that seems about right." Then they all would have reached into their wallets and paid the skinny, bald guy with the alligator on his shirt because he was the only one who thought I was that short.

In any case, my height—and, I'm sure, that of similarly lengthy people—is a topic of extreme fascination to people. I've always been amazed that people who never would consider asking how much you weigh or how old you are think nothing of inquiring about your height. Several tall people have told me they respond by asking the other person how much they weigh. That shuts them up in a hurry.

When we're born, it's the norm for our parents to tell the world that we're 21 inches long and that we weigh 8 pounds, 5 ounces. The weight thing never gets brought up again for the rest of our lives unless we play football, in which case it's listed in the game program every week so no one needs to ask. But the height thing gets brought up again and again and again. Racism, sexism and ageism and all sorts of other -isms are frowned upon in almost every society on the planet. Heightism seemingly is OK.

I am a fairly well-known sports columnist, and my picture appeared in the newspaper a few times a week over a period of more than 40 years and I frequently was recognized in public, but people consistently commented that they never knew I was so tall. "The picture in the paper is only that big," they say, holding their fingers about an inch apart.

So, you thought that was the actual size of my head? You expected me to be 1'7" with a face the size of a postage stamp?

The fascination with my height was, well, um ... heightened during a visit to Fort Wayne, Indiana, to cover a minor league hockey playoff game about 20 years ago. Some folks there were especially fascinated by my size.

As I arrived at the hotel at which I was staying, I noticed that special little ramps had been constructed at the base of the front desk. I was told that the hotel was hosting a little people's convention that week. The ramps made it possible for the convention-goers to be able to see over the counter and speak to the hotel clerks face to face.

I didn't see any of the convention attendees at that time, but when I returned later in the evening after attending the hockey game, it felt as though I had stumbled into Munchkinland. I got on the elevator to go up to my room and about 10 other people stepped in after me. None of them stood taller than my waist, and as the elevator doors closed, there was an awkward silence and a feeling of surveillance not unlike what I felt in the juice bar all those years earlier.

Finally, one of them summoned the courage to speak. "You're not here for the convention, are you?" he said. Everyone had a good laugh.

The next question was predictable: "How tall are you?" It was followed by the inevitable: "I'll bet you played basketball."

Fortunately, it was just about that time that we got to my floor and the elevator doors mercifully opened. I bit my tongue, suppressed my inclination to launch a smart-ass response, waded through the Lilliputians and made my getaway without saying what I wanted to say. "How short are you?" and "I'll bet you didn't play basketball."

What is amazing is that so many of the people we tall folks encounter on a daily basis express unabashed envy at our circumstance. They think it must just be a total blast to be gigantic. There is this standardized trilogy of questions. It begins with "How tall are you?" and it almost always is followed by "Did you play basketball?" The third question varies. Very often it's something like "Isn't it wonderful to be so tall?" Occasionally, it's phrased as a statement: "It must be great to be so tall." Then there are the really clever folks who ask about the climatic conditions up here 78¾ inches above the earth's surface.

It really wasn't all that clever the first 1,000 times I heard it, but the questioner always grins proudly as though he or she just came up with the most cute and original comment ever. Ralph Keyes pointed out in his 1980 book *The Height of Your Life* that tall people repeatedly told him that "it's not the incessant commentary about their height that is so annoying, it's the stupefying boredom of it all. Were anyone to say something original or witty or different in any way, the constant chatter thrown their way might at least be entertaining." He's right. I wouldn't mind the questions and comments at all if I ever heard one I hadn't heard 100 times before.

On the Internet, you can find a template for a business card that each of us should carry. You could hand it to everyone when they first embark on the three questions:

Yes, I am tall
You're very observant for noticing
6 FT 7 IN
(Yes, really)
No, I don't play basketball
The weather is perfect up here
I'm so glad we had this conversation

Anyway, let's go back to question 3A: "Isn't it wonderful to be so tall?" It might be the easiest one to answer.

No. Heck, no. It's not wonderful. Trust me on this. It can be pretty good at times. When your 5'4" wife needs help getting something off the top shelf, it's great. When you're standing 10 rows deep at the Fourth of July parade craning your neck to see, it can be useful. When you get separated from the aforementioned wife in a crowded venue, she never has a problem finding you. If you do play basketball and you get a multi-million-dollar contract to play in the NBA, then, yeah, it probably is a blast.

When it's time to buy clothes, ride in a bus, ride in an airplane, ride in a train, find an affordable car, sleep in most hotel beds, comb your hair in most hotel room mirrors, take a shower in a bathroom that was designed in 1965, pee in a really low urinal, ride in a roller coaster or the bumper cars at an amusement park, strain to hear what is being said by the 5'8" person standing next to you in a noisy bar, hold hands with someone 15 inches shorter than you while walking down the street, shop in the light fixtures section at your local home improvement store or walk through the doorway into the laundry room in your basement, it can really suck.

There is one doorway in our basement that is about 6 feet, 4 inches high, by the way. There's a big crack in the baseboard across the top. I don't always remember to duck.

There are all sorts of other issues that are less painful but annoying nonetheless. Elderly, undersized relatives you haven't seen in a while insist you've grown immensely since the last time you saw them.

"No, Aunt Rose, I'm pretty sure I'm the same size as the last time."

"But you seem so tall. I think you're bigger."

"Aunt Rose, I'm 68. I haven't grown since the Nixon administration."

Aunt Rose eventually walks away muttering, wondering why her favorite nephew is lying to her.

Being tall isn't just painful and annoying. It's expensive.

Tall people pay more for clothes, and since we can't really drive compact vehicles, we also pay more for cars. We're never truly comfortable in airplanes unless we fork over big bucks to fly first class.

In half the hotels in the country, our feet hang off the end of the bed and quite often the only thing we see in the bathroom mirror of those hotels is our belly button. In the urinals in half the public men's rooms in the world, we need to go into a well-rehearsed crouch in order to keep from splashing some pretty unpleasant stuff back onto that new pair of slacks that cost 50 percent more than what almost everyone else paid for their pants.

Sometimes all people see is our size. Many years ago, I was flattered when a local Jaycees club actively recruited me to be part of their organization. A few weeks later, I learned that they really just needed someone to serve as the Frankenstein monster in their annual Halloween haunted house fundraiser.

We're pre-destined to bump our heads hundreds, maybe thousands, of times in our lifetimes. Australian comedian Lewis Spears, who is 6'8", assembled a YouTube video listing 10 bad things about being tall—three of them involve the relentless basketball question—and I especially identify with item No. 2 on his list: "It is incredibly dangerous for me to walk into a light shop or any kind of shop that hangs shit from the roof."

We don't just hit our heads on light fixtures and low doorways, but things like ceiling fans really hurt when they're spinning at top speed. This isn't just painful; it's dangerous. Savanna Trapp-Blanchfield, who is 6'8½", actually had to end her basketball career at UCLA after one season because of multiple concussions, none of which occurred on the basketball court. She apparently forgot that for tall people, it's almost always duck season.

We can easily see over the top of people at concerts and parades. But the flipside of that is that we also are prone to blocking the view of others at concerts and parades and in movie theaters. As a journalist, I attended hundreds of news conferences through the years and I always had to make sure I took a seat on the outside of a row. If I sat in the middle, I was blocking the view of television cameras in the back of the room and I had angry TV reporters shouting at me to remove myself from their line of vision.

Amusement parks are distinctly unamusing for tall people much of the time. Roller coasters don't come with much legroom if you're allowed to ride them at all. I'll forever be scarred by a go-kart experience at the Wisconsin Dells in which I was unable to untangle my legs quickly enough to hit the brakes and ended up slamming into the kart in front of me. No one was injured but the glare from the woman I rear-ended is forever burned on my brain.

When we tall people walk into a crowded room, we're typically going to be the only person that people see rising above the throng. If your hair isn't combed neatly, everyone in the room knows it. There could be hundreds of bad hair days in the joint but yours is the one that everyone sees. There are times when perhaps it is nice to be noticed and recognized, but very often, especially when you're a teenager, you just want to blend in with the crowd. We can't. It's not possible.

I've never experienced this myself, but 7-footers have told tales about little kids coming up and kicking them in the shins to expose what they are sure must be stilts. Very tall women have stories of being mistaken for men and called "sir" by strangers they encounter even if they are wearing tight-fitting workout clothes that emphasize a distinctly feminine figure.

And then there's the question, that tired old basketball question. It seems every day we need to answer it. And then very often we also need to explain why it is that we didn't make third-team All-American at the college we attended because surely, being 6'6¾" should assure you of hoops greatness.

I've often thought of having a t-shirt made up that says "6'6¾" and yes, I played basketball ... but not terribly well." People still would ask, though.

Many people respond to the basketball question by asking the shorter person if they are a jockey or if they play miniature golf. One of the most unique responses to the "Do you play basketball?" query was one frequently used by 7'1" NBA star Artis Gilmore: "No, I wash giraffe ears."

Spears is really fed up with the basketball inquisition. "No, stop asking me," he pleads in his YouTube rant. "Every day I get three people asking me 'Do you play basketball?' No, I don't. Just because I'm tall doesn't mean I enjoy putting balls through hoops. Fuck off.

Everyone who is over 6'3" is sick of this shit. The next person who asks if I play basketball, I'm going to get down on my hands and knees and say, 'Good day, wee man, have you raced any horses recently?'"

One of the best expressions of the tall person's plight was put forward by Russell Baker, the Pulitzer Prize–winning columnist for the *New York Times*. Baker, who never specified his exact height in print as far as I can tell, wrote in 1978 that short people simply don't know how good they have it. "From down where they live, they can't see what misery is," he wrote.

Baker complained about "imbeciles" who asked about the weather up where he was. He groaned about the proliferation of short beds. He lamented the various derisive nicknames we get simply because we tower above others. He grumbled about having to lean over so far to kiss shorter people. He said he didn't really like being able to see all the dust that had gathered on top of his refrigerator.

He noted that tall people are expected to live their lives in "a perpetual stoop," always bending over to engage in conversations with others and ensure "social cohesion." He said there never was any attempt by shorter people to come up to his level during those conversations. "The long party stoops, and as the years of courteous, unselfish stooping begin to bow his back and permanently round his shoulders, people of less altitude deride him for bad posture," he added.

Baker went on like that for an entire column. He paused at one point to apologize (sort of) for the fact that diminutive folks will interpret his words as "a malicious whine." He assured his readers that was not the case. "Long people are not allowed to enjoy a healthy explosion of malice," he said.

I suspect that some may regard this entire book as being a tad whiny and tinged, as Baker said, with a pinch of malice. Please know that I harbor no enmity for those of you who are not of the beanpole variety. Some of my best friends are short. My wife isn't exceptionally tall. My mother is short. My maternal grandparents could have been extras in *The Wizard of Oz*.

And I'm certainly not going to tell you that there aren't a whole lot of really swell things about being taller than about 99.5 percent of the earth's population. Various medical studies through the years have indicated that tall people are smarter, less likely to suffer heart attacks, less likely to develop dementia, less likely to go bald and more likely to have an easy time with childbirth. We're also likely to make more money, be promoted more easily and be more successful in getting elected to political office. There also is some thought that we're more attractive to the opposite sex but that's a myth we will gladly explode at some point in the pages to come.

Suffice it to say that, yes, there clearly are many good things about being tall.

Just stop with the questions already.

2

Are We Still Growing?

Let's see if we can explain all of this in simplistic layman's language, without the use of too many 12-letter words. That's not going to be easy because it involves biology and genetics and all sorts of things that are beyond the intellectual grasp of even those of us with long arms.

But we're going to try to answer these questions: Why the heck does the world's population continue to get progressively taller? And is this trend going to continue indefinitely? Or has it possibly stopped already in some places?

There is a fistful of different factors that likely contribute to this trend of increased growth but it largely comes down to natural selection. In other words, people with a genetic tendency toward being taller than average frequently mate with other tall people and the end result is that they produce even taller offspring. You would think this might be balanced out by having short people mate with other short people, resulting in even shorter kids, but it doesn't seem to work that way. Natural selection appears to be a one-way street.

One thing is very obvious: The world has been getting taller for some time.

The consensus of scientists is that in most parts of the world, the average height of the populace has grown 4 to 6 inches over the past few centuries, with some places in Europe sprouting by as much as 8 inches over that span.

Harry Shapiro, a founding member of the American Association of Physical Anthropologists, estimated that early man probably was only 4'6" about a million years ago but we know the average in the United States was up to about 5'6" or 5'7" by the early 18th century. There have been a few ups and downs since then. Many scientists theorized the U.S. average probably declined somewhat between 1830 and 1880, then rebounded and continued to gain for about a century afterward. A 2018 report from the U.S. Department of Health and Human Services indicated that the average American male is about 5'9" although other sources say it is more like 5'10". The average U.S. female is somewhere between 5'3" and 5'4".

A 1954 study looked at 3,318 kids in Michigan and found that the average boy under the age of 9 was a half inch taller than he had been just 15 years earlier and that boys older than that were a full inch taller. The trend was similar for girls. Dr. Stanley M. Garns of the Fels Research Institute for the Study of Human Development said he thought Americans were gaining about a centimeter (roughly four-tenths of an inch) about every decade. The U.S. Department of Health, Education and Welfare released statistics that showed American kids in 1960 were close to 6 inches taller and 31 pounds heavier on average than their 1877 counterparts.

Along with that steady growth came a parallel increase in appetite. *U.S. News & World Report* reported in 1955 that food consumption was growing along with our bodies. The average American in 1924 ate about 59 pounds of beef and 318 eggs per year but 30 years later that had jumped to 72 pounds of beef and 405 eggs. There were even more precipitous leaps in the consumption of such things as fruit and ice cream.

There have been comparable trends worldwide. Historians at the University of Essex and the Institute of Labor Economics (IZA) studied soldiers from the United Kingdom who enlisted in World War I and concluded in 2014 that the average height of British adult men had risen four inches in the course of a century, going from about 5'6" to 5'10". Other studies conducted in several other western European countries arrived at similar conclusions.

There is some evidence that people were taller during the Dark Ages in Europe, but there also were reports that a majority of the men in Napoleon's army in the early 1800s were shorter than their commander, whose height is a matter of dispute but who probably was about 5'6".

The growth trend that continued through pretty much the entire 20th century is at least slowing down, if not coming to a grinding halt, in some parts of the world. Some countries, including the United States, have reported a small, almost imperceptible decline in the average height of the general population in recent years.

The United States was the tallest country in the world in the middle of the 19th century and that continued through the middle of the 20th century, but it seemingly hit a plateau, allowing the rest of the world to catch up. Countries in western Europe, Scandinavia and eastern Europe have passed us by in the height race, and the growth also is accelerating in Japan and other affluent Asian countries.

A 2007 report by John Komlos of the University of Munich indicated that the tallest people in the world now live in the Netherlands, followed by Denmark, the Czech Republic, Sweden and Norway. The growth spurt seemingly is continuing unabated in the Netherlands. In 2015, Dutch men averaged 6'0", making them 2 or 3 inches taller than Americans. Over a 150-year period from the early 19th century to early in the 21st century, it has been calculated that Dutch people went from being some of the shortest humans to being the tallest with the average height increasing by nearly 8 inches over that span.

Around the time of the birth of Christ, the average Dutch man is believed to have been about 5'9". They often were recruited to be guards for Roman emperors because of their size but then their height declined and leveled off for about 18 centuries as famine, pestilence and other environmental factors took their toll. By the 18th century, the Dutch were, on average, 2 to 3 inches shorter than their counterparts in North America. The average got back up to about 5'9" around the time of World War I and has shot up steadily since then.

A study of 42,616 people conducted by Gert Stulp, a behavioral biologist at the London School of Hygiene and Tropical Medicine, showed that taller Dutch men tended to have more children than shorter men and he concluded that natural selection was pushing up the national average in the Netherlands. His research also included looking at people in Wisconsin in the late 1930s and he found that the people having the most children there were average-sized men and short women. That could help account for the leveling effect on the American population.

Stulp, who is about 6'7" himself, said in 2015 that he has seen signs that this extreme growth pattern in the Netherlands is leveling off although he did not discount the possibility of Dutch men getting up to about a 6'3" average by the middle of the 21st century. "If we look at Paleolithic records—millions of years ago—we do find fossils that reach heights of 190cm (about 6'3") and that is much taller than many of the individuals in populations now," Stulp said. "That suggests that many populations haven't reached their evolutionary peak height ... but it is difficult to say."

Researchers have cited several socioeconomic factors as reasons for the past century of growth. The height of children, they found, can be impacted by the literacy of the parents, the number of siblings and the economic status of the family. Better educated and more affluent parents with fewer children tended to have taller kids. Health also is a factor in this. Scientists found that children who had frequent illnesses as infants also could end up being shorter as adults. (It's noteworthy that my 5'3" maternal grandfather often claimed that his growth had been stunted by a childhood bout with diphtheria. Since he had two brothers who were at least 6 inches taller than him, that's a very plausible deduction.)

It stands to reason, then, that extreme increases through the years in the literacy of the populace along with improvements in sanitation and hygiene combined with medical advances that have all but eliminated several diseases could have a profound impact on the height of people. It all sort of makes sense.

Komlos, a professor of economic history in Munich, wrote in 2007 that he believes poor dietary habits and an expensive and flawed American healthcare system might contribute to the recent lull in the U.S. growth spurt. Komlos and co-author Benjamin Lauderdale of Princeton University also found discrepancies in the heights of people who live in urban environments as opposed to those who live in rural or suburban communities.

The Centers for Disease Control's Behavioral Risk Factor Surveillance System reported evidence to support that phenomenon in 2022. It determined that people were slightly taller in 11 states in the United States and many of them were among the more sparsely populated states, including Montana, Wyoming, North Dakota, South Dakota, Nebraska, and Iowa. Conversely, states where the average height was lower included high-population areas such as New York, California, and Texas.

There also are all sorts of opinions on how our diet impacts our growth. In the early 1970s, researchers in Great Britain and Switzerland deduced that sugar intake contributes not only to greater weight but increased height. Noted dietician Nathan Pritikin said a high fat diet helps make us taller. Other studies have pointed to zinc as an important element in growth. Children who eat more meat, poultry and fish may be more likely to grow and those with a heavy diet of calcium might be less likely since calcium could interfere with the absorption of zinc into the system.

A 1978 study in Africa stated that "the most important nutrient for final height is protein in childhood. Minerals, in particular calcium, and vitamins A and D, also influence height. Because of this, malnutrition in childhood is detrimental to height.... Thus, adequate nutrition before puberty is crucial for height."

Environmental and dietary factors are only a part of the reason humans have grown in size in recent centuries. The biggest factor still seems to be genetics.

Scientists have identified at least 180 genes that have an impact on a person's height. Individually, they don't do much. Banded together, they are the single largest contributor to determining how tall someone is going to be.

Stulp's research certainly reinforces that point. Stephen Stearns, an evolutionary biologist at Yale University, said Stulp's study "drives home the message that the human population is still subject to natural selection. It strikes at the core of our understanding of human nature, and how malleable it is."

A 2017 article in *Scientific American* written by Dr. Chao-Qiang Lai offered the opinion that height is determined 20 to 40 percent by nutrition and other environmental factors and 60 to 80 percent by genetics. His conclusion was based on the heritability of human height. (We're starting to get into some of those 12-letter scientific words here. Heritability basically means how much of a person's growth is dictated by genes inherited from the parents.)

Peter M. Visscher of Australia's Queensland Institute of Medical Research studied 3,375 pairs of twins and siblings and determined that the heritability of height is about 80 percent. Another study of an even larger group of subjects in Finland pegged the number at 78 percent for men and 75 percent for women. Other studies have determined that the number is above 80 percent for Caucasians, perhaps a little less for other ethnic groups. A 2004 study at Hunan Normal University in China estimated heritability at only 65 percent based on 385 Chinese families.

Clearly, determination of a person's height is not a black and white concept. There are many shades of gray, a lot of mitigating factors that contribute to this equation. I had a 6'10" grandfather, Grover Cleveland Doxsie, who married an average-sized woman and their only son topped out at a mere 6'2½". They also had two daughters, one of whom was of average height, and the other was very tall, around 6 feet. That 6'2½" son (my father) may have had his height compromised by environmental factors. He suffered chronic ear infections as a child and his family was basically homeless for the better part of a year in the midst of the Great Depression, which undoubtedly led to some dubious nutrition. He then spent a few months in a foundling home funded by the Kellogg's company outside Battle Creek, Michigan, where the daily diet consisted of cereal for breakfast, cereal for lunch and cereal for dinner. He obviously got good nutrition there but perhaps not the sort that fuels extreme growth. (He also didn't eat cereal for the rest of his life, by the way.)

Grover Doxsie, the 6'10" grandfather of the author, with daughter Ruth and son David in the 1930s (author's collection).

He ended up marrying a fairly short woman and fathered four tall kids, the largest of whom (me) topped out at 6'6¾". My other two grandparents, by the way, were 5'3" and 4'11", but their short genes didn't keep me from having a 36-inch inseam because of the super-sized genes I inherited from good old Grover. It also didn't prevent me from having two very tall children with an average-sized wife. What I'm trying to say is these things are really hard to predict.

There also is this lingering question: Why are men taller than women?

Here is the best explanation I could find: A University of Helsinki study found that a genetic variant in Chromosome X close to ITM2A, a gene that affects the development of cartilage, is more common in short people. It found the more this gene is expressed, the shorter a person is likely to be, and it found the gene to be much more prominent in women, who have two copies of Chromosome X while men have only one.

Bear in mind there also are various other physical maladies that prompt people to grow to extreme heights, including Marfan Syndrome, acromegaly, gigantism, the presence of the XYY phenotype (we'd need some really lengthy words to explain that one) and other things.

However you explain all of this increase in height in the human population, whether it be in the Netherlands or Scandinavia or somewhere else, there are some folks who view this as a potentially disastrous trend. Anthropologist Ashley Montagu once said that the world has a "misguided pride" about having tall children and "an unwarranted feeling that we are producing a better breed of people."

Thomas T. Samaras, an engineer in California, has studied the ramifications of height for most of his life and published numerous books and articles on the subject. He has been saying for decades that the world has gone and gotten just too darn tall. "This widespread misconception about the benefits of taller stature," he said, "does not stand the test of scientific investigation."

Samaras' first book, published in 1994, was *The Truth About Your Height: Exploring the Myths and Realities of Human Size and Its Effects on Performance, Health, Pollution and Survival*, and in it, he expressed the theory that this is a perilous trend. "Increasing human size has a very high price tag," he wrote. "We suffer huge extra costs in relation to health, energy consumption, resource needs, pollution and economic progress."

Samaras cited research from dozens of experts, ranging from Harry Shapiro to Charles Darwin, to support his theories. He estimated that "the larger person creates about 73 percent more waste due to greater use of water, food, materials, and various products." He feels we need to find ways not only to control the number of people on earth but also the size of them. "Only this combination will result in reducing the harmful effects of billions of humans on the earth and the threat to the survival and happiness of future generations," he added.

He did not suggest that we all expose our kids to diphtheria to stunt their growth but he fell just short of suggesting that we somehow manipulate the genetic makeup of the population. He said we need to change the daily diet of our children, feeding them less animal protein, milk, fat and sugar, and raising them on a low-calorie, low-fat, primarily plant-based diet that hopefully won't create another generation of giants.

He really did propose we find ways to be shorter, just not too short. "It would appear that an average height of 4'0" to 4'6" would be the smallest we'd want to go," he added.

Samaras has a lot of valid points. He's a highly intelligent, very educated man who has invested his entire life into the study of this stuff. But I'm guessing the meat-packing and dairy industries and the NBA despise his theories, and to be honest, most of what he proposed regarding the reduction of height around the world is fairly unrealistic. It's sort of like global warming. A majority of people agree that it's a potentially disastrous trend, and that if it is allowed to continue, the world could be in big, big trouble. But we aren't doing nearly enough to counteract it. It's the same way with global growing. Very little, if anything, ever will be done about it until it's too late.

In fact, much more time and effort has gone into scientifically trying to figure out ways to make people taller instead of smaller. Numerous medical advances have been sought to stimulate growth although—and Samaras is probably relieved to know this—there is relatively little hard evidence that anything works.

As far back as the 1950s, people have wondered about human growth and contemplated ways to stimulate it. In 2003, the U.S. Food and Drug Administration approved the use of human growth hormone (HGH) treatments for children in the lower 1 percent of growth, constituting roughly 40,000 infants in the United States.

Those children were judged to have growth hormone deficiency (GHD) so the treatments gave them something they were missing in their systems. It not only can make them taller but assists in the development of organs and other tissues and can help regulate their metabolism and blood sugar levels.

Giving HGH to larger, healthier infants who do not suffer from GHD in the hope that they'll someday land NBA contracts is both dubious and potentially dangerous. That doesn't mean that many haven't tried it and perhaps had some small success in making their kids bigger, but it's a controversial topic. Most experts feel it's not a suitable course of action and should be used with extreme caution.

Charles Brook, who supervised a growth clinic in London, said many years ago that parents seeking to make their children taller with HGH could conceivably spend $10,000 a year to give their children daily injections for 10 years in order to help them be perhaps an inch taller. And they may end up doing more damage to them psychologically. "When children are being given human growth hormone, it is the parents who have to administer the injections," he said. "Each time they do so, they are giving the child the message that there is something wrong with being small. We have often had to provide a great deal of psychological support for those who have gone through the treatment."

There are other potential dangers to giving HGH to healthy kids. Some children who were given HGH in the 1970s and 1980s later developed Creutzfeldt-Jakob disease, a fatal brain disorder that has an incubation period of up to 20 years. Those kids received HGH that was drawn from the pituitary glands of deceased individuals and it has since been replaced by a synthetic version.

With any kids, HGH only can provide a small boost in height until they reach the end of puberty, which generally is before the age of 19 for boys and 16 for girls. Once they arrive at that point, their growth plates turn from cartilage to bone in a process known as fusion and further growth is no longer possible.

Despite that, there are all sorts of websites that appeal to adults who yearn to be taller even though there is widespread discussion about whether this is ethical or even possible. The general consensus is that once someone has reached adulthood, there is no way to make them taller. But the World Wide Web is littered with claims to the contrary. There are advertisements for nutritional supplements, apps, exercise regimens, special diets, devices and harnesses. Some claim to be able to make a person taller through hypnosis, subliminal messages or music to stimulate taller vibes.

Legitimate medical professionals are extremely skeptical of all of it.

A lengthy investigative piece by Gizmodo.com in 2018 quoted Dr. David Cooke of Johns Hopkins University as saying: "There's no food or nutritional supplement that has been proven to impact the final height of an otherwise healthy child."

It also included this opinion from Dr. Todd Milbrandt, the associate professor of orthopedics and pediatrics at Mayo Clinic: "No adult can increase their height without surgery, period."

Cooke also doesn't believe all the claims about music and hypnosis. "There isn't a mechanism I can come up with that has any foundation in physiology that would explain how that would work," he said. "The generic disclaimer is that many things are possible and until they are studied you just don't know.... The purist in me says, 'I don't know, show me the data.'"

It may be possible for adults to gain a small amount of height through stretching. In fact, most of us grow slightly while sleeping at night as the cartilage between the 24 movable vertebrae in our spine decompresses. Once we rise to an upright position, our body gradually reverts to its previous size. Astronauts in space have been known to grow a few inches because of the lack of gravity, but again, it's purely temporary. Once back on Earth, they return to their previous height.

Cooke admitted that it is possible for children with hormonal deficiencies to be helped by injections of synthetic HGH, possibly resulting in additional growth of an inch or two. But after peoples' growth plates disappear in their teens, fusion takes place and there is no way to get taller in any way except through surgery.

Amazingly, that is the one way in which adults can grow taller. And even more amazingly, some people are doing it. Some have opted for a limb-lengthening procedure in which the subjects have their legs broken with the bones then being induced to grow longer as they heal.

The technology for such a procedure—bilateral simultaneous leg elongation—has existed for nearly 80 years and was pioneered by doctors in the Soviet Union following World War II to treat wounded soldiers. It formerly was done with patients who had an arm or leg that was shorter than the other as a result of a birth defect or an injury.

It now is being done more and more on otherwise healthy patients purely for cosmetic reasons. People who feel the need to be taller for dating purposes or because they believe it will help them in the business world pay anywhere from $75,000 to $280,000 to have doctors surgically lengthen their legs by as much as five or six inches. There are at least two major centers for the surgery in the United States and it is being done in about a dozen other countries, including Germany, South Korea, India, Spain, Italy, Turkey and the United Kingdom.

The surgery is not only expensive but extremely painful and risky. The bone is severed and a rod is inserted that slowly moves the two severed ends apart, increasing the length of the leg by about a millimeter a day. At most of the centers now doing the surgery patients are issued a computer tablet and instructed to push a button each day that lengthens their leg by about an inch every 25 days. At the same time, the soft tissue around the bone—skin, muscles and nerves—also is stretched. After the desired height is reached, the bones hopefully heal back together and the patient goes through months of rehabilitation to regain their mobility.

Since all of these surgeries are being done in private institutions, there is no reliable data available regarding the success rate. However, Hamish Simpson of the British Orthopaedic Association said the potential for complications such as nerve damage, blood clots and lack of healing is daunting.

Inevitably, too, most patients end up losing some degree of athletic ability. So, anyone thinking they can use this to transform themselves into an NBA prospect probably is not going to succeed.

3

It's Tough to Grow Up as a Tall Guy

Perhaps nothing lends itself more to derisive nicknames than extreme height.

Stretch. High Pockets. Daddy Long Legs. Bones. Beanpole. Beanstalk. Legs. Stork. Stilts. Skyscraper. Marfan. Too Tall. Tree. Giraffe.

At various times through my life, I've been called at least half those names although it's probably been at least 80 pounds since anyone referred to me as Beanpole. Occasionally, strangers have simply addressed me as Big Guy or perhaps they used the sarcastic approach and called me Little Guy. Back in the days when I played a lot of shirts-and-skins pick-up basketball games, I had one friend who referred to me as Sasquatch although that may have been as much a reference to my considerable chest hair as my size.

None of those titles are designed to bolster self-esteem. And that's why we hear so many sad stories of people who struggled with their height growing up. Kids who are significantly taller than their peers often are bullied and demeaned, frequently made to feel uncomfortably conspicuous, just like kids who are extremely short. Many of them still become famous or prosperous in spite of that, but I think we can safely say that relatively few people who grew up tall grew up completely comfortable.

Ted Cassidy carved out a solid acting career playing mostly monster characters, but he was 6 feet tall by the age of 11 and already towered over his parents before he even reached junior high. "I had a miserable, unhappy childhood and wouldn't go through it again for anything in the world," he said in a 1965 interview with the *New York Daily News*.

Dave Rasmussen of Madison, Wisconsin, who grew to be 7'3" as a result of something called Klinefelter Syndrome, recalled in a 1999 documentary called *In Search of Giants* how much abuse he absorbed when he was growing rapidly as a kid. "Kids are cruel and when you're different, whether it's tall or short or fat or something, it's always the different person who is the one to make fun of," he said. "So, it was difficult as a child. It was upsetting at times. I imagine there are days when I went home crying."

Mark Piotrowski is 6'10" and is part of what has to be one of the tallest families in the world, which also was featured in *In Search of Giants.* His father was 6'8", he has brothers who are 7'1" and 6'8", plus a 6'0" sister, a 6'8" son, a 6'2" daughter and a couple of 7'0" nephews.

Piotrowski, who is a high school teacher in suburban Philadelphia, not so fondly remembers that it wasn't just the other kids who made life difficult during his childhood. Unfeeling, apparently unthinking, educators also contributed. He remembers a biology teacher telling his brother Tom that he was "a freak of nature."

Mark himself was the victim of some unreasonably high expectations from an elementary school teacher simply because he was tall. He had the audacity one day to yawn in class, and since his head stuck up above his peers, the teacher spotted it. She sent him to the principal's office. For yawning. His father was called to school as Piotrowski wondered what he had done that warranted such treatment. "The teacher said, 'Mark should be a role model for everyone else in the class. When we go to recess, he should be the first person in line and everyone should follow him. He needs to be tamed,'" Piotrowski recalled. "She really thought that since I was taller, it was my responsibility to be the best-behaved kid and be a model for everyone else."

Very often it isn't necessary for anyone to say anything to tall boys to make them feel uncomfortable and inadequate.

Rued Riis, a 6'8" Denmark native who writes a popular blog at tallsome.com, is now handsome, confident and accomplished in his early 30s, and he now sees his height as a clear advantage. "People associate that with authority or trustworthiness, respect, and the girls like it," he said.

But as with so many others, he struggled with his newfound height when he was in his teens. He just wanted to blend in and be part of the crowd but was unable to do that.

"You look different and it might sound kind of a little radical or harsh to say it, but you could almost compare it to race," Riis said. "For example, if you are the only Black kid or only white kid in a group of the other color.... It shouldn't matter but it does to the person who's different. I think it's the same if you're overweight or tall or whatever is different about you. It matters especially in those years when you're really insecure. You don't know what foot to stand on. You just grow taller than all of your friends and you just want to be normal."

The truth is that being tall makes a guy conspicuous and that can be extremely uncomfortable.

Michael Crichton became one of the most successful authors and screenwriters ever. He wrote *Jurassic Park* and *The Andromeda Strain* in addition to several other books and movies plus the hit TV series *ER*. He also earned a medical degree from Harvard although he never practiced medicine, opting instead to become what some have described as "the father of the techno-thriller." But as a teenager growing up on Long Island, Crichton was pretty miserable. He was 6'7" and only 125 pounds and felt like some sort of freak. "I wasn't comfortable," he said in a 1993 interview. "I remember thinking I must be the tallest person in the world."

Crichton, who ended up being 6'9" as an adult, felt bullied because of his height and he recalled in his 1988 memoir *Travels* that older kids would sometimes chase him home from school and knock him down. That led to a withdrawal of sorts. He became quiet and moody and suffered from depression later in life. On the plus side, it also made him determined to become successful. "I am smart, and I am going to show them all," he once wrote.

He wrote things under the pen name John Lange in order to help pay for medical school and became hugely successful using his real name while still in his 20s. However, the struggles with his height forever shaped his personality. He remained a soft-spoken, modest, unassuming man throughout his life, the sort of person who tried—usually without success—to melt into the background in a crowded room. "If he wasn't 9 feet tall, you wouldn't know he existed," said Michael Ovitz, his close friend and agent.

Crichton was not the only famous American writer who struggled to cope with his extreme size. Thomas Wolfe, author of *Look Homeward, Angel* and three other novels (not to be confused with the Tom Wolfe who later wrote such books as *The Right Stuff*), was either 6'6" or 6'8" and, by all accounts, hated his size.

"Wolfe's physical size was even more freakish in the 1920s and '30s than it is now," *Buffalo News* reporter Jeff Simon wrote in 1980. "It explains a good deal about his outsized, uncontrolled, logorrheic personality. I just don't think a man can grow up to be Wolfe's size without a fundamental physical alienation from the rest of us."

Long-time literary editor Malcolm Cowley wrote that he thought Wolfe, who died at the age of 37, had "the disposition of a morose elephant."

Alan Simpson, who for many years was the tallest member of the U.S. Senate, was a star athlete as well as inordinately tall but he also struggled early in life with the prospect of being 6'7".

"When you're a kid and you've got zits all over you, it's embarrassing, but as I got older and the zits disappeared and I had beautiful hair, which I have none of now, [being tall] is a comfort," Simpson said in a 2017 interview.

Albert Payson Terhune wrote a lengthy essay about this subject for *American* magazine in 1926, laying out the "Troubles of a Big Guy." Terhune, who was 6'2", said he was especially jealous of shorter men at parties.

"I envy them because they can walk or dance with a normal-sized woman without the spectacle making onlookers think of the Cardiff Giant and Little Eva," he wrote. "After I had watched a few men, as tall as I or taller, dancing with girls a foot shorter than themselves, I gave up dancing forever. A Big Guy is ridiculous enough, as Nature made him, without going out of his way to make himself more so by spinning around a ballroom with a girl whose nose comes no higher than his second shirt stud."

Terhune makes a good point: Many of the issues of tall men relate to their altitudinal proximity to the opposite sex. There remains a misconception that tall guys have some sort of monstrous advantage when it comes to dealing with women. There may be some small truth to that with some men. But not much.

There is a scene in the 2013 film *The Internship* in which there is an exchange between characters played by Will Ferrell and Vince Vaughn, both of whom are tall. Ferrell addresses the taller Vaughn as "Marfan's Syndrome" and then tells him: "I'm handsome tall. You're the type of tall where you walk through the airport, people stop what they're eating and look at you. You're like a freak."

Imbedded in the humor of the conversation is an underlying truth: When it comes to human attraction, it's possible to be too tall.

The old thing about girls hungering for someone tall, dark and handsome is essentially a myth. Handsome? Yeah, probably. Handsome is good. Dark? Maybe. Tall? Doesn't really mean as much as you might think.

Yes, it's undoubtedly more desirable to be 6'1" or 6'2" than to be 5'6". There is a sweet spot somewhere in there between 6'1" and 6'4" that definitely enhances physical attraction. But when you get to be 6'5", as Vince Vaughn is, you're almost getting to be too tall. (Not that most women don't find Vince very attractive. His boyish looks, curly locks, vibrant personality, droll humor and net worth are more than enough to overcome the fact that he is bordering on freak territory.)

Nevertheless, when you get to be that tall, people start to give you nicknames like Stretch. And Sasquatch. And Marfan's Syndrome.

Get to be 6'8", 6'9", and you're definitely getting into freak territory unless you happen to be a basketball star, which you obviously must be because height is a guarantee of basketball success, isn't it? If you're taller than that, your height becomes a genuine detriment when it comes to attracting members of the opposite sex. If you're 6'11", girls often look at you as though you just escaped from some sort of science experiment.

Our irreverent friend Lewis Spears doesn't necessarily believe that. He thinks his 6'8" frame gives him an edge in these matters. "I swear, being tall is a bit of a cheat code that tricks people's brains into thinking you're more attractive than you actually are," he said. "If I meet someone when I'm sitting down and then I stand up, I can literally see their perception shift in real time."

But it would seem that perhaps a man's height was regarded as more of a plus in male-female relationships by foregone generations. Syndicated columnist Erma Bombeck, who was short by her own admission, wrote in 1979 that her mother's first question about anyone she was dating was always "How tall is he?" Seemingly nothing else mattered. "It didn't matter if my prospective date had a 30-pound nose, dirt under his fingernails, and burned barns to release tension—if he was tall, he was acceptable," Bombeck wrote.

However, in a survey done by the *Village Voice* in the early 1970s on what physical features heterosexual women wanted most in a mate, tallness tied for sixth place behind a small, sexy butt, slimness, a flat stomach, nice eyes and long legs. A sleek set of biscuits actually was the runaway winner at 39 percent. Tallness was cited as the top asset by only 5 percent of the women who were polled.

In a parallel survey, men were asked what they thought women wanted and 13 percent said they thought it was most essential to be tall. Only 4 percent thought their derriere was of paramount importance.

Any role that tallness might have in physical attraction undoubtedly is superficial and very temporary anyway. A pair of graduate students, Alan Strathman and James Shepperd, demonstrated that with a study they did in the late 1980s. They surveyed 110 college students and found that height was a determining factor in selecting who they would date but that factor lessened considerably as the relationship progressed. "After dating, physical characteristics like height lose significance for women but not for men," Strathman said.

The idea that height is important in sexual attraction has been falsely reinforced by some experts. Thomas T. Samaras, who we already have mentioned as one of the leading experts in the study of height and human growth, fell back on a few generalities, stereotypes and assumptions in his 1994 book, *The Truth About Your Height: Exploring the Myths and Realities of Human Size and Its Effects on Performance, Health, Pollution and Survival*, stating that "tall men are usually more attractive to women."

He continued: "There's no doubt that most women are attracted to men who are taller than themselves. If we assume that personality, wit, humor, and style are equal for all heights, tall men have more opportunities to be lovers than shorter men. Because of more experience, they are probably better lovers."

This clearly was written by a 5'10" guy who has spent his life studying the tall rather than by someone who has spent his life actually be*ing* tall. I can honestly say I didn't get nearly as many "opportunities" in my bachelor days as I wanted. Being 6'6¾" was fairly worthless in that respect. I'm sure some would suggest that I just came up short in "personality, wit, humor, and style." More likely, I think some women were turned off because I stretched above the Vince Vaughn line. Samaras himself admitted his theory was derived from a study among women in France, where I suspect all people might receive more "opportunities."

Spears did mention in his YouTube video "Top 10 Things About Being Freakishly Tall" that he sensed a certain amount of desperation in tall women on the dating scene. Because he is 6'8", Spears said it seldom mattered what he looked like on that particular day. "A freakishly tall girl lowers her standards to the floor when they meet a freakishly tall guy." To be honest, though, I never experienced that phenomenon either. It might just be because Spears gets high marks in wit and humor.

Samaras provided some evidence that contradicted his assumptions, citing a poll of 200 women taken by the French magazine *Marie-France* that found tall men were not necessarily better in the sack: "The magazine reported their women readers, especially younger ones, equated short men with virility, power, and sexual experimentation." Samaras reasoned that short men may be more eager to please their female partners in bed because they are, well ... short. He figured we tall, good-looking studs tended to be complacent in bed because we get to do it so frequently.

A 2014 essay written by Adam Gropnik for the BBC reinforced that notion. Gropnik, who admitted to being short, said some sociologists have asserted that short men make good husbands simply because they are desperate and eager to please. "Short men live in a world of taller men and know that any advantage seized is better kept," he wrote. "Desperation makes short men good husbands."

There is all sorts of evidence, most of it anecdotal, to indicate that taller is not necessarily better and that men who reach the Vince Vaughn line generally will find their height to be more of a negative than a positive.

When "J" (real name Joan Theresa Garrity) published *The Sensuous Woman* in 1969, she included a list of the 10 sexiest men. No. 1 on it was talk show host Dick Cavett, who was 5'8". Her opinion was that women didn't care about Cavett's height (or lack thereof) but "are entranced by his wit, his intelligence, and his self-deprecatory charm." In fairness, there was no mention of whether or not he had a nice butt.

Since 1985, *People Magazine* has named a "Sexiest Man of the Year," and as of 2021, 27 of the 36 winners were between 5'10" and 6'1" with the average being almost exactly 6 feet. The four men who have won the award more than once—Brad Pitt, Richard Gere, George Clooney and Johnny Depp—all are under 6 feet tall. The tallest winner in all that time was former football player and professional wrestler turned actor Dwayne "The Rock" Johnson (2016), who is widely listed as 6'5" although many people feel he is nowhere near that tall. The Rock himself has hinted that his actual height has been exaggerated. The few other tall winners have been Blake Shelton (2017) and Ben Affleck (2002), both generally listed as 6'4", and Chris Hemsworth (2014) and Hugh Jackman (2008), who are 6'3".

The point is you seldom see anyone above the Vince Vaughn line being touted as sexy.

A 1979 article in *Ladies Home Journal* stated that among male celebrities who are viewed as sex symbols, height really wasn't a factor at all. "Women no longer feel the same need to look up to men," according to the author, Molly Haskell.

In an article in *Ebony* magazine that same year, titled "What Kind of Men Have Sex Appeal?," 10 prominent women spoke about what they found physically attractive in men. Only two of them mentioned height and one of those defined tall as being 6'0".

Mademoiselle magazine reported in 1987 that short men were becoming more popular with women, concluding: "Goodbye, tall, strong and silent; this is the era of short, cute and clever." (And apparently desperate.)

Diane Balson wrote in *Glamour* magazine in 1979—that was a big year for these types of stories—that perhaps short, dark and handsome is becoming more acceptable. "We do not discriminate against short men; we actually prefer them," she wrote. "Psychiatrists say that a preference for short men may result in anything from a mothering instinct to a desire to dominate."

She indicated that attitudes toward height have changed since the days of Erma Bombeck's mother, most likely because of the women's liberation movement, and she quoted psychiatric social worker Ellen Perlman Simon: "We're slowly freeing ourselves from stereotypes; our visual cues are changing. Women don't have to see men as big and powerful; men don't have to see women as helpless little playthings. Liberation works both ways. If a man is free to wash the dishes, he's free to be short."

More recently, Rocky Emerson, a 6'3" woman who bills herself as the world's tallest porn star, has said she actually doesn't find tall men attractive at all. "People taller than me freak me out because I'm not used to them," she said. "I get really, really uncomfortable. I'm actually less attracted to people who are significantly taller than me."

This shorter-is-better mindset is not a new development. In the 1940s, there was a group of 6-feet-and-over showgirls called the Glamazons who were nearly unanimous in thinking that short was better than tall when it came to the opposite sex. Bunny Waters, one of the tallest of the Glamazons, put it this way: "With very few exceptions, tall men are not nearly as attractive to us as short men. And you get so used to looking down every day that to date a man taller than yourself—if you can find one—gives you a pain in the neck from looking up. Then, too, tall men are more self-conscious and almost none of them are good dancers. And the bigger they are, the more they want to be babied."

4

It's Tougher to Be a Tall Girl

Gwen Davenport faced the challenge of being a tall woman of prominence in the 1940s and 1950s, and eventually she decided to try to do something to help others with the same challenge.

After having several great successes in writing fiction, including a book called *Belvedere* that spawned three movies and a television series, Davenport decided to take a shot at non-fiction on a topic very near and dear to her heart. We don't really know for sure how tall Davenport was. She apparently was sheepish enough about that not to be specific, but we know she was very tall. And she poured out all the advice she could muster in a 1959 book called *The Tall Girls' Handbook*, excerpts of which were thought to be important enough to be reprinted in several newspapers.

Some of her thoughts seem a bit outdated now. But some of them are every bit as pertinent as they must have been more than six decades ago.

Davenport said that as girls begin to sprout above their peers, everyone—friends, relatives, teachers, classmates—all seem to take notice and all seem to make them feel like they're Alice in Wonderland. "Young people, more even than all other people, hate to be conspicuous," she wrote. "A very tall person can never be anything else. Here is the making of a tragedy. However, as with any handicap, the first thing to do is to face it."

I'm not sure how I feel about her referring to excessive height as a "handicap," but Gwen still advised girls to "accept yourself as you are. Don't resent your size. You have only one life; don't let something you couldn't help spoil it. Just because you can't be little in physique, like your cute neighbor down the street, don't be little in spirit."

Author Gwen Davenport offered advice to young girls struggling with their height in a popular 1959 book.

Davenport said that although tall girls were likely to get their feelings hurt more often than others, they needed to take teasing "like a trooper." She did provide a few examples of snarky responses to the "How's the weather up there?" question. The best of them: "Why don't you grow up and find out."

"Anyone who makes sport of you because you are different from himself is an ignorant, unsophisticated person of narrow upbringing and limited experience of the world," she added.

She did say, however, that because tall girls are so noticeable, they need to be that much more careful about their appearance. "There is no charm in disarray on a grand scale," she wrote. "The dirty fingernail looks worse on a big hand. The unwashed or badly frizzed head that stands high above the crowd cannot go unmarked. Over long legs a sagging skirt hem or a safety pin will call attention not to your shapely limbs but to a slatternly disregard of appearance. Don't make the mistake of thinking that, if you are more or less six feet tall, nothing else about your appearance matters. It matters just that much more!"

We're not quite so sure about some of the advice she offered: She recommended that tall girls not be too assertive with members of the opposite sex. She recommended that they not wear too much makeup or use dark nail polish that might exaggerate the size of their hands or wear clothing that accentuates their height. And she strongly suggested that they go out for the basketball team. "You have a natural advantage in playing forward and center, and need not be a particularly good player to make the team...."

"Better than basketball is tennis," she added. "Boys like a girl who plays a good game of tennis."

Uh huh. We'll have more to say about the whole basketball thing in a later chapter. For now, we'll just say that it's a good activity for tall girls who really love the sport and who are committed to being good at it. If you're doing it just because everyone else expects you to do it, it can potentially make things worse. Better not to play at all rather than to play half-heartedly and badly. That can open the door to even more radical abuse and ridicule.

The mere fact that Davenport wrote a very popular book about the struggles of tall girls and that so many others have addressed the topic through the years in books and magazine articles leads me to suspect that's it's even tougher to grow up as a tall girl than it is to be a tall guy.

It makes sense. Women mature earlier than men with most of them reaching their full height by their mid-teens while men frequently continue to grow until they're 19 or 20. That means that as adolescents, girls routinely tower over their male counterparts. It's easy to see why they might be even more likely to become objects of ridicule and to encounter other problems created by their stature.

In many cases, extreme height is the first thing some people notice upon meeting a tall girl. All other positive attributes they might possess fall into the background. "When you're a tall girl it's the only thing people see," says the title character in the 2019 Netflix film *Tall Girl*. One of her classmates tells her: "You're the tall girl. You'll never be the pretty girl."

Tall women are prone to receiving all sorts of bizarre, backhanded compliments, such as the one that Donna Stocker received one day in an airport. A man she didn't know walked up to her and said "Wow, you're tall, but you're pretty!" Stocker, who is 6'1" and was named Miss Tall International in 2021 at the age of 58, wasn't quite sure whether to thank the guy or slap him upside the head. She didn't have time to do either because the man just kept walking.

"You just feel like you're sort of different because people are always pointing it out to you," Stocker said in a 2022 *Kelown Daily Courier* article. "Tall people sometimes are shy and they tend to hunch over. They don't want people to see them, yet they stand out. It's a blessing and a curse at the same time."

Chicago Tribune writer Mary Daniels summed it up pretty well in a 1976 piece: "Tall women have been funny and freakish to everyone but themselves. To be born tall and female, even if you were otherwise healthy, sane, talented, beautiful and intelligent, has been socially comparable to being born with multicolor skin or three legs and tentacles for arms."

You need not look any further than a poll question that was posed on the Facebook page for Tall Clubs International in 2022. It asked: "Does it bother you, or does it make you feel uncomfortable to be in the center of attention during events like your birthday party, your wedding or when you're being recognized for something in the group of people?" A little more than half of the respondents in the poll (51 percent) said they didn't really care one way or the other, but another 35 percent said they didn't like being in the spotlight because they were self-conscious about their height. About 11 percent said were very uncomfortable and couldn't wait for it to be over. Almost all of those respondents were women.

"A tall woman is usually treated like a circus freak ... or at least that's how I feel," one of the poll respondents wrote. "The attention you receive is not good, it's more like pointing and whispering behind your back. I hate it." Another added: "I don't like any attention on me at all. I would love to disappear in a crowd and walk outside without standing out."

People have been talking and writing about the problems of the tall girl for more than a century. An article in the *Seattle Times* in 1918 profiled a woman named Jobyna Howland and noted that "it isn't divine to be tall. It is diabolical." Howland was extremely attractive. She was one of a handful of women selected to pose for artist Charles Dana Gibson and be one of his "Gibson Girls." She went on to appear in 19 films, but she detested the fact that she was 6 feet tall. She desperately wanted to be 5'3".

Howland had all the same, familiar complaints about finding clothes and fitting into automobiles, but mostly she objected to the way men reacted to her. "No one is ever moved to coddle or pet or do things for the tall girl," Howland said. "No one will allow her to be a clinging vine. And no matter how tall she is, she wants to cling."

The author of the article, Ada Patterson, wrote that Howland also hated the fact that she could never be inconspicuous: "She is like the man on stilts who advertises something. Her generous inches advertise her wardrobe. If it is a poor wardrobe everyone knows it.

The tall woman in the shabby gown looks tenfold shabbier than a little woman would look in the same attire."

Although I can't speak from personal experience about this, I have a daughter who can. Emily is either 6'1" or 6'2"—she doesn't really want to be measured and have an accurate answer for question No. 1—and she had her share of issues in the dating world and also in finding clothes that fit and were fashionable.

Although she is beautiful—this is coming from Dad so I might be somewhat biased—she did not date very much in her teen years. She had no desire to be seen in public with a guy shorter than she was, which culled the herd of suitors considerably. And let's face it, that 5'9" guy really doesn't want to walk around with a girl who is 4 or 5 inches taller even when she isn't wearing heels. She was the second tallest person of any gender in an especially runty high school graduating class and she didn't particularly like the one boy who was slightly taller than her. She ended up going to prom with a group of other girls, some of whom also towered over the boys.

She faced similar problems when it came time to buy clothes. When she and friends went to the mall to check out the latest fashions, the friends were able to purchase items off the rack. Emily generally had to come home and check online to see if she could find something similar in her size. More often than not, she struck out. Even when she did find something and ordered it, she was rolling the dice on whether it fit properly because she hadn't been able to try it on. As for sharing clothes with friends, something that I'm told girls like to do, forget it. It never happened.

Fortunately, I don't know that she ever was bullied by other kids to any great extent because of her size. If she was, she chose not to tell her potentially over-protective dad about it. But there is ample anecdotal evidence that those things happen quite frequently to tall girls. Being a teenager is difficult enough, but when you look different from everyone else, when you stand out in a crowd, you can become an easy target for those with a cruel streak.

Julie Whitman Jones of Citrus Heights, California, is only moderately tall—about 6'0"—but when she was in the sixth grade, she already was 5'10" and taller than everyone in her school, teachers included. She said she was bullied constantly in every imaginable way.

When the kids played a playground game called Four Square, one particular girl always would throw the ball at her legs, then taunt her by telling her she was too tall. Dodgeball was an even worse experience. Jones said she always lacked self-confidence and felt awkward and, as a result, was extremely shy throughout her childhood. She feels it had a strong impact on shaping her personality for the remainder of her life.

"I hated being in school because I was being bullied," she said. "And it wasn't the guys who bullied me. It was the girls."

Sarah Hope, a 6'4" resident of Cambridge, England, said in a 1994 *London Independent* story that her high school years were a "nightmare."

"I was teased unmercifully, victimized and bullied. I could not get a school uniform that fitted, so I always looked odd, and people used to steal my books, steal bits of clothing and reduce me to tears," Hope said.

Actress/comedian Judy Gold, who had reached her full height of 6'3" by the age of 13, recalled other kids referring to her as "Sasquatch" when she walked through the hallways at school.

Actress Kristen Johnson, who is 6'0", said that throughout high school, she was "enormous, a monstrosity, a freak" and was made to feel like "an outsider."

There is an old Italian proverb—"Altezza e mezza bellezza"—which translates to "half of beauty is height" or "tall is beautiful." But you couldn't tell that to many women who were genuinely gorgeous as adults but were made by their peers to feel decidedly ugly as kids.

Actress Geena Davis, who I think we can all agree falls into the gorgeous category, felt very awkward as a child growing up in Wareham, Massachusetts, and became very introverted as a result.

"I didn't feel pretty growing up," Davis told *Parade* magazine in 1996. "I didn't have boyfriends in high school. I wasn't part of the crowd who went to parties. I had this fantasy that maybe I could go somewhere they never heard of me and don't know what a goon I am—and maybe for once I can be attractive."

Davis was immensely gifted at a young age. She played several musical instruments, wrote creative stories, made a lot of her own clothes. She has a genius-level IQ of 140 and is a member of Mensa. But when she got to about the age of 13, she was something of an outcast. She was "different," not a part of the social scene. "It was partly, well, greatly, my height," she said.

It all turned out fine in the end. Davis eventually became a model, then a highly successful actress, the winner of an Academy Award. But it was a struggle to get to that point.

It's a struggle that was very familiar to Gabriella Reece, a highly successful volleyball player, model, actress and sports commentator. She reached 6'0" by the time she was 12 and ended up being 6'3". She told *People* magazine in 2016 that "the worst thing you can be when you're going through puberty and those formative years is to be different," and it took her some time to adjust.

"It was a moment of, 'well, you're not going to fit in so are you going to be tortured or are you going to embrace the fact that you know who you are?'" she said in another interview with *Harper's Bazaar.* "So, I think I picked it up early. What was also very helpful for me was getting involved in sports; there were quite a few other girls like me. Sport also has the mentality of 'try to be stronger,' so that was really helpful at that time.... Once I got into sports that idea of being bigger was celebrated so it's that reminder of the notion of beauty is in the eye of the beholder—we need to define it for ourselves and think 'I'm going to celebrate who I am and not compare.'"

A woman named Maria Taylor went through a similar transformation on her way to becoming a topflight reporter for ESPN. Her adolescent years were one long, continuous struggle to cope with being different than her peers. "All you want to do as a kid is blend in and be accepted," she said in an interview with Thetallsociety.com. "Instead, I stood out and was taller than all of my friends and most of the guys that were around me. Some guys called me the Jolly Green Giant and at times I just wanted to curl up in a ball and hide but that is tough when you tower over everyone."

Becoming involved with basketball and volleyball at both the high school and college levels helped Taylor. She met others who were encountering the same struggles and she gradually accepted her size and gained the self-assurance necessary to alter her view of being 6'2". "The one thing that I felt was ruining my life when I was in middle school is now the characteristic that makes me unique and confident," she said.

Several decades before Reece and Taylor stubbornly rose above the potential obstacles presented by their height, a woman named Bess Myerson did the same thing.

Myerson wasn't quite as large—she was 5'10"—but that was very tall for someone growing up in the 1920s and 1930s.

Myerson remembered that any time she walked into a crowded

room as a teenager, she immediately sought out the first chair she could find so she could sit down and become inconspicuous. She wanted nothing to do with members of the opposite sex. "Our culture stresses the boy being taller than the girl so much that tall teenagers become very self-conscious," she said.

"Her height, she felt was something she had to endure, as if she had been born with one brown eye and one blue one," wrote Gwen Davenport, who held up Myerson as a role model for young girls in her book. She said Myerson viewed her height as a deformity or an affliction. "But it can be a deformity inside yourself—if you let it be," Myerson said. "I was eighteen when I suddenly said to myself, 'This is Me, and there's not one thing I can do about it.' I made up my mind to be the most attractive Me I possibly could."

She ended up as Miss America 1945, the tallest woman ever to win the honor at that time and also the only Jewish woman ever to do so. She became a well-known game show host, a regular panelist on the popular show *I've Got a Secret* and later held several government positions in New York City.

She was one of several oversized women to serve as positive role models for tall girls through the years.

Julia Child, who was 6'2", became one of the world's most famous chefs and cookbook authors, someone who frequently made light of her own size, and in doing so, made it much less of an issue than it could have been.

Maya Angelou rose from humble beginnings to become a prolific poet and author and influential civil rights activist despite growing up as a gangly 6'0" girl who never, ever thought of herself as being attractive. In a 1977 interview with Judith Rich, she said: "I was too tall. My voice was too heavy. My attitude was too arrogant—or tenderhearted. So if I had accepted what people told me I looked like as a negative yes, then I would be dead. But I accepted it and I thought, well, aren't I the lucky one?"

Russian model Ekaterina Lisina took a similar attitude, finally learning to embrace what she was and appreciate it. Lisina is 6'9" and has legs that are 52 inches long. In fact, she once was certified by the *Guinness Book of World Records* as having the longest legs of any woman in the world.

She began playing pro basketball at the age of 15 but said she was 24 before she ever had any inkling that she might actually be attractive. Her early life was filled with an endless stream of comments about her size. She heard about every nickname in the book at some time or another.

"It was a pretty difficult time at school, being so tall," she said. "I'd have to call my older brother to communicate with the boys."

She said she ultimately sought out the chance to gain certification from Guinness as a way "to be an inspiration to girls who are not very confident."

Cara Michelle grew up in Hawaii also thinking she wasn't remotely attractive because she was 6'2". She was proven wrong when she became the tallest playmate in the history of *Playboy* magazine. "I'm used to people staring and making comments about me," said Michelle, who was Miss December in 2000. "It bothered me when I was younger and less secure, but now I don't even notice."

It definitely has become more common since the days of Davenport's book for an extremely tall woman to be viewed as extremely attractive. Michelle, Lisina, Myerson, Davis, Reece and others provide ample evidence of that. But Thomas Samaras probably exaggerated about that a bit when he wrote in his 1994 book about human growth that "tall women definitely have the edge in getting modeling jobs and winning beauty queen contests."

A survey of the 32 women crowned Miss America from 1928 through 1960 showed that 29 were taller than average but the same concept holds true for girls as it does for boys: It's possible to be too tall. I don't recall ever seeing them get out a step ladder to place the tiara on a 6'4" woman as Bert Parks crooned, "There she is, Miss America." Sure, 5'9" or 5'10" is good, but there is a freak line there for women just as there is for men.

In fact, after the 5'10" Myerson won the Miss America pageant in 1945, it was 53 years before anyone taller than she has won. The tallest contestant in Miss America history was 6'2" Jeanne Swanner, who was Miss North Carolina 1963. She later carved out a career as a humorist under her married name, Jeanne Robertson, and frequently poked fun at her own size. She often pointed out that she had been voted Miss Congeniality, which she said is "the contestant who the others believe has the least chance of winning the title."

Samaras also said men are not at all turned off by a woman who is tall as long as she's not taller than they are, and with a few exceptions, he is right about that.

For decades, girls have tried to do things to make themselves look a little bit shorter when they're around guys.

Valerie S. Brown wrote in *Teen* magazine in 1988 that while short girls could make themselves look taller by wearing heels, there was almost nothing that tall girls could do to appear shorter. "Most tall teens eventually learn that crouching, slouching, hunching and bunching do nothing—except give them terrible posture," she wrote.

Author and actress Cornelia Otis Skinner wrote in *Reader's Digest* in 1957 that she learned to adopt something she called the "debutante's slouch" and recalled overhearing a friend of her mother's saying the poor girl looked like a croquet wicket. Skinner was only 5'7" but she still viewed her height as a "deformity," especially when it came time to go onto the dance floor with a boy. "At the proms I attended my dancing was less cheek-to-cheek than temple-to-jowl—and I needn't state whose was the jowl," she wrote. "I tried to mend matters by dancing with bent knees, or by putting myself into a sharp incline with chin propped on my hero's shoulder."

Mariah Burton Nelson wrote in *Ms.* magazine in 1987 that when she was 13, she already was 5'9" and she had a big crush on a boy who was 5'3". She wore desert boots every day to school to make her look a little less tall, even in the midst of a frigid Pennsylvania winter.

"I had already learned the delicate art of dislocating one hip in order to appear shorter, and my back was beginning to look like the women in today's calcium advertisements for avoiding osteoporosis," Nelson wrote.

Her mother, a physician, worried that Nelson's life might be destroyed by becoming obscenely tall and she was constantly measuring her daughter to see how much she had grown. She finally offered Mariah the option of taking estrogen pills to stimulate her menstruation cycle, thereby causing her bones to fuse and preventing further growth. (You remember all this from Chapter 2, right?) Nelson did it for a while but it apparently didn't work that well because she continued on to become 6'2". She went on to become a professional basketball player as well as an accomplished writer and editor, and she delighted in telling open-mouthed tall-gawkers that her growth had been stunted.

For what it's worth, the estrogen treatments were found in a 2009 study to probably do more harm than good. Any small gains that were made in improved body image for girls were more than offset by complications. The study concluded that "such treatment should seldom—if ever—be used in the future."

Albert Payson Terhune, in his 1926 essay in *American* magazine, sympathized with tall girls and said it always was easy to pick them out at a dance.

"Sometimes she is a chronic wallflower," Terhune wrote. "When she is not, she is likely to be the girl who is allowed to finish the whole dance with the same man with whom she began it. Seldom does any youth 'cut in,' to steal her from her original partner.... As a rule, few normal-sized or runty men care to make themselves seem ridiculous by dancing with her. Indeed, she is worse off than the Big Guy. You may see a tall man walking or talking with a short woman, without wanting to grin. The sight is too frequent for comment. But notice the covert smiles which greet the advent of the six-foot girl, strolling along with a five-foot-two man."

Cynthia Gorney wrote in *Seventeen* magazine in 1979 that this obsession with the man being taller stems from peer pressure. "In this society that thinks men should be taller than the women they love, a tall girl can feel out of things as she grows up," Gorney wrote. "Her head sticks up in P.E. class. Her shoulders stick out in dance class. She's called Highpockets, Stretch, Beanpole and is constantly asked what the air is like up there. She provokes raised eyebrows and funny looks until she feels like screaming. She may spend what seems like half her life looking for a boy who is at least her height and won't be put off by the fact that she can look him right in the eye."

This idea of tall girls feeling the need to find men taller than themselves is very prevalent. As mentioned, it's what kept my daughter from dating as much as many of her peers. Fortunately, she finally stumbled across a nice 6'5" engineer who has made her very happy.

Author Jane Smiley, who is 6'2", completely disregarded Gwen Davenport's advice about not being too aggressive with men. When she spotted Yale basketball player John Whiston, she immediately pursued him until he became her first husband. "It was important that I acted on my own instead of waiting for someone to find me," Smiley said.

Many women in an ongoing discussion on TCI's Facebook page complained that it is almost impossible to find a man taller than they are, even on modern-day dating apps.

"If you are looking for someone your height or taller, it is statistically improbable," one pointed out. "I am 6'2". I am taller than 98% of the men in the United States."

Actually, it's more like 99 percent.

There are a few dating apps especially for tall people including one called tallsingle.com. Another one called dateup.co is specifically for women seeking a taller mate. But the Facebook posters questioned how effective those sites are in helping them find big guys.

"It's tough when you're a taller woman," one of them said. "Most of my female friends who are under 5'5" still think they need a guy above 6'2"! Then tall guys have endless options strictly because of their height. I've seen so many men lead with their height in their bio.... It's that much of a draw. It's rough out there for a tall gal."

"You are treated differently as a woman when you date a man shorter than you and it is hard," another Facebook contributor added. "The struggle to find tall men is very real for tall women. It seems so many tall men go for significantly shorter women, for whatever reason."

Samaras reasoned that a woman's urge to find a taller mate is something that has been inbred through the centuries. "In primitive times, taller and larger men were valued for their greater strength because it allowed them to protect their mates and their children against other men and wild animals," he wrote. "Therefore, women would tend to select a larger male when they had a choice."

Although times undoubtedly are changing, it is relatively rare to find heterosexual couples in which the woman is taller. I know tons of people, and to be honest, I can probably count on one hand the number of happily married couples I know in which the man is significantly shorter than his partner.

"A couple who dared to marry outside the 'normal' male-female height proportions (the female being shorter even when wearing 3-inch heels) often had to be as strong as if their marriage had crossed racial, religious, social caste, or cultural lines," Mary Daniels wrote. "They often suffered teasing, taunting, snickering, and behind-the-back but not out-of-earshot jokes."

A woman who is taller than her mate sometimes gives the impression that she is the dominant figure in the relationship, according to experts. Dr. Morris Skalansky of the Chicago-based Institute of Psychoanalysis said: "A child is dependent on the larger parents, and this continues into the heterosexual relationship."

Another expert from the institute, Dr. Marion Toplin, added: "In early art, if they wanted to depict the importance of a king, they would make him very tall, and his wife and servants very small. This is a childlike idea of dominance."

Kae Sumner Einfeldt, who founded a club that was the forerunner of TCI in the 1930s, stated flatly: "We tall girls do not like the idea of being taller than most men."

The 6'3" Einfeldt recalled being asked out on a date by a guy who was 5'4", and although she suspected it was part of a fraternity initiation, she admired his spunk and said yes. But when the couple appeared in public, most people treated them as though she was the older sister being accompanied by her little brother. The guy didn't seem to care but it was their one and only date. After that, Kae went back to searching for someone her own size ... or bigger.

"Men want to be the all powerful, the all mighty, both mentally and physically," she added. "It isn't enough for them to know it, they've got to see it. This is unlucky for the tall girl. When a man has to look up to a woman, it ruins his illusion."

Many observers have encouraged women to reject the notion that height carries any importance whatsoever in a male-female relationship.

A 2018 article by Mariah Baylor called "The Tall Girls' Guide to Professional and Personal Perfection" said tall women should never allow their size to dictate who they date: "This is one of the silliest stereotypes that should have been exposed decades ago. If you are happy with someone, that's enough reason to date. People may still stare or make rude comments because ... well, they are people. Be confident enough in yourself and your relationship to realize they are placing their insecurities on you."

Valerie Brown added: "Aren't all these insecurities getting in the way of having fun? If the guy you admire is shorter, relax! While the tall guy/short girl ideal still exists, it's giving way to more modern thinking."

There are a handful of famous celebrity couples in which the wife is taller than the husband, but with few exceptions, it's only by an inch or two.

Tom Cruise, who is 5'7", has been married three times and all of his wives—Mimi Rogers, Nicole Kidman and Katie Holmes—were 5'9" or taller.

There really are men who want to be with taller women. Veteran actor Mickey Rooney loved statuesque women and especially enjoyed being seen and photographed with them. The 5'2" Rooney was married eight times and all of his wives were at least as tall as he was. A few of them appeared in photos to be at least six inches taller. He frequently referred to "the lumberjack urge to fell the tallest tree."

Arianne Cohen, the 6'3" author of *The Tall Book*, recalled running into this once when she went out with a man who insisted that she wear 4-inch heels on their first date. On the second date, he asked that she stand on a step stool in heels so she could "tower over him." There was no third date.

A tall woman with a shorter husband or significant other is still a rare sight. The times may be changing but they're changing very slowly.

There are some places in the world in which tall women are prized more than their shorter counterparts. As Cohen pointed out in her book, tall girls often can command a dowry of 80 to 120 cows among the tribes of South Sudan while an average-sized girl might only get 50 to 70.

Even Gwen Davenport, while advising tall women on how to cope with their size, wistfully pointed out that in ancient times, tall women were treasured.

"All through history, and in art, the admired woman has been the tall one," she wrote. "Of course, those admirers did not mean a woman excessively tall, and some of us may have gone too far and run it into the ground—or into the sky. If you are one of these, take heart. Find comfort in the knowledge that you may, indeed, involuntarily have gone too far—but you did it in the right direction."

A bolder, more modern approach to being tall as a woman comes from Alicia Jay, who is 6'6" and writes a blog on TallSWAG.com. Jay, 36, claims to wear 5-inch heels and said tall women need to be unabashedly proud of who they are and what they are.

Growing up, she not only was always the tallest person in her school but also one of the few Black kids, and she said the other students "always found a way to make the same comment hurt like a new one." She eventually gave in to the pressure to play basketball and found it helped her wade out of a sea of depression during her high school years.

"I grew out of my awkward stage, found my voice, embraced my uniqueness and built a house of confidence on the foundation my parents had been tirelessly fostering for years," she wrote. "I picked up all of the pieces and built an amazing me. I can't really tell you how it happened, I just know that I am now a strong, tall, beautiful woman that uses every word, good or bad, to empower my path. No matter how it happened for me, please know that it will happen for you too. The broken road you are traveling on leads right to the YOU that you want to be. Every crack, bump and pothole will be paved over with extraordinary confidence. Take knowledge from every word of the weak and use it to walk taller."

5

So, Where Do I Put My Legs?

As we're debating whether or not it's good to be tall, most of these questions admittedly are somewhat, well, ... debatable.

That applies to health benefits, success in business, success in politics, relative intelligence, human attraction and assorted other things. There is one area where there is absolutely no doubt: There is no question that when it comes to comfort in almost any sort of setting—and the accompanying cost—tall people get the short end of the stick.

That 5'5" guy probably never has had his knees bruised and battered and pushed up into his lap while riding on an airplane. He never has had to fold up his body into an uncomfortable, unwieldy pretzel in order to get into an automobile. He's never had his feet dangle off the end of the bed in a hotel. He never had urine splashed back on him because he neglected to squat slightly while standing at a urinal. He always has been able to buy inexpensive clothes straight off the rack in virtually any store. And all of the stuff he buys—clothes, cars, furniture, transportation—can be had for the normal price without needing to shell out extra in order to get something that actually suits his needs.

He probably doesn't realize just how lucky he is.

Even in the tallest country in the world, not enough is being done to comfortably accommodate the tall. According to a 2011 editorial in the British newspaper *The Guardian*, the Netherlands' Klub Lange Mensen (Tall People's Club) voiced loud objections, stating that "leg space on trains, trams and buses is insufficient. Airlines are not interested in delivering service to a minority group who have trouble sitting in their seats. The automotive industry is largely unconcerned by sitting comfort (for tall people); bicycle producers only serve tall people in their highest price range."

The Dutch government did alter its building codes to stipulate that door frames must be at least 7 feet, 6½ inches high, more than 10 inches higher than in the United States. And there have been some industries worldwide that have made small progress toward meeting the needs of those of us who are taller than average.

But there is one place where the quest to accommodate tall folks seemingly has taken backward steps. Some airlines, in a quest to make more money, have actually tightened the parameters inside their planes to squeeze in more people and make life even more miserable for those of us with elongated legs.

"As airlines around the world search for higher revenues and increased profitability, the effect on the passenger experience has not been overly positive, to say the least," Benjamin Zhang noted in a story on Businessinsider.com in 2016. "Even though airliners have not been getting any larger, their passenger carrying capacity has been growing steadily. Airlines have achieved this by cutting down the size of lavatories and the amount of room between seats."

The *Washington Post* pointed out the same thing in a 2014 story: "Airlines across the country have pushed for years for denser, more lucrative cabins—and jet makers are unveiling innovative new ways to cram more passengers into shrinking seats."

Seth Kaplan, an analyst for *Airline Weekly*, said that what he calls "densification" is a glaringly obvious trend in the airline industry. "And it's accelerated with the fact that flights are much fuller than they used to be," he added. "Back in the days when flights were two-thirds full, who cared how many seats were onboard?"

Unfortunately, it's an area where tall consumers have very little recourse. There are dozens—perhaps hundreds—of companies that now make clothes for tall people so there is plenty of competition there to compete for the tall person's dollar. It's a similar situation with the auto industry. Companies are endeavoring to improve the legroom in their vehicles in order to get into our pockets.

There are relatively few major airlines, so for those of us who are interested in flying somewhere, the airlines often have us over a barrel. (Or, more accurately, are trying to cram us *into* a barrel.) If you're flying to New York, Chicago or Atlanta, you have a fair number of airline options. If you're going to Syracuse, Spokane or Moline, you best be prepared to be icing your knees for a few weeks afterward.

This is a hot button issue with tall people. A random post about the lack of legroom in air travel on a site such as Reddit routinely gets hundreds of posts within a day or so. Over-heighted people quickly get over-heated when this subject arises. And there is very little reasonable recourse for us.

One alternative is to always fly first class or business class, where the space between the seats is ample enough to accommodate even the lengthiest of us. But you're also going to pay three or four times the cost for those seats. For most of us, that doesn't fit into our budgets any more than we fit into these planes.

Another way to get some extra legroom is to nab one of those rare exit row seats. However, those spots always seem to be snapped up by people who don't really need them. I can't tell you how many times I've had to try to jam my 6'6¾" frame into a seat with my knees up to my chin while the spacious exit row seat was occupied by some gray-haired 4'11" grandma who could have fit into the overhead compartment. I always cringe when the flight attendant comes around and asks those in the exit row if they're able to assist in the case of an emergency. You just know we're all going to die in that case because there is no way grandma is going to be strong enough to assist any of us.

I've heard tales of people paying extra to snag an exit row seat only to have the airline bump them back to a normal seat when someone paid more than them. Some tall people have tried to claim their height as a disability and maneuver their way into the exit row that way. There even have been people on social media who claimed to have success at getting into the exit row by subtly bribing or sweet-talking gate agents. They notice that the agent is sipping on a soft drink so they go and buy them a free one and try to finagle their way into a roomier seat that way.

From my experience, very little of that works most of the time. The airlines really don't care about me or my mashed knees.

At one time, it seemed the airlines were starting to look out for the big guy. In 1981, KLM Royal Dutch Airlines began offering extra legroom for passengers in its business class at no extra charge. It later allied with Northwest Airlines to offer the same thing in the United States, providing what it advertised as 50 percent more room. In the early 1990s, TWA became the first airline to develop something it called "comfort" class, which offered more legroom than regular coach class. Some of its competitors, including United, followed suit. It's what happens in the airline industry. If one of the big dogs does something that seems to be popular, all the other puppies follow along and do the same thing.

KLM also once had an agreement with Klub Lange Mensen to give tall people preferential treatment, allocating the seats with the most legroom for them. But it eventually did away with that practice after claims of discrimination from non-tall people.

There were a few other short-lived attempts to provide more spacious accommodations. Eva Air of Taiwan began offering what it called "evergreen class" or "elite class" in 1991 and a few other airlines copied that. In 2003, a new airline called MAXJet offered business class seating that provided an astonishing 60 inches of legroom with seats that reclined almost to a horizontal position. It was based at Washington-Dulles International Airport, only provided service to London, New York, Los Angeles and Las Vegas, and was very pricey, but it was an option. The airline survived for fewer than five years, filing for bankruptcy late in 2007.

Then the arrow started moving in the opposite direction.

Human growth expert Thomas Samaras, who has spent decades insisting that human beings need to find a way to get smaller, wrote in his 1994 book that an aircraft that held 200 passengers could—and presumably should—be modified to hold 110 more people just by reducing the space between seats. We're not blaming this on Samaras. Chances are, most airline executives never read his book, but in the years that followed most of them began doing exactly what he proposed. With the twists and turns in the economy and the growing popularity of air travel, there has been a horrifying trend toward less legroom in airplanes.

Henry H. Harteveldt, a travel industry analyst at the Atmosphere Research Group, said that in most planes the average pitch—the space between seats—dropped from around 33 to 34 inches before 2001 to about 30 to 31 inches. Some airlines now are down to 28 inches, which is the industry minimum. I can tell you from personal experience that even the 34-inch seats are a bit of a squeeze for someone who is 6'6¾". At 30 inches, one of my knees is jutted out into the aisle where the flight attendant can hammer it with her cart and the other knee is ... well, you don't want to be sitting next to me in that plane.

In 2017, it was reported that American Airlines was going to reduce the pitch in many of its economy class seats by a full two inches, down to an average of about 31 inches. In some of its Boeing 737 models, it was going to get down to 30 or possibly even 29, which allowed them to add about a dozen passengers to the plane. It also was reported that American was planning to cut down the size of its restrooms, which already were roughly the size of the linen closet in our upstairs hallway. (I suspect most tall people have learned to do what I do. Just before boarding the plane, I hit the restroom in the terminal. The last thing I want is to be forced to use the facilities in an airplane.)

Of course, with American making those changes, you know what was likely to happen. We don't really know how many other airlines followed along and also chopped down the pitch in their planes, but you can bet many of them did.

As Jon Ostrower reported on CNN.com in 2017, "As the big airlines match each other move for move, the risk is that 29 inches becomes the standard for flying economy in the United States."

Some smaller regional airlines already were cramming their customers into very close quarters, with some of them already offering that bare minimum 28-inch space.

Fortunately, Trip Advisor has an absolutely fabulous website called SeatGuru, which details the exact parameters for every plane being used on every airline. If you want to know the pitch on the Boeing 737s being used by Transavia Airlines, you can find it there, along with the width of the seats and any other available amenities.

According to SeatGuru, there were 16 airlines worldwide that had seats with that minimum 28-inch pitch in 2022. Most of them were small, regional outfits such as Wizz Air, based in Hungary, and Scoot, which is based in Singapore and operates only in southeast Asia and Australia. Both of those airlines had primarily 28-inch seats for their short-haul economy seats.

Almost all of those planes were Airbus A319, A320 or A321 models. It has been reported that the French-made Airbus A320 was originally designed to hold 150 passengers but was reconfigured to accommodate 186.

Those smaller regional airlines freely admit that their accommodations aren't as spacious, pointing out that it allows them to keep their costs down. It's like my wife tells me almost daily, you get what you pay for.

Former Spirit Airlines chief executive Ben Baldanza, whose airline had its share of 28-inch pitches, put it pretty succinctly in 2013:

"You don't get a Mercedes S Class for a Ford Fusion price. If you want more legroom—go pay for it at another airline."

Spirit later introduced special contoured seats that allegedly have more "usable" legroom. Current CEO Ted Christie, who is 6'2", said he thought seat pitch was an outdated measure of legroom and that he always has plenty of legroom when he flies on his own airline.

Fortunately, there did not appear to be any airlines anywhere in the world in 2022 that had a 28-inch pitch on any of their long-haul flights. Not yet, anyway.

Although American Airlines attracted some negative publicity for its decision to reduce the pitch in some planes in 2017, there doesn't appear to be much difference between the three big U.S. carriers—American, United and Delta. According to SeatGuru, all of them have some seats as tight as 30 inches but they also still have some in the 34 to 35 range and a few economy seats even roomier than that.

Like we said, though, if you're really tall, even that 34-inch pitch can be a pain. We're not going to be really comfortable in an airplane unless we spring for first class, where the pitch generally is more than double what it is in economy.

In 2015, the U.S. Department of Transportation held public hearings with a consumer advisory committee to determine whether there were safety issues in cramming too many passengers into planes. Some committee members pointed out that while there were minimum space standards for dogs flying as cargo, there were no such restrictions for humans. It doesn't seem as though the hearings accomplished much. Most planes are still veritable sardine cans for those of us who are tall.

As if things aren't already cramped enough for many of us on planes, we inevitably get seated behind some snot-nosed kid who insists upon reclining his seat, inflicting further damage on our knees. It has become enough of a problem that a few airlines, including Spirit, disabled the recline feature from their seats although most still allow it.

This unpleasant experience prompted a man named Ira Goldman to come up with one of the greatest inventions in human history: The Knee Defender.

Goldman, who was 6'4", traveled extensively as an aide to former California governor and U.S. senator Pete Wilson, and he grew tired of having his knees mashed. So, he devised a plastic block that prevented the passenger in front of him from reclining his or her seat. The Knee Defender worked only when the tray table was in the down position. It fit around the arm of the table, thereby restricting the seat from moving backward.

Goldman initially had 1,000 Knee Defenders made and quickly sold them for $10 apiece. He had more manufactured and began selling them for $21.95.

Needless to say, there were many people who objected to his innovation. The Federal Aviation Administration determined that the device did not violate any FAA rules and left it to individual airlines to judge whether or not to allow it. Obviously, since the tray table must be up during takeoffs and landings and when the plane is taxiing, it could not be used then and many airlines also eventually banned the Knee Defender from being used at all.

There was at least one instance of the device causing a major ruckus on a flight. A man used it on a United flight from Newark to Denver in 2014, causing the woman in front of him to become extremely angry when she could not recline her seat. When the man refused to remove his Knee Defender, the woman threw a cup of water in his face. The flight ended up making an unscheduled landing in Chicago, where both passengers were removed from the plane.

In the weeks that followed, there were more in-air incidents related to reclining seats. A flight from Paris to Miami had to be diverted as did one from New York to West Palm Beach.

USA Today published a travel piece in 2019 in which it implored air travelers to simply refrain from reclining their seats for the sake of peace and harmony, stating that it's "unacceptable because we're officially out of space."

"There's no space to recline," the story continued. "Airlines are trying to squeeze more passengers on a plane to make more money.... Airlines are stacking you into a plane like cargo—no two ways about it." The story also quoted retired Air Force inspector Larry Hickerson as saying that all airlines should disable the recline function on all planes, saying the tightened pitches set up "an untenable situation."

Airplanes aren't the only place where legroom is being trimmed. It also is happening in some places on buses, which never have been noteworthy for spaciousness.

But it would seem that, unlike the airlines, complaints are being heard and sometimes heeded by bus companies. When New York City rolled out a new fleet of express transit buses in December 2020, they were configured to accommodate wheelchair access. The result was a drastic reduction in legroom, especially on the driver's side of the bus. One woman who was 5'8" complained in an interview that she was bumping her knees on the seat in front of her. If the 5'8" person is squeezed, can you imagine what a 6'6¾" guy would be going through?

The MTA received enough complaints that it quickly moved to renovate 257 buses to restore them to the amount of legroom that was provided on older buses.

The Greyhound bus company, which dates back to 1914 and serves 2,400 destinations in North America, claims on its website that it has made an effort to increase legroom. It states that in its newest buses, an entire row of seats has been removed to permit a little extra space, adding parenthetically that "our bus designers must have been really tall."

We won't even get into the topic of school buses. If you've ever ridden on one as an adult, you know what we're talking about. It makes Wizz Air and Scoot Airlines seem spacious. School buses originally were configured to hold 41 people, but when some corporate genius realized they were being used primarily for children, most of them were expanded to 57 seats within the same amount of space.

It's actually difficult to find information about legroom for train travel but for lengthy trips it appears to be better than on airplanes. That's good because a trip that takes a few hours in the air can take days on the train.

We've seen various reports that the seat pitch in long-haul Amtrak trains is anywhere from 42 to 52 inches with local commuter trains obviously being considerably tighter. After Amtrak lost a reported $227 million in 2016, it hired former Delta Airlines CEO Richard Anderson as its new president and he hired several other former airline executives to fill high-level positions. That prompted fears that the pitch reductions that took place in the airline industry might also be enacted in trains, but it's not clear if that happened.

Meanwhile, legroom in automobiles seemingly is moving in the right direction as far as tall folks are concerned. Once upon a time, you had to buy an oversized sedan or a gas-guzzling van in order to have enough space for your limbs. But now legroom can be easily found in smaller, more fuel-efficient vehicles.

U.S. News and World Report's list of the best cars for tall people for 2022 didn't include any sedans or vans. Eight of the 13 vehicles on the list were SUVs of various sizes, all with more than 41 inches of legroom and 41 inches of headroom. Also included were four pickup trucks—two full-size and two compacts—and one crossover, the Subaru Ascent.

There also are plenty of sedans out there that offer ample room for tall people, including the Hyundai Sonata, the Chevrolet Impala, the Nissan Altima and the Kia Optima. (I actually drive a 2019 Sonata that has a whopping 45.5 inches of legroom and a respectable 40.4 inches of headroom.) You can even find really small cars that get 50-plus miles per gallon that are relatively height-friendly. The Kia Picanto has 42.1 inches of legroom and 39.4 inches of headroom. There are very few cars out there these days that won't accommodate a 6-footer with some degree of comfort, certainly nothing as suffocating as the Volkswagen Beetle my brother had back in the early 1970s.

There is one thing the auto industry has yet to address. While legroom and headroom seem to have improved, there still is a problem with the line of vision in some vehicles. Most of us who are tall have had the experience of coming to a stoplight and needing to crane our necks downward in order to see if the light is red or green because our head extends above the roofline. If we could sit lower or have the windshield extend higher, we'd be able to see the light with no problem.

All in all, though, the auto industry has responded much more to our needs and desires through the years than the airlines have.

Legroom obviously is an issue in more than just transportation. It also can be a problem in theaters, arenas, stadiums or almost any venue in which large numbers of people are crammed into a relatively small area.

When Moline, Illinois, opened a new civic center and arena in 1993, I was dispatched along with the shortest member of our newspaper staff to see how we fit into the seats. As it was a new facility, the legroom wasn't too bad but that was largely because of the incline of the seating. My knees didn't bash into the seat in front of me. They generally extended out *over* the seat in front of me.

Generally speaking, the older the facility, the better chance you have of needing to fold up your legs to wedge into a seat. As a baseball fan from way back, I had a chance to see games in a few of the old ballparks that no longer exist and had nightmarish experiences trying to sit comfortably in those places. Old Tiger Stadium in Detroit may have been the worst, even for the players. The roofs of the dugouts in that place were so low that if you were taller than about 5'6", you could not stand up straight without bashing your noggin. The legroom in the stands was equally painful.

The two old parks that have survived from that era—Fenway Park in Boston and Wrigley Field in Chicago—have been reconfigured somewhat so that they're not much tighter in terms of legroom than the new parks that are being built.

Bob Kaupang, who runs Bob's Baseball Tours out of Redwood Falls, Minnesota, is probably as familiar as anyone with the types of seating in major league stadiums and he said there actually are some newer sections of Fenway that are better than anything in many of the new parks. "If you don't want to feel as claustrophobic, get pavilion seating ..." he said. "There's less traffic all around you and there's more room."

Kaupang, who was once 6'4" but jokes that he now is closer to 6'2", said the legroom varies widely in the sport's newer ballparks and it's very often a case of getting what you pay for. If a tall person buys the cheap seats, he's likely to feel pretty miserable for most of the game. If you get the expensive seats, you may be able to walk out of the place without a noticeable limp.

There is one more area where we tall folks don't fit well and that's in the area of furniture, especially beds.

A standard double bed is 54 inches wide and 74 inches long, which obviously doesn't work if you're taller than 6 feet. That's why we now see more and more queen and king size beds.

Northwestern University made big news in 1960 when it installed new beds in its residence halls that were 80 inches long to replace its old 74-inch models.

Standard queen and king beds in the United States both are 80 inches long (6 feet, 8 inches) with the only difference being the width. A queen is 60 inches wide, a king 76. However, the dimensions may be slightly different elsewhere in the world. For example, a king in India is 85 inches long with other kings being as short as 75.

There also is something called a California king, which is four inches longer but four inches narrower than a standard king, at 72 by 84. The origins of the California king are subject to dispute but it appears they came into existence when a Los Angeles company began making extra-large beds for celebrity mansions in the 1960s.

At around the same time, one San Francisco hotel began putting a 7-foot long bed in every room with a number ending in 7.

Most mattress manufacturers now carry the larger sizes but a king size or California king mattress or box spring typically costs about 50 percent more than for a queen or double bed.

It is possible to get beds even larger than that. There is something called a Wyoming king, which is 84 inches by 84 inches. A Texas king is really great for tall people at 80 by 98. And there even is an Alaska king, which generally is 108 by 108. Of course, you better have a pretty spacious master suite to accommodate a bed that is 9 feet wide and 9 feet long.

Those special big beds are really pricey and often need to be custom made. You're not likely to find a Texas king mattress for less than $2,000 or an Alaska king for less than $4,000. And that's just for the mattress. You'll also pay extra for the frame, box spring, sheets, comforter, etc.

6

What Am I Supposed to Wear?

I like to refer to it as the great growth spurt of 1970–72. It changed my life, altered the way I thought and irrevocably tweaked my view of the world. It also did a total makeover on my wardrobe and, as a result, it put a big, fat, ugly dent in my pocketbook.

Up to that point, I always had been a tad on the short side. My parents started me in school when I was only 4 years old so I was younger than almost all of my classmates and typically a bit shorter than the average kid in the class. I never was the runt of the bunch but I was closer to that end of the scale than the tall end.

When I graduated from high school in 1971, I was 6'2" and 160 pounds, tall enough to retrieve things off the top shelf for my 5'3" mom but not so tall that I couldn't walk into pretty much any store and find all the clothing I needed in my size. Then I grew. A lot. It's as if I took off my cap and gown one day at 6'2", 160, and woke up the next morning 6'6", 220. Obviously, it didn't happen quite that quickly but it was a pretty radical growth spurt. When I enrolled in college the following fall, nothing fit. Pants that previously were down around my ankles looked like capris. I always looked like I was wearing three-quarter sleeve shirts. I used to roll up the sleeves so people couldn't tell just how short they were.

I didn't have a ton of money for new clothes—my father had died within the previous year—and I couldn't find clothes that fit me anyway. Where I previously could walk into Kmart or Zayre (anyone remember that chain?) and buy almost anything I needed, I couldn't find much of anything that worked on my suddenly oversized body.

I got through it somehow, but it wasn't easy. I learned the hard way that finding apparel for a taller-than-normal frame was very difficult. I had to take clothes that didn't really fit well and make them work. And when I did find something that fit reasonably well, I found out it was going to come with an extra cost.

New York Times columnist Russell Baker touched on this in his aforementioned malicious whine column of 1978. He said any time he went to buy a suit, sales clerks would show him endless racks of beautiful garments all tailored to fit normal-sized people while the one suit the store had that was even close to fitting him appeared to have been "cut from a horse blanket."

Arianne Cohen recalled in her 2009 book for tall people—*The Tall Book*—how challenging it was to find clothes for her 6'3" frame. She said her daily routine in high school involved "picking the eye-liner and earrings and scarves and nail polish that went with the man's pants." Her shopping strategy, she said, was "if it fits, I own it."

She at least had the option of finding some clothes large enough for her body even if they may have been designed for a different gender. That wasn't an option for the oversized man 50 years ago.

Fortunately, times have changed considerably. There now are thousands of options for tall people to find fashionable clothing in their size. Very often, the price still is steep but at least we have options.

There actually have been stores that catered to larger bodies for more than a century although it's only in the past decade or two that the market has blossomed as retailers learned that even though really tall people are relatively rare, it's a market in which they can make a few bucks.

An Ibisworld market research report in 2021 indicated that plus-size clothing stores were a $849 million industry and that only included brick-and-mortar facilities, not all the independent firms that have popped up on the Internet. *Women's Wear Daily* reported that just the men's big and tall industry was looking at about $10 billion in sales in 2021.

KingSize, now based in Indianapolis, was one of the first companies to offer clothing for "big and tall" men when it was founded in 1920. Probably the largest chain now is Destination XL (aka DXL), which is based in Canton, Massachusetts, and has more than 250 stores in the United States. It has its roots in a company called Designs, Inc., founded in 1976 by Calvin Margolis and Stanley Berger, and through the years it bought other similar chains such as Casual Male Big & Tall (in 2002) and Rochester Big & Tall (in 2004).

It opened its first store under the DXL flag in Schaumburg, Illinois, in 2010. For fiscal year 2021, it reported $505 million in sales.

But DXL president and chief executive officer Harvey Kanter told *Women's Wear Daily* in 2022 that the big and tall market in the United States is "highly fragmented. There are many retailers who dabble in big and tall, offering a piecemeal product here and there to a traditionally underserved customer," he added.

There are a few other big players in the market. Westport Big & Tall, founded by Tom Altieri and Bob Beausoleil in Westport, Connecticut, in 1989, reportedly now carries clothing from more than 20 countries and ships to customers in more than 200 countries.

But like DXL and KingSize, it caters to the "big and tall" market, and there is a reason the big comes before the tall in the company names. You can find pants on their websites for men with a 72-inch waist and shirts that are 9XL but sometimes the pants may only come in a 32-inch inseam. And even when items are marked as "tall," they are labeled as being for someone taller than 6'2". If you're really tall, like 6'6¾", they may not have much to choose from.

Many mainstream clothing companies now offer at least something for the tall person. You can find tall sizes—usually at higher prices—at a wide variety of stores. ASOS, Madewell, Nordstrom's, Target, Ann Taylor, Gap, J. Crew, Athleta, Bonobos, Chadwick's, Aeropostale, Old Navy, TJ Maxx, Banana Republic, New York & Company, Levi's, Land's End, Loft, Dillard's, J.C. Penney's and Abercrombie & Fitch all carry at least some taller clothing.

But few of them have clothing to fit someone who is very, very tall. Some of them define tall women as being between 5'7" and 5'10". One CEO in the industry said many mainstream retailers view the tall market as an "after-thought." That has spawned hundreds of smaller companies around the globe that have stepped into the niche to focus exclusively on what remains a somewhat underserved market.

The biggest development in the ease of procurement of tall apparel was the advent of the World Wide Web. Opening a store in the local strip mall that is only going to cater to perhaps 1 percent of the population just isn't cost-effective. But an independent operator can develop a website to sell apparel online for a fraction of the cost and reach the entire world in the process.

"If you go online instead of as a brick-and-mortar store, you can start as just two tall friends for a couple of thousand dollars and get a pair of t-shirts made and try it out to see if you can get some traction," said Rued Riis, who writes a blog called Tallsome.com that tries to keep track of all the new men's apparel companies that are popping up worldwide. "I think that's how a lot of these companies like Tall Slim Tees and American Tall, all these online stores got started. They began as an experiment to see if they could create a niche that is interesting enough to sell and then they go from there."

Riis has a vested interest in this. He is 6'8". Now in his early 30s, he began sprouting in his mid-teens and embarked on a career in marketing, developing skills in web search maximization. He originally began writing his blog in Danish but was convinced by a friend that he could reach a much wider audience if he did it in English. He kicked it off in 2014 and hardly a week goes by that he doesn't get an Instagram inquiry from some new company seeking a mention. He has seen an explosion in new companies although many of them are very small and somewhat limited in variety.

Denmark's Rued Riis has become an expert on the clothing options available to tall people and blogs regularly on the subject (courtesy RuedRiis.com).

"I think there's a pretty good supply of brands now but I think a lot of the brands have very similar clothing ranges," he said. "It's very often black, white and blue, and they start with very basic styles because they can't afford anything else. They don't have the huge mainstream markets to just test all sorts of patterns and designs and have styles flop. They can't afford that so because they're already a niche, they go for a very mainstream design that anyone wants."

Riis said the larger, mainstream companies sometimes offer more diverse styles even though they aren't strictly dedicated to the tall market. They have the financial backing to take more chances and possibly do things that are more colorful and daring.

There was a time, Riis said, when most tall customers were just happy to find a shirt long enough to cover their belly button and slacks long enough to cover their ankles. But the proliferation of smaller, boutique outlets has made them more selective. "Tall people know that there is a supply out there and they can get nice clothing that fits and is higher quality," he added. "So we're not as needy as 10 years ago."

There now are new sites popping up all over the place, many of which reflect the style indigenous to their part of the world.

Medium Tall began in Norway in 2015 making only t-shirts in the basement of the two co-founders, both of whom were 6'3". The company went full bore in November 2020 with the funding provided by 77 of their most loyal customers. All of them now own a piece of the business, which gradually has branched out into things other than t-shirts.

Highleytall.com launched in January 2011 in the Netherlands, selling mostly goods made by other companies. It branched out into women's clothing in 2013.

Son of a Tailor, based in Denmark, is a unique company that sells clothing made to order for the tall customer. CEO Jess Fleischer said that while many companies have done a good job keeping up with fashion trends, he feels the entire clothing industry is "100 years behind in supply chain innovation." There is a better chance that clothing from Son of a Tailor will fit, but it's also a little more costly.

A company called 2Tall began in Aberdeen, Scotland, in 2010, advertising apparel for men 6'3" to 7'4". The founder is 7'0" but the guy who runs the company on a day-to-day basis is only 6'9". "Just to make it clear, we're not a big and tall store," 2Tall says on its website. "We create clothing for slim and athletically built tall men. Clothing that makes a tall guy feel confident in how he looks. It's that simple. It shouldn't be a rarity to find clothing that fits."

A company called Navas Lab was named by the brother-and-sister co-founders after their pet cat. It claims to make clothes for men 6'2" and taller who weigh less than 250 pounds with all of its products being milled and manufactured in Canada.

Another relatively new company called American Tall also ironically is based in Canada. It was launched early in 2016 by the father-and-son duo Saul Rajsky and Jake Rajsky, who previously worked for other clothing companies but were frustrated by the resistance they met every time they suggested targeting the tall market. Against the advice of almost everyone they knew, they started their new brand with just a few styles, then gradually expanded their offerings, eventually getting into women's apparel. They carry slim-fitting clothes for men as tall as 7'2" and women as tall as 6'6".

"When your market consists of only 1 percent of the population, you can view that as an extremely difficult challenge, or you can take pride in the knowledge that your market is made up of the elite few who live above the masses, who appreciate simple pleasures that others take for granted," American Tall says on its website. "Simple pleasures like sleeves that extend all the way down your arms without being attached to a shirt that billows like a tent, or pants that fit your long legs all the way down, not just to the ankles."

All of those companies are online only. There are no brick-and-mortar locations.

For tall women, there seldom has been many brick-and-mortar clothing stores, even back in the old days. In the 1950s, there was a chain of women's tall shops called Over Five-Seven that was sprinkled across the United States, but they long ago disappeared.

But there may be even more relatively new online outlets for women's clothing than there are for men. Fit expert Jessica Couch said in a 2019 article in *Women's Wear Daily* that women often have been forced to choose between fit and fashion, seldom being able to find both.

"Tall is a tough problem," she said. "Because a lot of time when you think tall, you think, 'Let's just stretch it out.' That's not the best way to go. You have to really understand what type of bodies you're dealing with."

A company called Long Tall Sally began selling all types of clothes only for women 5'8" and taller in London in 1976 and opened a few dozen stores, mostly in Europe with a few locations in North America. "It's a really difficult niche to do well," president and CEO Andrew Chapin said in 2014. "The biggest issue is fit. The greatest challenge is finding pants that fit. We sell a lot more bottoms than tops."

The company has endured some tough times, especially during the COVID-19 pandemic. It announced in June 2020 that it was closing its doors, but then it was purchased by another company and remains in business today, doing much of its business now online.

New York–based Alloy Apparel has offered both big and tall clothing for women since 1996—where else can you get something that is 25XL or a dress that is 63 inches long?—and remains one of the big players in the industry.

In their wake, legions of smaller outfits have entered the market, most of them developed by individuals frustrated by their inability to find clothes that didn't just cover their bodies but actually fit in a flattering way.

Amalli Talli was started by sisters Amy Rosenthal and Alli Black, a pair of former college volleyball players. They began with an actual store in Minneapolis but now sell only online and claimed to have had a 300-percent increase in sales between 2018 and 2019. Amy, who is 6'4", recalled the anguish of trying to find a basic pair of khakis when she was in the marching band in high school. "I remember just having the biggest meltdown in the dressing room and telling my mom that there was just something really wrong with me," she said.

Another company, Simply Tall, also began as a physical store in Ohio in 2004, but five years later, it converted to selling only through its website. Founder Nicole Fox is 6'1" and was seeking a solution to "my shopping frustration combined with my desire to go back to work after the birth of my first child."

Talltique.com is the brainchild of another 6'4" woman, Helen Pappas. She is another of those brave women who thumbed her nose at the suggestion that she play basketball, and after many years of working in customer service jobs and struggling to find clothing she liked, she found her calling with her own company. She began selling clothes out of her home in 2011 and by 2013 had set up a showroom in Bethesda, Maryland. "My dream is not only to make tall women look, and feel, beautiful in their clothes. It is also to change how tall teens and women feel about their bodies, through allowing them to look fabulous in perfectly proportioned clothes," she said in a blog on the company's site. "Like so many other tall women, I grew up struggling to accept my body and my height. This discomfort came from the blatant stares of strangers, which was compounded by the fear that the ill-fitting and short clothes I wore only drew further negative attention."

Halfway around the world, another tall woman chose to create a company as a result of her shopping frustrations. Natalie Mathews, who is 6'3", grew up in Kent, England, then moved to Melbourne, Australia, in 2013 and struggled to find clothes that worked for her. She had taught herself how to sew her own clothes when she was 14, making her own dresses for school dances, and finally launched Height of Fashion a few years ago. "I understand how tall women can feel insecure about themselves," she said in a 2018 *London Daily Mail* article. "I know how women can shy away from expressing themselves in fashion because they are exceptionally tall. Too many tall women are feeling frumpy with bland fashion available but I want taller women to feel empowered by stylish clothes and to feel sexy.... There's lots of plus size clothing but I think they have forgotten about the tall women."

Finding larger-than-normal shoes, especially for women, is a whole other problem with even fewer options. Most of those new, emerging e-commerce sites haven't gotten into footwear. At least not yet. Companies such as Zappos and Nordstrom and websites such as bigshoes.com offer some extra large sizes and there are a handful of firms, including Nike, that will custom-make shoes of almost any size. As you can imagine, though, the price tag for those is steep.

There are a few sites that specialize in larger-than-normal shoes, including Apavi 40+, which has been selling online since 2010. The company also has a brick-and-mortar store, but to visit it, you need to go to Riga, Latvia.

Some women with exceptionally large feet even have gone to a site called Shoecup.com, which sells shoes for cross-dressers and drag queens. It carries feminine styles made to fit the feet of men. Sometimes you've got to do what you've got to do.

Kae Sumner Einfeldt, who founded the organization that became Tall Clubs International, identified one other solution in the 1930s. Three words: open-toed sandals. A precise fit wasn't as vital with those. Of course, Kae lived in Southern California. That solution wouldn't work as well for someone living in a colder climate.

7

You Must Play Basketball, Right?

Whenever I am asked question No. 2 of the standard trilogy, I have to pause and think about how I'm going to respond. "Did you play basketball?" The answer is sort of complicated.

Sometimes I say yes. Sometimes I say no. I used to try and concoct some big, fabricated tale about being a second-team All-American at Podunk A&M, but I've never been a very good liar. I usually end up telling the truth, which may be just as interesting anyway.

The short answer is yes. And no. Yes, I played basketball much of my life. We had a hoop on the garage in the alley behind our house when I was a kid growing up in the Chicago suburb of Maywood. I was out there all the time firing up shots that only occasionally went through the net. But no, I never really played on an organized team at the high school or college level even though I ended up being 6'6¾" and remain intensely interested in the game to this day.

This requires some explanation. As mentioned in a previous chapter, I was a notoriously late bloomer. In the eighth grade, I was a swarthy 5'3" and 97 pounds. At Roosevelt Elementary School, we had a lightweight basketball team and a heavyweight basketball team. If the sum of your inches in height and pounds in weight was more than 160, you were a heavyweight. I wasn't even the tallest kid on the lightweight team.

Maywood was a basketball-crazy town, home of Proviso East High School, which won the Illinois state title during my sophomore year. The star of that team was Jim Brewer, who went on to be the Big Ten's player of the year at Minnesota, a member of the 1972 Olympic team and a 9-year veteran of the National Basketball Association. His brother-in-law was Grady Rivers, who worked with my dad as a police officer and whose own son, Glenn (later known as Doc), was destined to take his place in the pantheon of Proviso East greats. I used to walk down 19th Avenue to Winfield Scott Park and watch Brewer play pickup games but I was a slow-footed shrimp who never would have dreamed of getting into those games. Playing on the same court with Brewer in those days was about as realistic to me as taking a weekend trip to Saturn.

During high school, we moved a few miles west to another suburb, Elmhurst, but it was more of the same. York High School was a mammoth school—enrollment 3,600—with a splendid basketball tradition, only a notch below that of Proviso East. I was 6'2", 160 when I graduated and was only a part-time starter for my intramural team. Trying out for the varsity basketball team wasn't even a consideration.

Then the aforementioned growth spurt kicked in and I sprouted during the summer like an overnourished weed. When I was registering for classes at the local junior college—the College of DuPage—in the fall of 1971, an assistant coach spotted me towering above the other kids and asked question No. 2. He didn't ask if I had played for my high school basketball team. He just asked if I played. I couldn't lie. I said yes. He then asked if I wanted to try out for the squad being assembled by new head coach Dick Walters and I eagerly agreed.

Walters was one of those firebrand coaches cut from a similar cloth as one of his contemporaries, Bobby Knight, and he was scrounging up every warm body he could find and grab every edge he could get. I became part of a special, invitation-only "intramural" league that began playing about the time school began. It was a thinly-veiled way to circumvent the rules and get in six weeks of extra practice before the season started. I was thrown in against even bigger, much more experienced players and generally got the crap beat out of me. I never got to play in an actual game, never even suited up for one.

After that brief experience at DuPage, I realized I never was going to play in the NBA and focused my time and energies on writing about basketball rather than playing it. I was much better at that although that short stint with the team at COD made me a much better basketball player in later years after I filled out and reached my full growth of 6'6¾". Just ask the guys who played against me in a recreational league in Woodstock, Illinois, in 1977 and 1978. I dominated there.

Anyway, that's my answer to question No. 2. I told you it was complicated.

It illustrates the fact that just being tall, even if you have very little else going for you, opens doors in the sport of basketball.

It all makes sense. Basketball is all about putting a ball through an iron hoop that is 10 feet off the ground. To do that, you need to shoot upward so if the obstacle in front of you is 6'6¾" instead of, say, 5'10", it becomes infinitely more difficult. And after you miss the shot, the taller guy has a certain advantage in rebounding the errant shot. Excessive height can mask deficiencies in speed and skill and as such always has been at a premium in the game.

But size doesn't just open doors in basketball. It sometimes forces people to walk through those doors whether they really want to or not. There is an inherent expectation that just because you're tall, you *must* play basketball.

If you dive deep into the internet, you can find a WordPress blog from many years ago in which the writer stated that any man who was 6'6" or taller who was not a professional athlete was a WOH—a waste of height. He referred to a 7'0" basketball player who did not begin playing until his junior year of high school and only played a few games in the NBA, and said, "For that, his parents should be ashamed." That's the sort of twisted mindset many tall folks encounter. It's not OK to pursue your individual interests and passions. Basketball is an obligation, not a choice. By that blogger's definition, I was a WOH.

My daughter had plenty of experience with this. She was asked almost every day of her high school years if she played basketball and when she said no, question No. 3 very often was "Why not?" She loved dancing and when she suffered an ankle injury in that endeavor one day, we took her to our friendly neighborhood orthopedic surgeon, who immediately assumed she had gotten hurt throwing up a skyhook or taking a charge. She told the doctor she didn't hurt it playing basketball so he went for an alternate question No. 3: "Oh, I guess it is more volleyball season, isn't it?"

She did actually play a little basketball and volleyball in junior high, mostly to humor Dad, I suspect. But she ultimately put her focus on dancing. That's what she had done since the age of 3 and that's all she really wanted to do. It was her passion and she was very good at it. She became the only girl from her high school to make Iowa's All-State Honor Dance Team three times and her photo now hangs in the lobby of the school gym even though she never nabbed a single rebound. That still didn't defuse the basketball questions. It didn't help that the girls basketball team at her high school went 0–19 in her senior year. People made her feel as though it was her duty to play the sport and I'll forever admire the way in which she politely thumbed her nose at those expectations.

I know plenty of other kids who haven't been as successful at repelling the expectations. During my years of writing about sports, there was a young man at West High School in Davenport, Iowa, named Eric McPherson. Great kid. Wonderful kid. Big-hearted. Bright. Talented, especially musically. He sang in the chorus at his high school and in church. He played the trumpet in the marching band.

He didn't really know or care very much about sports, but when he was 5'11" in the seventh grade and then grew 10 more inches the following year, he really didn't have a choice. The world around him wasn't going to let him *not* play basketball.

He thought it might be fun so he tried it. He had grown so fast that he was very uncoordinated. It happens a lot with people who go through rapid growth spurts. It sometimes takes years for their natural coordination to catch up with the radical transformation of their bodies. Their skeletal framework grows at an accelerated pace and their muscles struggle to develop as quickly as their bones, making them very clumsy and sometimes prone to injury.

"It was really hard in the beginning," McPherson told me for a story I wrote about him in 2000. "I grew so fast that my coordination was completely thrown off. They had me doing special drills just to try to get my coordination."

McPherson, who topped out at 7'3", worked tirelessly in the gym to do even the most basic things, like dribbling and making a layup. He gave it everything he had but never really got to be very good at it. I vaguely recall that he scored just a handful of points in his entire high school basketball career and was ridiculed—seldom to his face but very often behind his back—because he never became very proficient at something I suspect he never really wanted to do very badly anyway.

His story is hardly unique. A lot of people who didn't really view basketball as the doorway to their future were pushed through it, and some of them actually prospered in it more than McPherson did.

Case in point: George Mikan. As a kid growing up in Joliet,

Illinois, in the 1920s and 1930s, he gave some thought to becoming a priest and really yearned to cultivate a career as a concert pianist.

He never got close to either of those goals and at least part of the reason was the fact that he was huge. As he walked through his neighborhood to go to the Joliet Conservatory of Music for lessons during his boyhood, Mikan frequently was taunted by other kids because of his ungainly size. On at least one occasion, he got into a fight with one of his antagonists and the other boy was momentarily knocked unconscious when he fell. Mikan, who never wanted to be seen as a bully, was horrified. It was the end of his piano career. "I was foolish enough to let myself get laughed out of it," Mikan admitted in a story by Dick Joyce in *The Sports Immortals.*

Over the course of time, he tried to do things to make himself a little less imposing.

"I remember how I used to stoop all the time to make myself look shorter than I really was," he said. "I became round-shouldered, ungainly and so filled with bitterness that my height nearly wrecked my life."

There was a nun at the school he attended who would see Mikan slouching, trying to conceal his height, and she would whack him forcefully on the back to make him stand erect, shouting "Straighten up. The good lord gave you this body. Make the most of it."

Mikan eventually did that but it took some prodding. He didn't begin playing basketball until his junior year at Joliet Catholic High School and he only did it then because his younger brother Ed, who was considerably shorter, loved the sport and coaxed him into it. Mikan eventually transferred to Quigley Prep, a Catholic seminary in Chicago, but one of the priests there recognized that the kid, who by then was 6'7", was simply trying to run away from all the taunting and the other problems that his height caused. While at Quigley, Mikan played for a Catholic Youth Organization basketball team and began to be noticed by some college scouts. He ended up enrolling at DePaul University, where new coach Ray Meyer saw great possibilities in him.

Meyer put Mikan through an intense regimen to enhance his coordination and make him more graceful. He had him skip rope and shadow box for hours at a time. He improved his pivoting skills by placing folding chairs around the basket. If Mikan pivoted the wrong way, he would bang his knees on a chair. Meyer had Mikan do a drill in which he put up layups alternating between his left and

George Mikan (No. 99) overcame insecurities about his height to become the first dominant big man in the sport of basketball (courtesy DePaul University Athletics).

right hand for long periods. The exercise has stood the test of time. Many decades later, University of Iowa center Luka Garza credited the "Mikan drill" with helping him become the national player of the year.

Meyer even made Mikan attend school dances and ordered him

to pick out the shortest, smallest girls he could find to steer around the dance floor, according to a 1999 story in the *Minneapolis-St. Paul Star Tribune*. Meyer figured the kind-hearted big guy would be so conscious of trying not to step on girls' feet and crush them with his size that it would improve his footwork.

All of it clearly helped because Mikan became an All-American at DePaul, leading the country in scoring in both 1945 and 1946, and he embarked on a history-making career in professional basketball. "Once I got rid of my obsession that my height was a frightful bugaboo, I came to realize that for every shortcoming of an oversized body, there is a plus quality to compensate," he said.

Mikan ended up becoming one of the first dominant big men in basketball's formative years of the middle of the 20th century. He had a devastating, unblockable hook shoot and was an imposing force on defense, helping the Minneapolis Lakers become the NBA's first dynasty. He probably provided the impetus for more basketball rule changes than any player ever. The NBA made its lane wider to prevent big men like Mikan from camping in there for too long and it outlawed the practice of goaltending, jumping up to block shots that were on their downward arc. After the Fort Wayne Pistons decided to just hold the ball to keep Mikan from scoring at will in a 1950 game that ended with a 19–18 score, the NBA eventually instituted a 24-second shot clock.

The effectiveness of Mikan and his college rival, 7'0" Bob Kurland of Oklahoma A&M, showed the world what supersized men could accomplish on the basketball court and it opened the door to decades of dominance by big men in the sport. Following in their footsteps was another giant named Wilt Chamberlain, who became even more of a dominating force on the court. But as with so many other oversized basketball players, Chamberlain took up basketball with a bit of reluctance.

Chamberlain not only was very tall—the one and only time he allowed himself to be measured, he checked in at 7 feet, $1\frac{1}{16}$ inches—but he was astonishingly strong and extremely athletic with endless stamina, prompting one observer to call him "the most perfect instrument God made to play basketball."

He scored 100 points in a game during the 1961–62 season and averaged 50.2 points and 25.7 rebounds per game in that campaign, almost certainly the most eye-popping one-year run of any athlete in any sport. He dominated the NBA from 1959 through 1973, averaging 30 points and 23 rebounds per game for his career. His endurance is demonstrated by the fact that he averaged 45.8 minutes played per game in his career. An NBA game is 48 minutes long. Obviously, Chamberlain spent very little time resting on the bench.

And yet, he admitted in his 1973 autobiography that were it not for his extreme size, he probably never would have even considered a career in basketball. As a kid, he viewed basketball as a "sissy" game. Unlike McPherson and Mikan, he had elite athletic gifts and loved track and field. He envisioned himself as someday being an Olympic sprint champion or perhaps a Philadelphia lawyer or race-car driver.

But Chamberlain's body defied genetics and totally altered the path that his life took. His parents both were about 5'9", and although he had one brother who was 6'5", none of his other seven siblings were over 6 feet. He did supposedly have a grandfather who was 7 feet tall, although Chamberlain said he never met him or saw any photos of him and doubted the stories of his height were true.

Chamberlain himself was 29 inches long when he was born and claimed that he grew four inches over a period of less than two months while he was in junior high. He used to get mad when he went to the movies because all of his friends would get in at the children's prices but the ticket sellers never believed Chamberlain when he told them how old he was. He always ended up paying the adult price.

He was 6'11" by the time he enrolled at Overbrook High School in Philadelphia although he only weighed 202 pounds and seemed to be all legs. He had a 41-inch inseam. That led to a lifelong nickname: Wilt the Stilt. As his growth spurt kicked in, he was prone to bumping into things and friends joked that he had to constantly dip down to avoid hitting his head on doorways. That led to another enduring nickname: The Dipper. It helped that Chamberlain's father was a handyman. He eventually renovated the family's home, raising all the light fixtures to accommodate his son.

Although he eventually came to embrace and enjoy his height, Chamberlain may have bristled as much as anyone ever at the mention of questions No. 1 and No. 2.

He really wanted to just blend in with the populace but never was able to do that and hated it when people called attention to his height. A New York hotel once had a 9-foot bed built especially for him and Chamberlain was invited to come to a special public unveiling of it. He turned them down flat. He gladly accepted the bed but refused to become part of the public spectacle.

"What is it with people anyway?" Chamberlain once said. "They see someone extra big and somehow all politeness is off. They seem to think nothing of just grabbing me or walking right up and breaking into a conversation. When I'm eating, they just stand there and watch me eat. I think they regard someone unusual as public property."

Chamberlain ranted about the fascination of height for several pages in his autobiography, talking about the "rude stares and smart-ass questions."

"It's something I've never been able to understand," he said. "Otherwise intelligent people will come up to me in an airport or a restaurant or on the street and ask me, 'How tall are you?' or say, 'Gee, you're sure tall.' They wouldn't in a million years dream of going up to an obviously overweight guy, someone about 300 pounds, and say, 'How much do you weigh?' or 'Gee, you're sure fat.'"

Chamberlain sometimes ignored the questions. Sometimes he would tell people he was 6'13". When they asked if he was a basketball player, he often would tell them he was a jockey. More often, he would just become sullen at the endless questions, leading to a reputation for moodiness.

And it wasn't just the ordinary man on the street who called attention to his size. Chamberlain despised reporters who did so and who cracked jokes about it, especially *Los Angeles Times* columnist Jim Murray.

It even happened sometimes on the basketball court. When Chamberlain played at the University of Kansas, the Jayhawks went up against North Carolina in the 1957 national championship game. Tar Heels coach Frank McGuire sent 5'10" Tommy Kearns out to jump center against Chamberlain to begin the game, a psychological ploy to mock Wilt's size. It seemingly may have had some impact as North Carolina won the game. (Ironically, McGuire was Chamberlain's coach in the NBA during his remarkable 1961–62 season and Kearns later became his stockbroker.)

"As you can see, I feel pretty damn strongly about this whole height question," Chamberlain added in his autobiography rant. "But I don't want to give you the idea that I'm unhappy about being 7 feet tall. I'm not. I'm only distressed by those who make such a big deal out of it, using it to intrude on my privacy and demean and degrade my dignity as a human being."

He said he ultimately found it was mostly fun to be tall and he actually wished he could have been slightly taller.

Following Chamberlain in the succession of ultra-dominant basketball big men was Kareem Abdul-Jabbar. Jabbar, who was born with the name Lew Alcindor, was not as long as Chamberlain was at birth—he was a mere 22½ inches—but he weighed 12 pounds, 11 ounces. The doctor who delivered him allegedly took one look and exclaimed, "Here's a basketball player."

Like Chamberlain, Jabbar attracted often unwanted attention because of his size for his entire life and, according to some reports, was depressed about it as a kid. Over time, however, he defused the depression with an acute deadpan sense of humor. He loved to tell a story about his first day in a new class in elementary school when he did what all tall kids do: He took a seat in the back of the room. The teacher looked out across her class, pointed to him and said, "You, there, sit down." Jabbar's response: "I *am* sitting down."

He was smarter than Chamberlain in at least one respect in dealing with his extreme height. When he went to the movies with friends, he made sure he carried a copy of his birth certificate to prove to ticket sellers he was young enough to get in for the reduced price.

Jabbar didn't immediately take to basketball, trying sports such as baseball, swimming and skating, but with his height, he inevitably was pigeon-holed into basketball and grew to love the game. His story has some parallels to that of Mikan in that he grew up playing in Catholic Youth Organization programs and improved his agility by skipping rope.

By the time he started playing at Power Memorial High School in New York, he was 6'10". He also ran extremely well and had great hands, and he quickly evolved into the most coveted recruit in the country by leading Power Memorial to 71 straight victories. He continued his career in the powerhouse UCLA program, leading the Bruins to an 88–2 record in three years and being named the national player of the year three seasons in a row.

As with Mikan, opponents' inability to stop Jabbar led to rule changes. Following his record-breaking sophomore season in 1967, the NCAA outlawed dunking. Modern-day basketball fans may be flabbergasted to learn that dunking was illegal at both the high school and college levels for 10 years before the rule was reversed in 1977.

Jabbar, who topped out at 7'2", went on to a lengthy career in the NBA, becoming the league's career leader in points scored, being named the MVP six times, and making 19 All-Star teams. He did much more than collect a lot of points. He also made the NBA's all-defensive team 11 times.

But Jabbar constantly resented the notion that he was just an oversized jock. Basketball became his pathway to fame and fortune, but he really yearned to be known for such things as writing, music and social activism. He chose not to try out for the U.S. Olympic team in 1968 as his way of protesting the way Blacks were treated in the United States, and when he made the jump from college to the NBA, he changed his name from Lew Alcindor to Kareem Abdul-Jabbar. He actually converted to Islam when he was still in college but didn't publicly take his new name, which is Muslim for "noble servant of the powerful one," until he turned pro. He dabbled in martial arts and acting, wrote several books about Black history and became an ardent activist for cancer research, earning the Presidential Medal of Freedom in 2016.

Jabbar shared one other thing with Chamberlain. Both men wrote in their autobiographies that their excessive height raised expectations so high that nothing they did on the playing floor seemed to be enough. Both worked very hard to maximize the impact of their God-given physical stature but seldom received full credit for that. Reporters sometimes wrote that Chamberlain underachieved and didn't play hard enough—50 points a game apparently wasn't good enough—and Jabbar faced similar treatment. When he dominated games, some scoffed and said it was only because he was so tall. When he didn't dominate, he was bashed.

It's a fate that plenty of other 7-footers have encountered. Veteran NBA writer Terry Pluto once wrote: "When you're 7-foot and play a game where the accent is on height, fans naturally expect very big things from the biggest men." He added: "A center is supposed to play bigger than life because he seems bigger than life."

Bill Russell, who was Chamberlain's chief rival and who won a record 11 NBA titles in his career, said, "When you're a Big Man, you're expected to do more."

Another NBA writer, Bill Livingston, pointed out in 1983 that some of the sport's most accomplished centers, including

Chamberlain, Bill Walton, Moses Malone and Ralph Sampson, all developed some sort of speech impediment, possibly because of the unreasonable expectations placed upon them.

Jabbar, to his credit, had a droll sense of humor about the whole thing. You've seen the scene in the classic comedy film *Airplane*, right? Jabbar plays the role of co-pilot Roger Murdock and he's chatting with a kid who visits the cockpit and recognizes him as the star center of the Los Angeles Lakers. Jabbar tells the kid he's mistaken but the kid insists he's right.

"I think you're the greatest, but my dad says you don't work hard enough on defense," the youngster tells a visibly agitated Jabbar. "And he says that lots of times, you don't even run down the court. And that you don't really try ... except during the playoffs."

Jabbar responds by grabbing the kid and pulling him closer.

"Listen, kid, I've been hearing that crap ever since I was at UCLA," he snaps. "I'm out there busting my buns every night. Tell your old man to drag Walton and Lanier up and down the court for 48 minutes."

It's a hilarious scene, in part because there are threads of truth running through it. Jabbar and other giants of the game often have been held to a higher standard because of their size. Nothing they did ever was good enough for some critics. They were predestined to be viewed as underachievers.

The game of basketball has changed in the decades since Wilt and Kareem, who almost certainly rank among the top 10 players in the history of the sport. The advent of the 3-point field goal has deemphasized the value of height in basketball. Why continually jam the ball inside to a 7-footer for two-point baskets when a 6-footer standing 23 feet away can get you three points instead? It has become more of a positionless sport in which everyone—even the 7-footers—are expected to be proficient at handling the ball and shooting from the perimeter. Size is still a valued commodity but the average height of a player in the NBA has dipped slightly from a peak of 6'7" from 2000 through 2005 to a fraction of an inch less than that now.

The ensuing years have given birth to even taller players in the NBA, but none of them have dominated the way that Mikan, Chamberlain and Jabbar did.

The two tallest players ever to play in the NBA are Manute Bol, who played from 1985 through 1995, and Georghe Muresan, who was in the league from 1993 through 2000. Both were generally listed at 7'7".

There have been at least seven other players who were either 7'5" or 7'6": Slavko Vranes, Shawn Bradley, Yao Ming, Chuck Nevitt, Pavel Podkolzin, Tacko Fall and Sim Bhullar. The influx of foreign players into the league is evident on that list. Only Nevitt and Bradley were raised in the United States.

Although those players were tall, they weren't anywhere near as good as Chamberlain and Jabbar. Ming is the only one of the 7'5" and over group who ever made an All-Star team in the NBA. Vranes played only one game in the league, Bhullar three, Podkolzin six.

Nevitt, who was the tallest player in NBA history when he first came into the league in 1982, hung around for 10 years and played in 155 games but never was a starter. Some people labeled him the "Human Victory Cigar" because he usually did not appear on the court until after the outcome of the game had been decided. The former North Carolina State player was well aware that his place in the NBA was based solely on the size of his body. He proudly had vanity license plates that read "7 FT 5" and he actually looked forward to fielding question No. 2.

"Do you play basketball?"

"Some people say I do," Nevitt would say with a smile, "and some people say I don't."

Bol, who claimed that his father was 6'8" and his mother was 6'10" and that he had a great grandfather who was 7'10", replaced Nevitt as the league's tallest player in 1985 and had one of the most unusual careers ever. At 7'7" and 200 pounds with an 8'6" wingspan, he really had only one skill of real value. He could block almost anyone's shot. In 624 games spread over 10 seasons, he averaged only 2.6 points per game (despite the fact that he could dunk without jumping) but had a very impressive 3.3 blocked shots per game.

It's possible Bol also was the oldest player in NBA history although we'll never really know for sure. When Cleveland State University coach Kevin Mackey recruited Bol out of his native Sudan, he really had no idea how old the big center was so he fabricated a birthday for him in order to get him into school: October 12, 1968. After Bol died of kidney failure in 2010, Mackey admitted he had no clue about Bol's actual age and suspected he may have been in his 40s when he played at the college level.

Muresan was as much of a curiosity as Bol and an even bigger project. His extreme growth was the result of a tumor that pressed on his pituitary gland, but we may never have heard of him were it not for a toothache. Muresan grew up in the small town of Tritenii in the Transylvania region of Romania, the son of a factory worker. The family of seven, none of whom was over 6 feet tall other than the kid everyone called Ghita, was extremely impoverished, living in a home with no heat, no electricity and very little food. Despite that, Muresan grew to be 6'9" by the time he was 14. It was around that time that his mother took him to the capital city of Cluj to see a dentist who also happened to serve as the dentist for the Romanian national team. When the dentist saw how big Muresan was and heard he was only 14, he put in a quick call to the coach of the national team.

"I stayed that night," Muresan said in a 1995 *Sports Illustrated* profile. "I never went home."

He ended up playing for a team in Pau, France, where head coach Michel Gomez set about trying to mold that monstrous body into a basketball player, much the way Ray Meyer did with Mikan. Gomez worked with Muresan on a trampoline and had him do tumbling drills. "Physically, he did not accept his size," Gomez said in that 1995 *SI* piece. "The first thing I did—before any basketball—I taught him how to walk. He walked like an old man, all hunched over. I taught him how to stand straight, to be proud of his height."

The Washington Bullets took a chance on Muresan in 1993, selecting him in the second round of the NBA draft despite the fact that he was facing a major operation to remove the pituitary tumor. The Bullets' gamble paid off. Although Muresan never became a superstar, he played in 307 games over a six-year NBA career, averaging 9.8 points per game and becoming one of the most popular players in the league because of a buoyant personality.

There have been a handful of equally tall players who competed at a very high level but never made it to the pro ranks. Ri Myong-hun, better known as Michael Ri, was a 7'8½" player who starred in North Korea in the late 1990s but was denied the chance to play in the NBA because of a U.S. ban on trade with his native country.

Kenny George, whose growth also was accelerated by a pituitary tumor, was 7'7" and 360 pounds with size 28 feet when he played at UNC Asheville from 2006 through 2008 although some published reports listed him as tall as 7'9". Sadly, George was unable to finish his career after he developed a staph infection in his right foot during the summer of 2008 and had to have part of the foot amputated.

George Bell was a 7'7" center at Morris Brown College who lamented in a 1980 article in *The Sporting News* that he sometimes wished he was short and that there was no such thing as basketball. "It's an awful thing for people to walk up to you and say you ought to be playing basketball just because you're tall," he said. "But when you're tall, that's all people talk to you about."

One of Bell's contemporaries, 7'6½" John Hollinden of Indiana State University Evansville, told *The Sporting News* he actually liked the interplay with curious strangers, saying it was "fun" at times. "Sometimes I just answer people by saying 'No, I'm not a basketball player. I'm studying to be a doctor,'" said Hollinden, who was 6'8" and 138 pounds in the ninth grade and who, like Mikan, was an aspiring pianist. "Or I'll say 'I'm a musician.' If you tell them something unexpected, they don't know what to say. But they usually don't believe me anyhow."

Obviously, there have been plenty of extremely tall women who also made a name for themselves in basketball.

Poland native Margo Dydek is generally considered to be the tallest women's basketball player ever, at 7'2". She was a two-time All-Star in the WNBA, and during a career that stretched from 1998 through 2008, she blocked more shots than any player in the history of the league. Dydek, who had two younger sisters who were 6'6" or taller and also played basketball, died tragically at the age of 37 in 2011 while she was pregnant with her third child.

Uljana Semjonova, a 7-footer from Latvia who wore a men's size 21 shoe, helped the United Soviet Socialist Republic to Olympic gold medals in women's basketball in 1976 and 1980 and is a member of the Naismith Basketball Hall of Fame. Two 6'10" women—Zorana Todorovic of Serbia and Bernadett Hatar of Hungary—starred on the international basketball scene.

The tallest American-born player to play in the WNBA is 6'9" Brittney Griner, who starred at Baylor and with the Phoenix Mercury and was one of the standouts of the U.S. team that won an Olympic gold medal in 2021. Griner said in a 2015 interview with *ESPN the Magazine* that her feet are bigger than those of Jabbar and her hands are larger than those of NBA star LeBron James. She has been able to palm a basketball since her freshman year of high school and was one of the first female players to dunk in a competitive game.

But she also endured excruciating leg pain during her childhood growth spurts along with more than her share of gaping stares and bullying. She doesn't love always standing out in a crowd. "For me, it's a very tall world," she said. "Just walking around, it's kind of like being on display at a museum, like being on display 24/7."

Another WNBA star, 6'8" Australian native Liz Cambage, has been very open about the mental health issues she has experienced throughout her career, some of which have their roots in her height. She admitted she began getting "blackout drunk" at the age of 15 and occasionally has missed games during her pro career because of mental health struggles, including pulling out of the 2021 Olympics.

"Growing up and being bullied, it's not a sad story for me," Cambage told *The Women's Game* in 2020. "It's defined me and what made me so strong."

Griner and others have admitted that basketball became a path to acceptance after being taunted and bullied so much as kids. "All that teasing stopped when I started playing basketball," she said. "You become that cool person when you start playing sports and you prove you're good at it.... I love being different. If everybody was the same, it'd be a boring-ass world."

Griner is not the only basketball player who has grown to appreciate their size. Shawn Bradley, who parlayed his 7'6" stature into a very solid NBA career from 1993 through 2005, said, "My mom taught me at a young age that she loved me and God loved me. When you're a little different, they make fun of you in school. That's just the way it is. But when that happened, I didn't let it bother me. I just take the negative things and put them in the rubbish bin.... I don't know how other people feel who are 7'6", but I love being 7'6". If I were 7'10", I'd love that. I like who I am. I love my height."

8

It Doesn't Help in All Sports

While extreme height clearly is a plus for someone who aspires to play basketball, if you really think about it, there is a large number of sports in which height is much less of an advantage.

I never harbored any ambition to be a gymnast or a jockey, but if I had, I would have been screwed. My height also didn't do me much good in other sports that I attempted in my lifetime, such as golf and bowling.

Really, the only other sport besides basketball in which tallness is an absolute, no-doubt-about-it, clear-cut advantage is volleyball. For many years, at the high school level, the best girls basketball players also were the stars of the volleyball team. The skill sets are so similar. The advent of specialization has cut into that trend a little bit with many young athletes opting to focus on one of the two sports over the other.

If anything, height has become even more of a factor in volleyball than in basketball over the past few decades.

When the United States won the Olympic silver medal in women's volleyball in 1984, the players on the roster averaged just under 6 feet tall with the tallest being 6'5" Flo Hyman, one of the legendary players of the game's developmental years. The average height of the U.S. team in the 2021 Tokyo games was a full two inches higher at 6'2". There was no one as tall as Hyman—6'7" Kathryn Plummer was an alternate on the team—but 10 of the 12 squad members were 6'2" or taller.

The upward trend was similar on the U.S. men's national teams in those years. In 1984, the average U.S. men's player was 6'4" with Craig Buck being the tallest at 6'7½". In 2021, the average was up to 6'6", including a pair of 6'10" players, Matt Anderson and Max Holt.

There are even taller players out there around the world. Dmitriy Muserskiy, who is 7'2", helped Russia win an Olympic gold medal in 2012. American Phil Dalhausser, a 6'9" former basketball and tennis player, has become an Olympic champion in the relatively new sport of beach volleyball. And 8'1" Morteza Mehrzadselakjani has become a dominant force playing sitting volleyball in the Paralympics, helping Iran to gold medals in both 2016 and 2020.

Russia also has provided some of the tallest Olympic caliber women's players. Ekaterina Gamova, who was generally listed as either 6'8" or 6'9", starred for Russian national teams from 1999 through 2016 and competed in four Olympics, while one of her contemporaries, Nelly Alisheva, was about an inch taller than she was.

However, the first player who achieved fame for her volleyball dominance because of her size was Hyman, whose career ended tragically at the age of 31. During a match in Japan in 1986, she collapsed and died from what initially was thought to be a heart attack. She later was found to be suffering from Marfan Syndrome, one of several ailments that can cause accelerated growth and which often can lead to aortic aneurysms. Hyman had suffered from fainting spells and had been tested for cardiac problems but never was tested for Marfan while she was alive. Her death led to more extensive caution and testing of extremely tall athletes.

In that respect, Marfan Foundation president Carolyn Levering referred to Hyman as "a game-changer. Even today, when we have conversations with people, they talk about her."

As with basketball, extreme height opens doors for athletes in volleyball just on size alone. Twins Ann and Claire Recht, both just a shade over 6'7", are believed to be the tallest female twins ever and that led to them receiving volleyball scholarships to American University in 2006 even though they had only played volleyball at a high school level for two years.

The Recht twins had parents who were 6'5" and 6'3" and they had two older brothers who were even taller. When they joined the American University squad, teammates such as 5'4" Cynammon Burns weren't sure what to think. "I didn't even know girls could be that tall," she said in a 2006 *Washington Post* story. "It's kind of like, 'Hey what's it like up there?' They're in a different world and see different things than I do down here."

There are no other sports in which there isn't a place for people of average or below average height. Thomas Samaras wrote that "a small or average sized person has little chance of participating in basketball, football and baseball," but that's not true at all. It's mostly true in basketball and size certainly helps in football, although not necessarily in terms of height as much as weight. In baseball, there have been plenty of major league baseball players of average or below average height. Ichiro Suzuki, Greg Maddux, Wee Willie Keeler and many others certainly weren't impaired in their quests to carve out Hall of Fame careers.

Height definitely can be a great benefit in football although this is another of those instances in which it's possible to be too tall, especially at certain positions. There is a reason you don't see 6'5" running backs and 6'6" defensive backs in the NFL, where the average height of a player is 6'2".

"In very simple terms, too much height creates a bigger target," NFL Hall of Fame executive Bill Polian told *The Sporting News* in 2005. "Generally speaking, tall people tend not to be real good knee benders and real quick in their movements. The axiom I've always followed is beware of too tall rather than beware of too short."

There always are exceptions. Harold Carmichael became a stud receiver with the Philadelphia Eagles in the 1970s but he felt being 6'7" was as much an impediment as it was an advantage. "I don't think size determines ability," Carmichael said in a 1979 *Chicago Tribune* article. "If being big is all it takes, why don't more guys quit basketball and take up football? I'm a big target for the quarterback but I'm also a big target for the cornerbacks. They may be a foot shorter, but they all have elbows and knees and know how to use them."

Another exception was Ed Jones, a 6'9" defensive end who registered 106 sacks and made three Pro Bowls during a 15-year run with the Dallas Cowboys. His nickname, fittingly, was "Too Tall." The story was that in Jones' very first practice at the high school level, he came onto the field wearing pants that were way too small for him, eliciting the ridicule of teammates for being too tall for the sport. The name followed him all the way to the NFL.

Most of the really tall players in the modern-day NFL are offensive tackles who are able to use their wingspan to ward off speedier pass rushers. There have been a few really good 6'9" offensive linemen, including Baltimore Ravens Hall of Famer Jonathan Ogden. It's hard to find an offensive tackle in the league who isn't at least 6'5".

There also has been a trend in the NFL over the past several decades toward having taller players at the most visible position: quarterback. The star quarterbacks of earlier generations often were only a little more than 6 feet tall. Fran Tarkenton, who held the NFL's career passing record until 1995, may not have even been that tall. Now, QBs who are 6'4" or 6'5" are the norm although it may be possible to be too tall at that position too. The six QBs in NFL history who were 6'7" or taller all had very nondescript careers with the tallest quarterback in league history being one of its most notable busts. Dan McGwire, the 6'8" younger brother of major league baseball star Mark McGwire, was the first quarterback selected in the 1991 draft but he played in just 13 games in five years and threw for only 745 yards and two touchdowns, 506 less than Brett Favre, a 6'2" QB who was chosen in the second round in the same year. When McGwire was a freshman at the University of Iowa, head coach Hayden Fry claimed he could throw the ball 90 yards but a lack of accuracy and mobility held him back.

In fact, most of the tallest players in NFL history never made it big. The tallest of all time was 7'0" Richard Sligh, a defensive tackle who played sparingly in just eight games with the Oakland Raiders in 1967. The Raiders let Sligh go to the Cincinnati Bengals in the expansion draft following that season and he told the *Dayton Journal Herald* that summer that he thought he was still growing. "I love being large," he added. "It opens a lot of opportunities—things like television appearances and movies. I'm thinking I might wrestle after the season." There is no evidence that Sligh ever appeared in any films or TV programs or that he ever took up wrestling. He never played in another NFL game either. The Bengals cut him in training camp.

Cincinnati had a 6'11" offensive lineman, Matt O'Donnell, many years later but he never appeared in a single game in two years with the team. In more recent times, Detroit had a 6'10" offensive tackle named Dan Skipper, who played in just 13 games in four years.

The only player 6'10" or taller who ever saw regular action in the NFL was Morris Stroud, who played tight end for the Kansas City Chiefs from 1970 through 1974, starting 49 games and catching 54 passes. However, Stroud became best known for something else. When opposing teams lined up to kick field goals, Chiefs coach Hank Stram sometimes positioned Stroud below the goalposts and had him jump up to try to block kicks before they cleared the crossbar. He never succeeded in blocking a field goal that way—he never really came close—but the NFL still enacted a rule change making such tactics illegal, stating that it was "palpably unfair" to try to block a field goal that way.

Height in the sport of baseball is much the same as it is in football. It can be beneficial but it's largely a positional thing. It's great to be tall if you're a pitcher and it's usually pretty good if you're a first baseman. It's not all bad if you're an outfielder either but 6'5" catchers and 6'4" middle infielders are pretty rare.

My son, Ryne, found that out the hard way. As his Little League manager, I knew the kid was going to be tall and I had every intention of grooming him to be a pitcher-first baseman. When he was 8 years old and playing in Little League minors, we had two other kids earmarked to be catchers. But in the first inning of the first game, one of those kids took a sharply hit foul ball off his leg and laid there in the dirt crying. I motioned for the other kid to come into the game but he sat frozen on the bench, gripped in fear at what he had seen happen to our other catcher. He basically refused to strap on the gear and subject himself to the physical abuse that came with the position. I was left with a quandary: I had two catchers who no longer wanted to catch and I had to expose some other kid to the perils of the position. There was no way I could put in some kid who never had even practiced there without risking considerable wrath (or even a lawsuit) from a parent. I did the only thing I could do: I put my own son back there.

He loved it, took to it immediately. He liked the fact that he didn't need to run as much as you did at other positions. It's something he could basically do sitting down. He also liked the cerebral aspect of being totally involved in the game and more or less being the quarterback of the team, and he didn't seem to mind the fact that he was inevitably going to get nicked and bruised in the course of doing his job. He was a catcher for the next 10 years and even procured a partial scholarship to a small college based purely on his skills behind the plate. The coach who recruited him offered him the scholarship before he ever saw what he could do as a hitter. But for years, Ryne—who topped out at 6'5"—heard the same refrain from many coaches: "You're too tall to be a catcher." He had to continually prove people wrong.

It all makes sense, of course. Catchers need to be able to get low to block pitches in the dirt and they need to be able to manipulate borderline pitches to make them look like strikes to the umpire crouching behind them. All of that is understandably easier to do if you're 5'11" instead of 6'5".

As a result, there were very few really tall catchers at the major league level until the 21st century. Players such as Sandy Alomar, Jr., Joe Mauer and Matt Wieters—all 6'5"—have helped pave the way for taller catchers although Wieters was frequently criticized for his lack of pitch-framing skills. However, Alomar was a six-time All-Star and Mauer won the American League's Most Valuable Player award while playing primarily as a catcher in 2009. The Pittsburgh Pirates' 6'5" Jacob Stallings further blazed the trail when he won the National League's Gold Glove for his defensive skills in 2020.

There have been three 6'6" catchers in MLB history but none of them had lengthy or distinguished careers. Don Gile started four games behind the plate during a four-year career with the Red Sox from 1959 to 1962 and Pete Koegel started four games with the Phillies in 1971. More recently, Grayson Greiner saw extensive action at catcher for the Tigers from 2018 to 2021 although he never became the team's full-time starter.

It would seem barriers also are crumbling for oversized middle infielders. Oneil Cruz, who is 6'7", became the tallest shortstop in MLB history when he debuted with the Pittsburgh Pirates in 2022.

The tallest players in baseball history obviously have been pitchers. Hurlers who are 6'5" or 6'6" are commonplace in the major leagues and there have been at least five who were 6'10" or taller. The tallest player in major league history was 6'11" Jon Rauch, who pitched for eight different teams during an 11-year career from 2002 through 2013.

The most noteworthy really tall pitcher was 6'10" Randy Johnson, who won 303 games and struck out 4,875 batters (the second most ever) during a Hall of Fame career from 1988 through 2009.

But Johnson didn't become a Hall of Famer because he was 6'10". He really got to be that good in spite of his size. It was an obstacle he had to overcome on his way to stardom. He always could throw. He recalled firing tennis balls against the garage door of his family's home in Livermore, California, so ferociously as a kid that his father would come out with a hammer and tell his son to pound in the nails he had loosened. But one scout used the word "gawky" and referenced Ichabod Crane from Washington Irving's *The Legend of Sleepy Hollow* after his first glimpse of Johnson. His control and mechanics were that bad. Johnson worked very hard to regulate his God-given ability. Once he did, he became a frightening sight for hitters. "He's right on top of you," Chicago Cubs hitter Mark Grace told the *Contra Costa Times*. "It looks like he's about 20 feet away once he releases it."

"Obviously, my height was to my advantage but only until I was able to harness my ability," Johnson admitted many years later in an interview with the *Sacramento Bee*. "Being 6-foot-10 and all arms and legs, obviously there weren't too many power pitchers like me. So, I didn't have a blueprint to work with."

Many teams tried to use Johnson as a template to develop even taller pitchers in ensuing years. Ryan Doherty, a 7'1" former Notre Dame star, spent three years in the Arizona Diamondbacks' farm system before finding stardom in another tall man's sport: beach volleyball.

And the Minnesota Twins signed a 7'1" pitcher from the Netherlands named Loek Van Mil who also did not come close to reaching the major leagues. Van Mil actually started out as a catcher before being converted to pitching, where his overhand fastball, according to Twins director of baseball operations Rob Antony, looked as though "it's coming out of the sky." Van Mil, who later died as a result of a hiking accident, liked to have fun with people about his height and over the fact that he didn't play another tall persons' sport. He wore a t-shirt that said, "Don't ask" on the front. On the back it said, "7-foot-1. No, I don't play basketball."

The search for the next Randy Johnson continues. In the 2022 major league draft, the Baltimore Orioles used their 13th-round pick on 7'0" Jared Beck, an unheralded pitcher from Saint Leo University.

Among non-pitchers, the tallest players in major league history have been a pair of 6'8" first basemen: Tony Clark, who had a solid 15-year career from 1995 through 2009 and now serves as the executive director of the Major League Baseball Players Association, and Nate Freiman, who had a much shorter and less significant career with the Oakland A's in 2013 and 2014.

There also have been a few 6'7" outfielders. Frank Howard, a former Ohio State basketball player, spent 16 years slugging home runs in the majors from 1958 through 1973 although he probably didn't have the speed to play the outfield in today's game. Howard stole just eight bases in 16 MLB seasons. Two modern-day 6'7" outfielders—Yankees star Aaron Judge and Astros prospect Taylor Jones—are much more athletic. In fact, Judge said in an *ESPN the Magazine* package in 2016 that he thinks his size helps him defensively, noting,

"In the outfield, it takes me three strides to get in the gap. If I want to rob a home run, I just have to get to the wall."

Tall athletes have found considerably less success in the other major team sports.

In hockey, for example, there have been relatively few really tall players, especially at the offensive end of the ice. The average National Hockey League player is just 6'1" with the tallest ever being 6'9" Zdeno Chara, a highly successful defenseman with the Islanders, Senators and Bruins from 1997 through 2020. Chara, who was about 7'0" when he strapped on a pair of skates, was steered into hockey by his father, who was a Greco-Roman wrestler back home in Slovakia. His size probably has helped him in one respect: At the 2012 NHL All-Star skills competition, he recorded the hardest slap shot in hockey history, 108.8 mph.

Chara, who used a 67-inch stick, didn't really look like a hockey player off the ice and endured the same daily gauntlet of questions that all tall people face: "How tall are you? Do you play basketball? Were your parents tall?" Chara once told *Sports Illustrated*: "I was thinking of getting a hat that says, 6'9", NO, NO."

There have been a handful of other players in the NHL who were 6'8". They're all defensemen: Andrej Sustr, Tyler Myers, John Scott and Joe Finley.

There is a trend in the league toward taller goaltenders. It probably began in 1979 when the Montreal Canadiens played the New York Rangers in the Stanley Cup finals. Montreal's Ken Dryden told the *New York Times* he was sure there never had been a finals series matching such tall goalies. He was 6'4" and the Rangers' John Davidson was 6'3".

It was unusual then but not anymore. In fact, during the 2021–22 season, the average NHL goaltender was 6'3" and none of the regular starters in the league were under 6'0". Ben Bishop was the tallest goaltender in the league at 6'7".

Dryden said 40 years ago that he didn't think being tall gave him any advantage because the goal is only four feet high and six feet wide. But the consensus now is that tall goalies are better able to block shots with their long legs and have an advantage in seeing over players in front of the net so they're not as likely to be screened out when a shot is coming their way.

Changes in equipment have had an impact on the size of goaltenders too. Hard as it is to believe, there still were goalies who did not wear face masks as late as 1974. The addition of masks and larger leg pads facilitated what is known as the butterfly style of goaltending. Goalies now crouch more and keep their knees closer together so they can kick their skates out to block shots, meaning a larger goaltender has an advantage in defending the corners of the net.

One team sport in which height generally is less of a factor is soccer although even it has a few more tall players than it used to. As with hockey, most of them are goalkeepers. There are several goalies at the higher levels of the sport who are in the 6'7" to 6'10" range with Kristof Van Hout of Belgium-based Standard Liege believed to be the tallest.

Most of the players out front who score goals and grab headlines are around 6 feet tall if not shorter. The tallest professional soccer player who does not play in goal is 6'8" Stefan Maierhofer of Wolverhampton in the English Premier League. Peter Crouch, who had a long career as a 6'7" forward in the Premier League, had a lifetime of being asked why he didn't become a basketball player. Crouch finally had cards printed up that he handed to people who asked him such questions.

There are relatively few individual sports in which there is much benefit to being tall although you see many tall athletes in swimming. The greatest Olympic swimmer ever, Michael Phelps, is 6'4", and there have been two swimmers who won four or more Olympic medals—Gustavo Borges of Brazil and Matt Grevers of the United States—who were 6'8". At the 2021 Tokyo Olympics, there was only one men's swimming medalist who was shorter than 5'11" and only two female medalists shorter than 5'7".

Being tall also can be beneficial in some track and field events. There are very few short high jumpers.

And in recent decades, there has been an influx of some taller athletes in the sport of tennis. Ivo Karlovic, a 6'11" player from Croatia, created a bit of a sensation when he burst onto the pro tennis scene about 20 years ago. Karlovic, nicknamed "The Leaning Tower of Zagreb," had a powerful serve that was clocked at as much as 156 mph but he sometimes was overmatched by smaller, more skilled players. As he himself admitted in a 2010 interview with the *Palm Beach Post*, "Tennis is a fast game and I'm slow." Karlovic still won a handful of pro events but never got as far as the semifinals in any of tennis' four major tournaments.

American Reilly Opelka also played on the pro circuit at 6'11" but his serve wasn't nearly as freaky fast as Karlovic's and he won only two pro tournaments. No player taller than 6'6" ever has won any of the four Grand Slam men's tournaments. Juan Martin Del Potro of Argentina won the U.S. Open in 2009 and Croatia's Marin Cilic, also 6'6", won the same event in 2014.

Taller players have become much more prominent in women's tennis over the past few decades. Until the 1980s, the top women's players in the world were of average height, perhaps even a bit on the small side. Chris Evert, Billie Jean King and Martina Navratilova all were in the 5'4" to 5'8" range.

That changed with the arrival of 6'2½" Lindsay Davenport, 6'0" Maria Sharapova, 6'1" Venus Williams and 5'10" Serena Williams, all of whom blended rocket-like serves with long reaches to become great players. "There are some disadvantages in tennis to being tall," long-time tennis coach Nick Bollettieri said in a 2005 interview with the *Cincinnati Post*. "But if I had a choice, I would certainly take a big, strong, flexible athlete over a smaller athlete if everything was in order in terms of mentality and work ethic. I think you have more of a chance with a bigger girl."

While Serena Williams has made her case for being the best women's player ever, Davenport provided one of the big breakthroughs for tall girls when she won the 1998 U.S. Open. Davenport, whose father was 6'8", struggled with her size as a kid. She sprouted six inches between the ages of 14 and 16 and just wanted to fit in as one of the girls but she frequently was ridiculed, even by her fellow tennis players. As S.L. Price wrote on CNNSI.com in 1998, tennis is "the closest thing sports has to a gossipy, clique-ridden high school."

"I wasn't a perfect thing at 17. I didn't have confidence," Davenport said in Price's story. "I was hunched over and real embarrassed, and I didn't want to be in the limelight. But it changed over time."

Her success on the court ultimately bred confidence. She never totally overcame the self-consciousness about her height—she once turned down a chance to appear on the *Late Show with David Letterman* because she knew he was likely to make jokes about her size—but she did finally come to terms with her size on the court and take advantage of it.

Height can be an impediment if your goal is to play some other individual sports.

There have been very few really good tall golfers at the highest level of the sport. Tiger Woods, who has won more tournaments than almost anyone in history, is only 6 feet tall, and Jack Nicklaus, Ben Hogan, Arnold Palmer, Tom Watson, Sam Snead and almost anyone else who would rank as an all-time great is even shorter than that. One of the few exceptions is Phil Mickelson, who is 6'3".

It makes sense from a physics standpoint. A long swing arc allows a golfer to hit the ball a longer distance, just as it helped Karlovic with his serve and Chara with his slap shot. But the longer the swing, the less control the player has over where the ball is going. And precise ball placement is everything in golf.

"Not a lot of guys are tall," admitted Jordan Hahn, a 6'8" former University of Wisconsin golfer who played in his first PGA Tour event in 2021. "There's a lot more room for error, but then again, you get a lot more speed and power."

Because of that lack of precision, you don't need a lot of fingers to count the PGA Tour victories by really tall men. Phil Blackmar, who was 6'7", is the tallest player ever to win on tour and he did it just three times (in 1985, 1988 and 1997). There are a few more tall players showing up on tour now. In addition to Hahn, Great Britain's Jon Thomson is 6'9" and Craig Smith is 6'8".

The *Guinness Book of World Records* lists Germany's 6'9" Marcel Pickel as the tallest professional golfer ever. He played on the PGA Tour of Germany from 2010 through 2013.

One of the problems those players face is finding the proper equipment. They can't just walk into a pro shop and use the same clubs utilized by a man a foot shorter.

Thomson, who gravitated toward golf when a childhood bout with leukemia precluded him from competing in contact sports, said his clubs are 2½ inches longer than normal, "which is kind of the longest you can go legally. Equipment has been a huge challenge for me. It's always been difficult finding the right stuff, for the boys to fit me."

There has been at least one all-time great women's golfer who was extremely tall.

Carol Mann, who was 6'3", won 38 LPGA Tour events including two majors. She won 10 tournaments in 1968 and eight in 1969, when she was the leading money-winner on tour. She might have won even more had she not begun experiencing chronic back pains in the 1970s, which forced her to alter her swing. She was never the same after that.

Early in her career, Mann confessed to being very self-conscious and shy because of her size, but she eventually became a vocal leader in the sport, serving as the president of the LPGA. Free-spirited and self-effacing, she frequently told people she actually was 5'15" and she poked fun at her own stature by having the likeness of a giraffe printed on her business cards.

The latter-day generation of female golfers includes at least one tall player. Michelle Wie is 6'0" and hits the ball far enough that she twice received sponsor's exemptions into a PGA Tour event, the John Deere Classic. But she admitted that she views her size as perhaps more of a detriment than a help. "Longer arms means more leverage and speed, but it's harder to hit consistent shots," Wie said in that 2016 *ESPN the Magazine* feature. "I got all my distance from my height, but it's harder to balance in windy conditions."

While you don't see many really good tall golfers, you see even fewer long-legged bowlers.

Again, it all sort of makes sense. Tall bowlers need to radically bend their knees to get lower and roll the ball along the floor. They're not likely to be as smooth in their delivery. "Ninety-five out of 100 bowlers will tell you, 'The smaller the bowler, the better the bowler,'" Professional Bowlers Association official Jerry Levine told author Ralph Keyes in his 1980 book.

Steve Cook, who was 6'7", 260 pounds, was one of the few exceptions. He won 15 PBA events and is in the sport's Hall of Fame. Another very successful pro bowler of recent times was 6'5" Wes "Big Nasty" Malott of Fort Wayne, Indiana.

We probably don't really need to tell you that you can't be tall and make it as a great gymnast or as a jockey in horse racing, right?

Gymnastics is basically the 5'6" and under league. Probably the greatest male gymnast ever, Japan's Kohei Uchimura, was 5'4". Russia's Nikolai Andrianov, who won a record 15 Olympic medals in the sport, was 5'5".

The size thing is even more pronounced among women. After 4'11" Olga Korbut made a big splash at the 1972 Olympics, there was a trend toward even smaller gymnasts with some eastern European countries allegedly even doing things medicinally to delay puberty for girls. Many of the best in the sport since then have been super tiny. Simone Biles is 4'8", Mary Lou Retton 4'9".

If you're looking for a reason why there are not more tall gymnasts, consider this explanation in a 2021 Quora blog from Joel Gheen, a financial wizard with considerable experience as an athlete and runner: "As you increase the length of a body, the mass increases in a cubed ratio. In other words, all else equal, doubling in height of a body is 8× the mass, or 8 times 'heavier.' Additionally, if you review moment physics (and think about levers), it becomes intuitive that longer bodies undergo massively increased stress as they rotate while also requiring much higher velocities at the extremes.... What's easier to toss and flip in the air and catch? A broomstick or a 6-foot 2×4? A pencil or a telephone pole? The larger bodies are much harder to rotate and are far more likely to break because there's so much more force and velocity, not to mention requiring higher altitude for a similar rotation."

I have no idea if Gheen knows what he's talking about but it all sounds very plausible.

As for horse racing, that's easier to explain. You simply want a lighter, more compact load for the horse to haul around the track, right? There actually has been a handful of tall jockeys. Manute Bol, who we mentioned in a previous chapter as a 7'7" basketball player, actually rode a horse in an exhibition race at Hoosier Park in 2003 but it was just a publicity stunt to raise money for war refugees in his native Sudan. The tallest known professional jockey was Australian Stuart Brown, who was 6'2" and who fought for his entire life to keep his weight down. In the film *Seabiscuit,* much is made of the fact that the famous horse's jockey, Red Pollard, was much larger than normal riders. Pollard was 5'7". That's generally about the max for jockeys.

One sport where you wouldn't think height would be a factor is auto racing, but even in that sport, there have been relatively few tall competitors, in part because of safety factors. The tallest NASCAR driver ever was 6'6" Buddy Baker, whose 19 career victories included the 1980 Daytona 500 and who is a member of NASCAR's Hall of Fame. Michael Waltrip, who won Daytona in 2001 and 2003, was 6'5".

There have been a handful of other drivers who were 6'4", including Elliott Sadler, who said in *ESPN the Magazine* that the biggest challenge he faces is just getting in and out of the vehicle. "The first thing I check is where my head is. In a crash, you don't want your head banging against the roll bars or the roof."

9

No One Roots for Goliath

It's all spelled out right there in Samuel I, Chapter 17, Verse 4 of the Old Testament.

"And there came out from the camp of the Philistines a champion named Goliath, of Gath, whose height was six cubits and a span."

A cubit was measured in biblical times as roughly the length from a normal man's elbow to the tip of his extended fingers, about 18 inches. A span was about 9 inches. So, we can calculate that Goliath was supposedly 9 feet, 9 inches tall. Big guy. Andre the Giant and Hulk Hogan likely would have quaked in fear at the sight of this man.

And he apparently wasn't the proverbial gentle giant. The Bible further tells us: "Goliath stood and shouted to the ranks of Israel, 'Why do you come out and line up for battle? Am I not a Philistine, and are you not the servants of Saul? Choose a man and have him come down to me. If he is able to fight and kill me, we will become your subjects; but if I overcome him and kill him, you will become our subjects and serve us.' Then the Philistine said, 'This day I defy the armies of Israel! Give me a man and let us fight each other.' On hearing the Philistine's words, Saul and all the Israelites were dismayed and terrified."

All except one. Goliath's eventual opponent that day back in the Ellah Valley of ancient Israel was a stripling named David. The Bible doesn't tell us how many cubits and spans he was, but it notes that he was "little more than a boy." We can assume he was somewhere between normal sized and qualifying for that convention I infiltrated all those years ago in Fort Wayne.

We skip ahead to Samuel I, 17:49: "And David put his hand in his bag and took out a stone, and slung it, and struck the Philistine on his forehead; the stone sank into his forehead, and he fell on his face to the ground."

According to Greek mythology, a similar scene played out on a battlefield in 1203 BC when the competing armies of Thessaly and Mycenae each decided to send out their best warrior to decide the outcome of a battle. Thessaly chose Boagrius, a huge, hideous mountain of a man to oppose Achilles, who was fairly ordinary in size. If you've seen the opening scene of the film *Troy*, you know how this came out. Achilles (played by Brad Pitt) takes a flying leap toward Boagrius (portrayed by 6'8" former pro wrestler Nathan Jones) and slays him with one thrust of his sword. Theater audiences across the country undoubtedly erupted in delight when they saw it.

The fact is, it always has been human nature to root for the little guy against the big guy. Always. Always. The big guy is always the bad guy. The big dog is never an underdog. Even those of us who are very sizeable in stature root for the Davids of the world when they go up against the Goliaths. I myself watch the film *Rudy* and root for Sean Astin to show up those Notre Dame behemoths every time. I end up on my feet cheering with tears of joy when he is triumphantly carried off the field at the end of the movie.

Wilt Chamberlain put it very succinctly: "No one roots for Goliath."

It's irrepressible, undisputable human nature. But that doesn't mean it's fair. Wilt the Stilt endured a lifetime of people wanting to see him fail simply because he was 7'1" and many of the rest of us have had moments when those around us wanted to see us get cut down to size.

Albert Payson Terhune's 1926 essay in *American* magazine, "Troubles of a Big Guy," deals extensively with this topic. Terhune, who was only 6'2" but still taller than most of his contemporaries, said people of average size or less viewed a tall man "with a deathless hatred. They hated him as they hated unjust taxes or earthquakes, or any other irresistible force they must submit to."

He pointed out that in fairy tales and other stories the villain is always the big man and he inevitably is put to death. "You will find that, from the story of Ulysses and the Cyclops down to the saga of Jack the Giant Killer. Always in those tales the Big Guy was the wicked aggressor. Always, soon or late, he came to grief at the hands of some of the Little People."

Famed writer Albert Payson Terhune articulated many of the problems of being tall in a 1926 essay, "Troubles of a Big Guy," which appeared in *American* magzine (Library of Congress, Prints and Photographs Division).

At the very least, there is a built-in feeling of fear or trepidation, a wariness, in the relationship between tall and short.

Ted Evans, who made a living as a sideshow giant in the circus in the 1940s and 1950s, recalled coming across a pretty girl in a railroad station one day. Like any red-blooded male, he snuck a peak at her and she immediately recoiled in horror, whispering to a companion, "Let's get away from that monster."

Evans, who admittedly was much taller than the normal man, well over 7 feet, still was alarmed at how threatened many people were at the mere sight of him. "It seems that most everyone's ideas about men who are unnaturally tall have been twisted by nursery stories, old wives' tales and Greek mythology, in which the giant is forever damned as the hulking villain in need of comeuppance," he wrote in a 1952 magazine article.

Remember Eric McPherson, who we told you about as a very tall high school basketball player back in Davenport, Iowa? He became a target the few occasions he did get to play in games, with opposing players intentionally ramming into him at times. It even happened sometimes in practice with his own teammates. But off the court, he encountered a completely opposite reaction from people who were significantly smaller.

"A lot of smaller people seem to be afraid of me," he said. "They ask a lot of questions mostly. I hear the same questions day after day. How tall are you? How's the weather up there? They keep coming up to me and asking."

In 2016, *ESPN the Magazine* conducted a poll of NBA players with 52 percent saying they thought people felt threatened by them because of their size. One player in the anonymous poll noted: "If I'm standing behind someone in Chipotle, they kind of take a glance at me and they're like, 'Oh gosh.' They scoot forward. That lets you know."

Robert Cornegy, Jr., a 6'10" member of the New York city council, told *USA Today* he needs to be careful not to stand too close to constituents lest it cost him votes the next time he's up for reelection. He said it makes normal-sized people uncomfortable and intimidated.

Many tall people have told me that shorter people are almost afraid to speak to them, perhaps because it's difficult for them to make eye contact from way down there.

Lewis Spears, the extremely tall and totally unfiltered comedian from Australia, has experienced a similar phenomenon, as evidenced by item No. 5 on his YouTube video of "10 things I love about being freakishly tall." He said when he walks into a busy area, people just magically get out of his way. "Whenever I'm in the city, I feel like Moses parting the Red Sea except instead of parting the Red Sea, I'm parting like a really weird mix of office workers, crackheads and really rich Korean kids wearing designer clothes," he said.

This feeling of wariness isn't really that awful. As Spears implied, it might even be useful if you're trying to get someplace in a hurry on the city streets.

But very often, as Terhune indicated, the short man's attitude toward his taller counterpart descends into outright hatred. That becomes more of an issue.

Novelist D. Keith Mano penned an angry essay for *Esquire* in 1978 in which he said "being five four stinks from here to West Mephitis." He admitted to occasionally fantasizing about taking a swing at tall men in barrooms. The entire piece seethed with enmity and disdain for tall men. Mano said if he had been 6'2", he would have written only one novel in his life instead of six. (He went on to write nine.) "Tall men don't have to *do* anything: stand up now and then, perhaps." There also are tinges of envy in Mano's manifesto. "Face it, there is something more sincere, morally better, implied (or perceived as implied) by tallness. It may relate back to the Protestant concept of election: we are justified visibly by success, growth. Tall is good. Honest. Open. Blessed. More American. And more marketable."

Most of us who are 6'6¾" or thereabouts have run into guys like Mano from time to time in our lives. When I was in high school, I worked for a local fast food restaurant at which my manager was a feisty little guy named Mike, who probably was no more than about 5'5". I hadn't yet reached my full growth—that age-17 growth spurt hadn't kicked in—but I still was the tallest of his underlings and he made my life perpetually miserable with his abuse. Seemingly nothing I did met with Mike's approval. He constantly referred to me as Dipshit Donald. The term bullying hadn't come into popular use yet, but as I look back, that's what was happening. Mike may have treated all his employees that way but I don't remember that. I only recall the way he made me feel, seemingly because I was significantly taller than he was.

Many of us also have had moments when some liquored-up David approached us in a barroom and decided he wanted to make us his Goliath. I've had guys come up to me, crane their necks upward, breathe heavily on my chest and try to instigate a confrontation. You face the choice of squashing them like a cockroach or backing off. It's always a no-win situation. If you choose the squash option, you look like a bully. If you retreat, you look like a coward.

Mark Piotrowski, who is 6'10" and lives in the suburbs of

Philadelphia, has faced the same thing throughout his life, even running into it as a kid.

"There was always a small kid trying to prove themselves," he said. "I was kind of a gentle giant as a kid growing up and I definitely got picked on by smaller kids."

He recalled one incident in which he strolled onto the playground in elementary school and suddenly went tumbling to the ground. He looked back to see three small kids who had tripped him. There hadn't been any provocation. He hadn't had any run-ins with these kids before. "They were just looking to prove to their friends that they could beat up a big guy," he said.

Piotrowski did what so many of we gentle giants have been forced to do. He just walked away.

New York Times columnist Russell Baker, a fellow tall guy, wrote that people of extreme stature are almost required to back off in those situations, lest they soil their reputations. He said short people were allowed to be—or actually expected to be—"cocky" or "scrappy" while tall people had to be "Lincolnesque" in their demeanor. That is, they had to be calm, gentle, demure and careful not to crush the spirits of the people around them.

"As one of the long people, I can tell you that we, too, secretly yearn to crush a spirit now and then," Baker said. "But woe be unto the person of great altitude who comes out of the closet and does so. He will not be hailed for a lovable, cocky, little scrapper, but regarded with suspicion and loathing as one who has failed Abraham Lincoln."

Former Wyoming politician Alan Simpson, who at 6'7" was the tallest member of the U.S. Senate for a long time, admitted he faced a few of those bully-or-coward quandaries in his lifetime. He always strived to be as "Lincolnesque" as possible. "Sometimes little guys—and I don't mean this in a denigrative fashion—I was 6 feet 7 inches in college and played football and basketball, and especially when I was drinking beer, which I did quite frequently in college, people would come and say, 'You're a pretty big shot, aren't you?' You had to handle that."

Terhune wrote in his 1926 piece that after centuries of smaller people being bullied, he felt the roles had reversed and short men had free reign to try and bully bigger people. He said he actually envied short and average-sized men "because nobody hates them or has a yearning to punch them, unless they have done something to merit it."

"That sounds absurd, does it?" he added. "Think it over, you men of five-feet-ten, or under. Can you say honestly that you never thought, on seeing some very tall man, 'I'd like to take a punch at that big stiff. I believe I could lick him.' I doubt it. Yet you don't feel that way about other Little People. Why feel so about a harmless Big Guy? It's an ancestral throwback."

Terhune said he puzzled over this phenomenon for years, wondering why short men somehow had a compulsion to prove themselves against tall guys. "I couldn't understand their vicious craving to take a punch at a man much larger than themselves," he said. "Though they don't yield to this craving—being for the most part a prudent folk, and fond of keeping out of the hospital—yet the yearning is there. To me it used to seem a cruelly perverted desire."

Then Terhune was introduced one day to a sideshow attraction who billed himself as the Oklahoma Cowboy Giant. This man was 8'4" (or at least that's how he was advertised) and towered over the 6'2" Terhune, who found himself visualizing what it would be like to take a poke at the big cowpoke. It suddenly occurred to him that there was "a normal human complex, bred of subconscious envy at the greater size of the other fellow."

Fortunately, those confrontational situations seldom come to actual violence. As Terhune indicated, when push almost comes to shove, not all little guys have the bravado of David.

Nancy Jacoby, a 6'0" paralegal, noted in a 1991 *New York Times* story that her height frequently defused contentious situations. "If I'm at a bar and I'm sitting on a bar stool and getting hassled, when I stand up it quiets them down and they'll walk away. It's a presence," she said.

George Mikan told a story in *The Sports Immortals* about how he was driving in Minnesota one day and the driver in front of him slammed on his brakes with Mikan's car crashing into the rear bumper of the other vehicle. "The driver rushed at me, fists clenched and shouted, 'Get out of that car,'" the 6'10" Mikan recalled. "I stepped out slowly and drew up to my full height. The driver's face paled and he backed away. 'All my fault,' he mumbled. 'Guess I shouldn't have stopped so short.'"

Mikan told another story about an episode in his teenage years when he won his neighborhood's marbles championship. This apparently was a huge deal back in Joliet, Illinois, in the 1930s. Mikan was very proud of his accomplishment. But he was subsequently chastised for it by adults who felt it was a case of a big kid taking advantage of the little kids. Mikan's height later helped him succeed in basketball but it's hard to imagine it gave him any sort of edge in shooting marbles. Heck, it might have even been a handicap. Can you picture a guy that big crouching down to get his knuckles on the ground in order to flick his marble? It had to be tough. But people despised Mikan for his victory nonetheless.

The antipathy of smaller people against tall guys can take many forms. Some of the NBA players in that 2016 ESPN poll indicated that they felt their size even turned referees against them. A total of 56 percent said they thought they received fewer favorable calls from officials because of their size.

Some exceedingly tall lawyers have expressed fears that their height might antagonize short people on juries, prompting the attorneys to do things to make themselves tall enough to be attractive and commanding but not so tall that they're intimidating.

Some feel that some small men develop what has come to be known as a Napoleon complex, a proclivity for taking on an aggressive, domineering, sometimes cocky personality in order to compensate for their lack of stature. That would help explain why Terhune felt short people somehow had gotten the upper hand through the years.

Ian Fleming, author of the hugely popular James Bond 007 books, wrote about this in *Goldfinger*, indicating that his signature character had a low (pardon the pun) opinion of diminutive men: "Bond always mistrusted short men. They grew up from childhood with an inferiority complex. All their lives they would strive to be bigger than others who had teased them as a child. Napoleon had been short, and Hitler. It was the short men that created all the trouble in the world."

Hitler, at 5'9", actually was of fairly average height. But Josef Stalin was 5'5". Francisco Franco was 5'4". And Benito Mussolini was 5'7". None of those insidious mid–20th century dictators were big guys.

Then again, Osama Bin Laden was 6'5". It's not just the pint-sized world leaders who aren't trustworthy.

For what it's worth, most psychologists don't believe there is any such thing as a Napoleon complex or a short man's syndrome. "For every hard-driving, ambitious short man there are 100 who are well-adjusted," Dr. Joyce Brothers said.

A University of Central Lancashire study in 2007 also declared this a myth. In a study of 10 short men and 10 men of average height, it found that the larger men reacted more aggressively by having their knuckles rapped with wooden sticks. However, I'm not sure how much stock to put in a study that involved only 20 people, none of whom were of above-average height.

Sidney Portnoy, a psychologist at Temple University, developed a test in the 1970s to correlate a person's height with their personality. He wanted to gauge how a short man reacted to another short man as opposed to how he might react to a taller man. He found the short men grew stubbornly defiant when confronted by disagreement with tall men. "They get their backs arched up when they're with tall people," he said. "They become very defensive. I thought they would feel threatened and conform more with a tall man, but they were threatened and conformed less."

Very few things have done as much to fuel the hard feelings that short people have toward tall people as a song written and performed by Randy Newman in 1977. Newman's song, titled "Short People," is catchy and clever but pretty harsh. It talks about how short people have "little hands" and "little eyes" and suggests that they "walk around tellin' great big lies." It undoubtedly infuriated some height-challenged people by mentioning that some of them wear platform shoes on their "nasty little feet" and it ultimately concludes that "short people got no reason to live."

The song struck nerves all over the country. Isaiah Dixon, a 5'5" member of the Maryland House of Delegates, proposed a bill calling for the song to be banned from the airwaves in his state. The state's attorney general quickly pointed out that would be a blatant infringement on the First Amendment.

Several radio stations in Wisconsin declined to play Newman's tune following protests from officials in the Madison school district, one of whom had a son who was a dwarf. The officials claimed the song was "a derogatory comment on people in general" and was "messing up" kids in the district who were short of stature.

Not everyone hated it. The song reached No. 2 on the Billboard Top 100 charts and it was boffo in Buffalo. One disc jockey in that city defiantly played it 18 consecutive times on the radio, and when Newman held a concert in Buffalo, the crowd implored him to sing "Short People" as an encore even though he already had performed it earlier in the concert.

Newman, who was barely 6 feet himself, was dismayed by the backlash, insisting that it was a satire intended to poke fun at people who are short figuratively, who are small-minded in their thinking. He was frustrated that so many people didn't get the joke and misinterpreted his words as bigotry. "I would never write a song to make fun of someone or something," he told the *Chicago Tribune*. "What I'm making fun of is people's callousness and insensitivity."

There is no question that there remains a lingering animosity between people of divergent heights. A few years ago, there was a social media campaign promoting "National Kick a Tall Person Day." People who were 5'4" and under were encouraged to kick a tall person in the shins that day. In fairness, it appeared to be a reaction to "National Throw a Short Person Day."

But there are some signs that the way in which tall and short people view each other is softening, evolving toward less envy and hatred. A 2004 research study surveyed 956 students in grades 6 through 12 to gauge how they viewed other students based on height. The kids were not told the purpose of the study and were asked to assign their classmates to play parts in an imaginary dramatic play. The expectation was that the tall kids would be portrayed as leaders or villains and the short kids would be stereotyped as clowns or heroic underdogs, but there ended up being no evidence of any sort of bias of any kind.

It's encouraging. Perhaps the lines between tall and short are being blurred. Maybe we'll all be able to get along more amicably in the future. Maybe the D. Keith Manos of the world will be able to have a beer with the Albert Terhunes without harboring fantasies of physical mayhem.

Maybe. It would be nice.

10

We're Smarter ... Just Ask Us

In one of the early scenes of the 1948 film *Good Sam*, Sam Clayton (played by Gary Cooper) is sitting in church and is asked to help take the collection. He agrees to do it but his wife (played by Ann Sheridan) says, "You can't take the collection. You're too tall. You'll look silly. You're too clumsy."

Sam agrees to do it anyway, and predictably, he drops the collection plate, spilling loose change all over the place and eliciting laughter from the gathered flock. One more stereotype perpetuated.

It's another example of tall people being portrayed in popular culture as clumsy and stupid.

If you're familiar with John Steinbeck's classic story *Of Mice and Men*, you know it's about two men who travel the countryside together. George is short and smart. Lenny is tall and feeble-minded.

Look at the inept crooks in the *Home Alone* movies. Although neither of them is especially bright, the short guy (played by Joe Pesci) is the brains of the outfit and the tall guy (Daniel Stern) is the buffoon.

Who is the tallest Disney character you can think of? Probably Goofy.

Think of how tall people are portrayed in various television series, especially those in the 1960s, 1970s and 1980s. There is Jethro Bodine on *Beverly Hillbillies*, Gomer Pyle on the old *Andy Griffith* series, Dauber on *Coach*. All tall, all clumsy, all stupid.

We can't really debunk the clumsy part of the stereotype. There may be some small threads of truth to that. Just ask my wife.

But as for the stupid part, that's total BS. You short folks may want to sit down for this one, not that you aren't already pretty close to the ground anyway: Numerous studies through the years have shown that we tall folks actually are smarter than you.

Nearly every attempt to scientifically quantify this thing—and there have been dozens—has come up with the same conclusion. There isn't a single study that has come up with the opposite conclusion to support what is frequently depicted in popular culture. Scientists struggle to explain the phenomenon in terms that even super-smart tall people can fully understand but the conclusion is clear. Close the case. Drop the mike. Etch it in stone: Tall people generally are smart and short people are, well, not quite as smart.

It's not universally true, of course. There have been plenty of highly intelligent people of meager height and we all know a few really tall dufuses. But in the aggregate, there is a noticeable trend toward a relationship between altitude and aptitude.

Scientists have been studying this hypothesis for centuries. Probably the first to dig into it in any detail was Sir Francis Galton, an eminent and astonishingly versatile scientist in Victorian England. Galton, a distant cousin of Charles Darwin, visited just about every corner of the scientific world at one time or another. He devised the first weather map. He was the first to prove that no two sets of fingerprints were the same. He dabbled in biology, psychology, meteorology, mathematics, statistics, forensics, genetics, and eugenics. He actually coined the term eugenics. He was a pioneer in the concept of correlation, authoring such books as *Hereditary Genius* in 1869 and *Natural Inheritance* in 1889.

Mingled among all of those scientific explorations and discoveries, Galton expressed the opinion that there was a definite correlation between how tall you were and how smart you were. He lived before the advent of IQ tests—Alfred Binet and Theodore Simon devised the first one in 1905—so he measured intelligence with reaction times to sounds. He contrasted those results with measurements he collected in his studies of heredity and identified a pattern.

Since then, there have been numerous attempts to either deny or confirm Galton's theories. While some have questioned how pronounced the pattern is, no one has come to the conclusion that smaller people are superior intellectually.

Donald G. Paterson, a professor at the University of Minnesota, came the closest to doing so. He conducted his own study many years later and concluded in a 1931 book, *Physique and Intellect*, that there is no significant connection between physical traits and mental ones.

He didn't say that short people were more intelligent, but he said that Galton's evidence was "wholly unconvincing."

"Our survey has demonstrated that prevalent notions regarding an intimate relation between bodily traits and mental development have been greatly exaggerated," Paterson said. "Structural characteristics such as height and weight seem related to intelligence to only a slight extent.... Hope of finding positive relationships of greater magnitude by employing complicated indices of body build seems to vanish when carefully controlled investigations are made."

As proof of his theories, Paterson identified two male students at Minnesota who were at opposite ends of the height spectrum, with a 20-inch difference in size, and found them to be very comparable in intellect. Hopefully, his conclusions were based on a sample size of more than two people. In any case, his is perhaps the only study that has not supported the hypothesis that more height equates to more intelligence.

Just a year later, in 1932, Dr. Shepherd Dawson offered contradictory ideas in a report called "Intelligence and Disease" that was produced for the Medical Research Council of Great Britain. In a survey conducted at two hospitals in Glasgow, he found that "children of a higher intelligence tend to be slightly taller than other children." His study involved 1,000 poverty-level children and detected "clear evidence of a correlation" between height and intelligence, finding that the correlation was even stronger with boys than with girls.

Dr. Meinhard Robinow, a pediatrician and anthropologist in Yellow Springs, Ohio, offered his thoughts on the subject in 1969, expressing the opinion that intelligence goes along with having a larger brain. He concluded that it was reasonable to think that bigger people had bigger heads and bigger brains and were smarter as a result. Many decades earlier, anthropologist Ales Hrdlicka determined that taller people generally do have slightly larger brains.

More extensive and more credible studies in more modern times have reached similar conclusions.

A group of researchers at Stanford University, headed by Dr. Darrell Wilson, found proof of "a small but significant association between relative height and IQ scores" in children in 1986.

The Stanford study looked at 13,887 kids between the ages of 6 and 17 and was detailed in an article in *Pediatrics*, the journal of the American Academy of Pediatrics. It suggested that the intelligence gap between tall and short could be environmental, speculating that adults may tend to treat smaller children differently, babying them more than they do tall kids. "Perhaps people treat shorter children as if they were younger than they really are," Wilson wrote.

It does make sense that a tall kid might be given more attention and more responsibility, especially in a classroom setting, and that he may also be challenged more by teachers, thereby elevating his intellectual potential. Wilson's study also threw out the idea that height and intelligence might be linked in that they could be equally impacted by intrauterine or postnatal malnutrition. It also found that the results of the study were not impacted by such things as birth order or the size or affluence of the family.

Wilson, who was 5'5", admitted to being surprised by his own findings. "I actually thought that short people would do better, but I was proven wrong," he said.

A study done by University of Illinois researcher Lloyd G. Humphreys in the mid–1980s expanded on this analysis and expressed the opinion that any correlation between height and intelligence is based on standing height.

That idea was echoed by Arthur Jensen and S.N. Sinha, a pair of psychologists who co-authored a 1990 paper on the subject. Jensen and Sinha attempted to pull together data from all previous studies and correlate IQs with all sorts of physical attributes, not just height but also weight, brain size, vision, eye pigmentation, age at the onset of puberty, blood chemistry, allergies, metabolism and even the subjects' ability to curl their tongues.

They ended up with the same conclusion as Humphreys: The best indicator of intelligence is having long legs. In other words, the height of a person when they're sitting down is a non-factor in determining intelligence. It's how tall they are when they're standing up. Their explanation is a little complicated and seems like a reach, but they speculated that attractive women with very long legs are most likely to mate with men with high incomes and high IQs, thereby creating a connection between long legs and high IQs. Jensen and Sinha pretty much admitted they were guessing, but they were hard pressed to find any other logical reason for such a connection.

There have been tons of other studies done around the world, all trying to get at the roots of this phenomenon.

A study in the Netherlands between 1985 and 2005 looked at height/intelligence correlations in twins. A 1991 survey in Denmark involved 76,111 subjects. There was another one in Sweden in 1999 that studied 32,887 men who were 18 years old. In 2005, scientists in Norway looked at 1,181 identical twins and 1,412 fraternal twins and found that 59 percent of the height-intelligence correlation could be attributed to environmental factors. Genetics, they said, only accounted for about 35 percent.

A study performed on 6,815 unrelated people in Scotland between 2006 and 2011 by Edinburgh University's Institute of Genetic and Molecular Medicine in conjunction with researchers from University College London came up with the same conclusion: Shorter people are less likely to be intelligent than their taller counterparts although it stated that there was only a "small association" between height and intelligence.

One of the most intriguing assessments of the topic was done in 2009 by evolutionary psychologist Satoshi Kanazawa, who published his findings in *Psychology Today.*

Kanazawa stated flatly that men are more intelligent than women. (We don't know if he was married, but if he was, we're betting he slept on the couch for a while.) He determined that this is likely just because men are taller. He admitted he honestly can't explain precisely why tall people come up with higher IQs in all these studies but he threw out two possible theories.

One is pretty simple. It's that "both height and intelligence may be indicators of underlying health. According to this view, people who are genetically and developmentally healthier simultaneously grow taller and become more intelligent than those who are less healthy, producing the positive correlation between height and intelligence."

His second theory is much more complex and states that a combination of factors add up to this phenomenon. He said it could be a product of "assertive mating" between tall men and beautiful women, compounded by the mating of smart men and beautiful women. It's what he termed "extrinsic correlation."

One other potential factor cited by Kanazawa is that taller parents are more likely to have sons. "So, over many generations, more sons will inherit their parents' genes inclining them to be taller and more intelligent, and more daughters will inherit their parents' genes inclining them to be shorter and less intelligent."

Kanazawa is not the only scientist ever to suggest that men are smarter than women. J. Philippe Rushton, a professor at the

University of Western Ontario, made the same contention in 2006 and he actually said much more controversial things prior to that. He authored studies in the 1990s that contended Asians were superior intellectually to whites and that whites were superior to Blacks. Those findings were loudly and vociferously denounced and prompted many to also dismiss his 2006 statements, which were based on a study of the SAT scores of 100,000 teenagers. That study found boys had IQs 3.63 points higher than girls.

There has been one other study with very intriguing results, which may at least partially refute the notion that tall people are smarter because of the way they are treated by teachers in school. The study, done by Princeton University economists Anne Case and Christina Paxson, was published in the University of Chicago's *Journal of Political Economy* in 2006 and actually was intended to determine why tall people are more successful in the business world.

Case and Paxson concluded that it may simply be because they're a little bit smarter. They studied children born in the United States and the United Kingdom and found there were signs that the tall kids were smarter as early as the age of 5 in terms of "conceptual maturity, visual-motor coordination, and vocabulary." In other words, they already were displaying signs of higher intelligence before any teachers got a hold of them.

They speculated that kids who were smarter were better fed and better nurtured and came from more affluent backgrounds, implying that their cognitive ability and their size both had their roots in prenatal and early childhood care.

When the findings of Case and Paxson were released, the report generally was applauded by academics as ground-breaking and revealing. Then the Reuters News Service published a small story about their findings under the glaring headline "Taller people are smarter—study."

The story provided only a tiny sliver of a 51-page block of research and focused on an aspect that echoed what had been found many times previously in other studies, but it resulted in a firestorm of criticism. Case and Paxson were showered with emails, most of them hostile and many of them profane, accusing them of prejudice and bigotry and offering anecdotal evidence that there are highly intelligent short men in the world.

It also accused them of bias based on the fact that both women were a bit on the tall side. Paxson was 5'9", Case 5'8".

"The idea that we would have written it any differently had we been five feet two is frustrating," Paxson said. "It's sort of like if you're driving and somebody thinks you did something wrong and they give you the finger. You know you didn't do anything wrong, but you also feel, like, how could they think that of me?"

So, are tall people really smarter as a whole? Maybe. Like we said, there is no disputing that there are some very bright short people and some dim-witted giants. But it does seem as though many of the genetic markers that make people tall also make them intelligent.

I sort of like what Jack Marshall, a 6'9" resident of Marin County, California, told us. He said he isn't really sure if tall people have a higher level of intelligence so much as they seem to have "a heightened sense of awareness."

11

We May Not Be Quite as Healthy

Doctors have been dissecting and debating this question for generations. Ask 100 different medical experts whether it's better from a health standpoint to be tall or short and you may get 100 divergent answers.

There are pros and cons each way. It's probably a split decision. A lot of people will tell you that it's a little bit healthier to be just a little bit short. Then again, someone who is 6'6¾" (and who never attended a day of medical school) might have a contradictory opinion.

Thomas T. Samaras definitely thinks it's healthier to be short. And to be honest, he may be in a better position to make this call than almost anyone we know.

Samaras grew up in New York as the son of Greek immigrants who weren't very tall. They stuffed their kids with all sorts of meat and gravy and a couple of quarts a milk a day, and Thomas sprouted all the way up to 5'10". But as an adult, he came to realize that all those protein-soaked food products that made him taller than his parents weren't likely to keep him on this earth for very long. He became a vegetarian and has devoted more than six decades to the study of human growth and longevity, becoming one of the world's foremost experts on the subject. He has written a couple of books and several articles for the National Library of Medicine on the subject, and his research has been quoted by more than 2,000 scientists in studies of their own.

He's not a doctor either, by the way. He's an engineer. But since he is extremely average in height, he probably doesn't have a built-in bias in either direction. When he says that the world would be better off if more of us were just a little less tall, that carries a lot of weight.

But it's definitely debatable. Here is the abridged assessment: It's generally agreed that tall people are less susceptible to heart disease, diabetes, Alzheimer's disease and strokes. Tall women also appear to be better able to handle childbirth and tall men seemingly are less likely to go bald. (That may seem like a trivial item to some of you, but I like it.) On the other hand, taller than average folks also may be somewhat more vulnerable to cancer, lung ailments, blood clots and atrial fibrillation. They also might be more likely to suffer backaches and possibly even headaches.

Who lives longer? Tall people or short people? You can find studies that lean both ways on that one.

Samaras teamed with researchers at the University of California San Diego to study deceased veterans at the San Diego VA Medical Center. A survey of 373 men found that those who were 5'9" or shorter lived an average of five years longer than those who were taller than 5'9".

Another study of 1,700 deceased men and women in Cuyahoga County, Ohio, also found that taller men had shorter lifespans. Every inch they were over normal height translated to 1.2 fewer years on their lifespans.

In his 1994 book, *The Truth About Your Height: Exploring the Myths and Realities of Human Size and Its Effects on Performance, Health, Pollution and Survival,* Samaras cited similar trends with baseball players, basketball players, football players, celebrities, U.S. presidents, boxers, strongmen, giants and famous British people. He admitted in one of his earliest interviews, in 1978, that a lot of his opinions are based on his "gut feeling" and it's easy to be skeptical of some of his findings.

For example, some of that research, especially with the presidents, represented a very small sample size. Samaras did at least exclude the four presidents who have died as a result of assassination, which obviously would have greatly skewed his research. Some of the giants he studied undoubtedly suffered from gigantism, acromegaly and Marfan Syndrome, and people with those afflictions frequently don't live beyond their 30s. His study of football players predated revelations about chronic traumatic encephalopathy (CTE), which has demonstrated that the long-time health of many football players is impacted by repeated head injuries.

It's easy to see how any of those things could distort his research in favor of short people. He also cited a Cornell University study that indicated that small rats lived longer than large ones. We'll concede that perhaps tall rodents are destined to die early. We've tried to confine our own research to human beings.

However, we need to give Samaras the benefit of the doubt based on more than a half century of expert analysis of data on this subject. His conclusions undoubtedly have merit.

Some of the studies he has factored into his theories make loads of sense. He cited multiple surveys of professional basketball players and one on West Point graduates that both showed the shorter men tended to live a few years longer. Since the subjects in those studies had what he called "similar homogenous qualities and lifestyles," the results would seem to be much more valid.

Samaras repeatedly points out that pure height is only one small slice in a whole loaf of factors that dictate how long people live. He thinks things such as lifestyle, diet, stress, body type and body mass are much bigger slices.

His 1994 book does provide some evidence of contradictory trends, which point to the idea that taller people might live longer. There was one study of 1.8 million people in Norway in 1984, another on 12,000 male civil servants in 1990 and one on men in England and Wales in 1990 that all indicated tall folks have greater longevity. A study of 12,695 people in Sweden in 1980 found that the tallest subjects lived 20 percent longer than the shortest ones.

A 1921 study that tracked 2 million recruits during World War I was fairly inconclusive. It did find that tall men were more vulnerable to certain ailments, but it reflected no significant difference in lifespan.

There definitely are certain corners of the globe where it seemingly pays to be short. Some of the shortest people in the world live in Okinawa, a prefecture of Japan that is comprised of about 150 islands in the Pacific. The average adult male there was reported to be 4'9" in 2015. Okinawa also has about seven times as many centenarians per capita as any other place in the world. The people there have amazingly low rates of cancer and heart disease and they live much longer lives, apparently because they have a very low-calorie diet almost entirely free of any sort of fat. They eat mostly vegetables, grains and fish, drink tons of tea and imbibe regularly a type of rice liquor called awamori that is crammed with antioxidants.

It's very clear that their diet and lifestyle are the major contributors to their longevity because Okinawans who have moved to the

Japanese mainland or other places don't do nearly as well. So, it's not really because they're short. It's because of their environment.

By the way, remind me to see if awamori is available at my local liquor store.

There is no question that there are some health factors that favor the tall. At the very least, it seems clear that people of above normal stature are less likely to drop over dead from a heart attack, even though that is what happened to both my tall father and my very tall grandfather.

A couple of different studies in Boston showed 30 years ago that there definitely is a correlation between height and the risk of a heart attack. A Boston University study in 1990 showed that short women are more susceptible to heart attacks and further research demonstrated the same conclusion in men. That study, conducted by Harvard University researchers, began in 1982 and compiled data from 22,000 doctors over a five-year period, looking at men between the ages of 40 and 84. In the ensuing five years, 378 of the men suffered a heart attack for the first time and an alarmingly high number of them were short guys. The conclusion was that men who are 5'7" and shorter have a 60 percent higher risk of suffering a heart attack than men 6'1" or taller. For every inch someone is over 5'7", their risk drops by 3 percentage points.

A more recent study published in the *New England Journal of Medicine* studied 200,000 people and found that every 2.5 inches of additional height meant they were 13.5 percent less likely to develop coronary artery disease, most likely because of "shared biologic processes that determine achieved height and atherosclerosis development."

(We're going to be throwing a lot of those sort of complex statistics and some really big words at you over the next several pages so forgive us if your head begins to swim. Do what you can to at least tread water.)

The logical explanation for tall people's reduced vulnerability to heart ailments is that short men have narrower coronary arteries and smaller blood cells, which could make them more susceptible to clots or blockages. Smaller men may also suffer from smaller lung capacity, limiting their ability to supply oxygenated blood to the heart.

A 2016 paper published in *Lancet Diabetes & Endocrinology* indicated that for every 2½ inches of height a person has, they have

6 percent less chance of dying from heart disease, possibly because their lungs and hearts may simply be bigger and stronger.

Samaras also cited studies that indicated tall people, who tended to also be higher on the economic scale, were inclined to smoke and drink less than their shorter, less affluent counterparts. That could contribute in some small way to this trend.

USA Today reported in 1995 that clot-busting drugs benefited big and tall men more than short men, allowing them to more effectively survive heart attacks. This study was massive. It covered 1,081 hospitals in 15 countries and involved 41,021 patients. It showed that not only did tall men have a better survival rate but they also experienced fewer side effects such as bleeding complications caused by the drugs. Again, the speculation was that it was a result of bigger men simply having bigger arteries.

There has been other research, however, that seemingly contradicts some of these findings.

A 16-year study concluded in 2017 pointed to the possibility that tall women might be as much as three times more likely to develop atrial fibrillation, a disruption in the rhythm of the heart.

Another 2017 study published in the journal *Circulation: Cardiovascular Genetics* found that taller people may be more likely to develop venous thromboembolisms, blood clots that are the third leading cause of strokes and heart attacks. In a survey of more than 2 million Swedish siblings, it was determined that men shorter than 5'3" had a 65 percent lower risk of developing such clots than men who are taller than 6'2". They found the same trend in pregnant women, who are susceptible to thromboembolisms. Women shorter than 5'1" had a 69 percent less chance of getting one than women 6'0" and taller. Dr. Bengt Zöller, associate professor at Lund University and Malmö University Hospital, said it may just be a product of gravity. "It could just be that because taller individuals have longer leg veins there is more surface area where problems can occur," he added.

Looks like another split decision, doesn't it?

There is a lot less disagreement about diabetes.

Another study: A look at 2,662 adults in Germany between 1994 and 1998 found that tall people were at a significantly lower risk of developing type 2 diabetes. The risk declined by 41 percent for every 10 centimeters (just less than four inches) of additional height for men and 33 percent for women in the study, which was published in *Diabetologia*.

It's possible that the same high protein diets in childhood that make people tall might lead to increased production of a hormone that helps the body control cholesterol and blood sugar levels. The German researchers pointed to "higher liver fat content and a less favorable profile of cardiometabolic risk factors."

Researchers admitted they weren't entirely sure how to explain this revelation. Dr. Matthias Schulze, head of the department of molecular epidemiology at the German Institute of Human Nutrition Potsdam-Rehbruecke, wrote: "Supporting a role for diabetes, it has been reported that taller people are more insulin sensitive and have better beta-cell function, which might partly be a result of less ectopic fat storage (e.g., in the liver). Recent Mendelian randomization studies support that height is associated with cardiovascular risk and that this risk might at least in part be mediated by cardiometabolic risk factors relevant for type 2 diabetes, namely (blood pressure), blood lipids and inflammation. However, the relevance of liver fat and cardiometabolic risk factors as potential mediating factors linking height and its components to diabetes risk remains largely unknown."

Ectopic? Randomization? Cardiometabolic? Hopefully, you're still treading water.

On the topic of tall vs. short where dementia and Alzheimer's disease are concerned, it again looks as though it's preferable to be big.

A 2014 study published in the *British Journal of Psychiatry* determined that shorter people are more susceptible to these afflictions. This research analyzed 180,000 medical records collected from 1994 through 2008. The conclusion of senior researcher Dr. David Batty: "Short height in itself of course does not 'cause' dementia. Rather, height captures a number of early life factors, including early-life illness, adversity, poor nutrition, and psychosocial stress, and so allows us to examine the effect of these factors on dementia more closely." One clue is that growth hormones not only are linked to how tall someone is but they also impact something called hippocampal function and cognition.

Another research project done at Case Western Reserve University in Cleveland in 2007 found that the tallest group of men had a 59 percent lower risk of developing Alzheimer's.

And a 2005 study done jointly by researchers in New York and Israel also found that men who suffered from Alzheimer's and dementia tended to be shorter. They reasoned it was most likely because of childhood nutrition and other obstacles in their early development, which also impacted their lack of height.

Yet another deep dive into this topic in 1998 showed men 5'1" and under had a 25 percent chance of suffering from dementia. For men 5'9" or taller, it was only 9 percent.

While undernutrition may, in fact, lead to tall people suffering fewer problems with dementia, there is some thought that overnutrition could lead to a slight inclination toward cancer.

That same 2016 *Lancet* report we mentioned earlier indicated that people have a 4 percent greater chance of dying from cancer for every 2½ inches taller they are than their peers. I know that's a really small number—really too minuscule to even worry about—but it is one for the short folks' side of the ledger.

The speculation is that the same animal proteins that made people tall could leave some cells in their body vulnerable to mutations.

German researchers also suggested that the larger the organ the more likely it is to get cancer. Some other studies indicated that tall men might be more susceptible to prostate cancer—I overcame that myself in 2004—and that tall women could have an inclination toward melanoma.

Speaking of tall women, here is one more check mark for the high side of the ledger: There is considerable evidence that the taller a woman is, the more easily she is likely to handle childbirth.

A 1988 study done in Canada and reported in the *American Journal of Obstetrics and Gynecology* assessed 781 first-time mothers and found women 5'2" and shorter were almost twice as likely to have "difficult labor" as women 5'5" and taller. Difficult labor was defined as being in labor for more than 15 hours or requiring a Caesarian section. It happened with 10 percent of tall women compared to 27 percent of short women.

Molly Thomson, an epidemiologist from Victoria, British Columbia, told *Parenting* magazine that for every inch taller a woman is, the more likely she is to have an easier labor.

As with so many of these things, the experts can only speculate about the reasons but they think this one might have something to do with shorter women having smaller pelvic openings.

There obviously are some physical attributes that make it better to be short. For one, tall people generally endure more back problems, especially in the lower lumbar region. This is easier to explain than most of these other things. All of us have the same number of vertebrae in our back whether we're 5'2" or 7'2". It stands to reason that with those vertebrae spread further apart, they can be more easily stretched and strained. We oversized folks seem destined to have dysfunctional posture. As we bend over to type on a computer, slouch to make ourselves look shorter, contort our bodies to get into a car or airplane seat or bend over to hear what the short guy next to us is saying, we're placing wear and tear on the back muscles. We don't need some elaborate medical study or a litany of 14-letter words to tell us that.

There also seemingly is some truth to the old adage "The bigger they are, the harder they fall."

Tall people have a higher center of gravity and therefore may be more prone to taking spills. Remember how we told you a few chapters ago that NFL teams don't want 6'5" running backs? That's because a 5'8" guy with a bowling ball body has a much lower center of balance and is infinitely more difficult to knock off his feet.

And when we fall, we're a lot further from the ground than you short people and therefore more likely to suffer serious injury.

That image of Gary Cooper taking a tumble and spilling the collection plate all over the place in *Good Sam* isn't a myth. We probably are more clumsy and injury-prone. Score one for the short guys.

There also is a school of thought that tall people may take a bit longer to heal those bruises and broken bones. There are studies to indicate that since our nerve impulses have more ground to cover the healing process may be slightly more tedious.

However, here is something you might not have thought about: Tall people may have a better shot at surviving an automobile accident because of one modern-day factor: airbags. A 1997 study found anyone sitting too close to an airbag when it inflates could suffer serious head or neck injuries. Someone sitting further away or higher generally won't be hit by the airbag until it is fully inflated and thereby will be helped by it rather than being hurt. Dr. Tilman Jolly, chairman of the National Conference on Medical Indications for Air Bag Disconnection, cited statistics implying that perhaps very short people would be wise to disconnect their airbags to avert injury in the event of a crash.

It has been shown that larger people probably also have larger organs although the size of their hearts, livers, kidneys, lungs and brains seemingly is more affected by their weight than their height.

I did have a doctor tell me many years ago when I got my first colonoscopy that I had one of the longest colons he had ever seen. It was so lengthy that the instruments available to him at that time were not long enough to reach the very end of my colon and, as a result, he subjected me to a barium enema afterward so that he could check out the portion he could not inspect during the colonoscopy. In terms of looking at the pros and cons of things, that was a really big con. The enema was 10 times worse than the colonoscopy. In any case, the size of my colon apparently had little to do with the fact that I'm tall. Just the luck of the draw.

(For a long time, I had an alternate theory. Just before the doctor put me under for the procedure, he and I engaged in some amiable banter about football, and upon hearing that I was a Chicago Bears fan, he informed me that he was a Green Bay Packer backer. I vaguely recall making some sort of wisecrack about Brett Favre. I wondered for a long time if the doctor, who was very short, didn't decide right then and there that this guy was getting a barium enema.)

For centuries, there has been an urban legend about the correlation between the size of a man's body and the size of one specific male-related body part. You know the one I'm talking about.

Women have speculated for years that they could discern the size of that body part by the man's height or by the size of his feet, hands, thumbs or possibly even by his race.

The St. Louis-based research team of William Masters and Virginia Johnson spent 24 years studying all aspects of sexual relations between men and women, and their conclusion was that any correlation between a man's height and the size of his penis was pure mythology. They performed a study in 1966 in which they measured the penises of 312 men in their flaccid (unstimulated) state and couldn't find any connection. In fact, the largest piece of equipment in their study belonged to a man who was 5'7" and the puniest was on a 5'11" guy.

Although there is very little real scientific evidence to back the big guy/big equipment myth, Dr. Paul Turek left open that possibility on his website, Theturekclinic.com, in 2018: "In actual fact, the only consistent scientific correlation described is between penis size and a man's height, and it's a weak one at that."

The *British Journal of Urology* also did a 2015 study on this. Researchers measured the penises of 1,521 men—how would you like that assignment?—and found that all the urban legends about the size of feet and hands and thumbs matching up with the size of their genitals were baseless. But they indicated there may be some small threads of truth to the height-penis correlation.

It's a very small connection, though. As blogger Lucy Tiven wrote in 2016: "Swiping right for tall dudes doesn't guarantee you a bigger package."

There are a few other fairly insignificant medical pros and cons relating to our height.

A 2017 study in Great Britain indicated that tall people may be more likely to be bitten by mosquitos. The feeling is that our larger body surface leads to more carbon dioxide output, thereby making us more attractive targets for those insidious bugs.

And a German study, also in 2017, determined that short men probably are more likely to go bald than their taller counterparts.

The research, conducted at the Institute of Human Genetics at the University of Bonn, looked at more than 22,000 men from seven countries and demonstrated that many of the same genetic markers that lead to a lack of height also are linked to male-pattern baldness. They identified 63 alterations in the human genome that are linked to a tendency for men to lose their hair. The same study found correlations with light skin color and increased bone density. The reasons for this have yet to be determined but there is some thought that it is tied to early puberty and the premature fusing of growth plates.

The good news for we tall guys is that when all of you short guys do go bald, we'll notice it before you will.

12

We Make Good Leaders

Some experts are inclined to chalk this up to something called evolutionary psychology. Since the days of the caveman, the largest and the strongest always have been the dominant figures, the warriors, the leaders, the protectors of those who are smaller and weaker, so we're conditioned to think that bigger is better.

Others think this is something that is inbred in all of us. As children, our parents and all adult authority figures are larger than us so we're conditioned to look up—both literally and figuratively—to people who are taller than us.

Whatever theory you subscribe to, it's clear that taller, more imposing people frequently take the leading role in business, the workplace and personal relationships. And it is especially evident in government and politics.

"Not to get too psychological about this, but some of it has to do with looking up at daddy and assuming power and size go together," said Dr. Henry Biller, a psychology professor at the University of Rhode Island who co-authored a book titled *Stature and Stigma* with David Myers and Leslie Martel in 1987.

History obviously is filled with tall people who had great leadership qualities. Some had a natural shyness or sheepishness about their height and may have been reticent to accept a leadership role, but they had it thrust upon them nevertheless and actually blossomed in that capacity.

That was the case with arguably the two most revered presidents in American history: George Washington and Abraham Lincoln.

Washington is generally thought to have been either 6'2" or 6'3" at a time when the average adult male was about 5'6". There is a story that Washington often ordered clothing from a tailor in London and described himself as being only 6 feet but the clothes he received were too small and needed to be altered, lending credence to the notion that he was taller than that. There was another report that a doctor measured Washington's corpse after his death and found him to be 6'3½". Whatever his exact height, it was clear that our first president was significantly taller than almost everyone else in his era.

Although he had a burning passion and a combustible temper, Washington generally was viewed as being outwardly humble. Upon being named the commander of the Continental army in the early stages of the Revolutionary War, he said: "I am truly sensible of the high honor done me in this appointment, yet I feel great distress from a consciousness that my abilities and military experience may not be equal to the extensive and important trust."

But it was inevitable that he gravitated toward leadership roles at least in part because of his size. He is frequently described as having had "a tall, commanding physical presence." There is a great line in the 2008 HBO mini-series *John Adams* in which Adams refers to Washington as a "natural leader" and Benjamin Franklin responds: "He's always the tallest man in the room. He's bound to end up leading something."

Lincoln also seems to have had mixed feelings about his height. According to a 1992 *New York Times* article, someone once asked him how tall a man should be, and he said, "A man should be tall enough so that his feet touch the ground."

The best source we have for Lincoln's size is portrait artist Francis Bicknell Carpenter, who was curious about Abe's actual stature one day. He had the president stand next to a large canvas and he marked how tall he was and then measured it. He determined that Lincoln was 6'3¾' in his stocking feet, which would tie him with Lyndon Johnson as the tallest president in American history.

Lincoln occasionally made fun of the fascination with his height although he apparently was quite proud of being much taller than the average 19th-century American male. Often, when encountering another tall man, Lincoln would stand back to back with the other man to compare and see who was taller. He also poked fun at the difference in height between himself and his wife Mary, who was only 5'2". He would tell people, "I'm the flag pole and Mrs. Lincoln is the flag."

Lincoln's father, Thomas, was of no more than average height and we know very little about his mother, Nancy Hanks, but we do know that by the time he was 17 Lincoln was 6'2" and he continued to grow a few more inches after that.

Most of Lincoln's height was in his legs, and one of Lincoln's many biographers, Stephen Oates, wrote that he felt he was "gawky" looking because of his height and as a result was very standoffish around members of the opposite sex as a young man. Oates noted that he occasionally was made fun of by young girls.

One of Lincoln's contemporaries, statesman and journalist Carl Schurz, said Lincoln had problems finding clothes that fit properly. (E-commerce was more than a century away.) After watching Lincoln in the sixth of his famous debates with Stephen Douglas at Quincy in October 1858, Schurz wrote: "His lank, ungainly body was clad in a rusty black dress coat with sleeves that should have been longer, but his arms appeared so long that the sleeves of a store coat could hardly be expected to cover all the way down to the wrists. His black trousers, too, permitted a very full view of his large feet."

Lincoln's long legs and lanky frame worked to his advantage in the wrestling matches in which he loved to take part and he also took advantage of his size once when challenged to a duel by political adversary James Shields.

A dispute between the two men arose in 1842 when the Illinois State Bank went bankrupt and opted to no longer accept paper currency that it had issued. Shields, a Democrat and the state auditor, was among the biggest supporters of the decision. Lincoln, a leader in the opposing Whig party, allegedly wrote a scathing letter to the editor that was published in the *Sangamo Journal* under the pen name "Rebecca." There is some speculation that Mary Todd, who eventually became Lincoln's wife, actually wrote the letter. In any case, the piece not only criticized Shields' politics but also attacked him personally, mentioning his Irish ancestry and suggesting that perhaps he should go back to where he came from.

When Shields was informed that Lincoln probably was the author of the letter, he challenged the 33-year-old state legislator to a duel, which was to be fought across the border in Missouri, where dueling was legal. Lincoln was allowed to choose the weapons, and in order to take advantage of a huge reach advantage over a man seven or eight inches shorter, he selected cavalry broadswords. In truth, he didn't want to kill Shields any more than he wanted to be killed himself. When the duel commenced on the morning of September 22, 1842, Lincoln quickly reached up and with one swipe cut a branch off a willow tree above the head of Shields, who immediately recognized that he had no chance against such a tall opponent. He backed off and the two men reached a truce.

Because Lincoln's parents were not exceptionally large, there began to be speculation in the 20th century that Lincoln's extreme size might have been the result of Marfan Syndrome, a disorder that affects the connective tissue in the body and can lead to excessive growth in extremities, among other things.

Lincoln not only was very tall but had extremely long fingers and toes, an apparent deformity in his chest and hollowed eyes. He also was stoop-shouldered and may have shuffled somewhat as he walked, all signs that would point to Marfan.

Marfan victims also frequently suffer from circulatory problems, have a high-pitched voice and are clumsy and non-athletic. None of those was the case with Lincoln, who was an expert wrestler and, according to some accounts, a very fast runner. Also, people who suffer from Marfan seldom live to the age of 50. Lincoln was 56 at the time he was assassinated in Ford's Theatre in 1865.

Nevertheless, researchers sought to study strands of hair and blood stains preserved from Lincoln to test his DNA and they received permission to do so in 1991. The hope was that if they could prove Lincoln had Marfan, it could inspire and enhance the self-esteem of people who suffer from the affliction. They never found any evidence to support their speculation, however.

Washington and Lincoln are not the only tall men to serve as president. Of the 45 men who have held the office, 24 were more than 6 feet tall, led by Lincoln and Johnson. Donald Trump frequently has said he is 6'3" although a public records search by Politico.com found that he billed himself as being 6'2" on his 2012 driver's license.

Only two presidents—5'4" James Madison and 5'6" Benjamin Harrison—were shorter than the average adult male in their era. No president since the advent of television has been shorter than 5'10" and every president elected since 5'7" William McKinley in 1900 has been taller than the average American male at the time of his election.

Unlike Washington and Lincoln, who seemed to downplay their height, Johnson consciously used it to his advantage for political purposes. There are many photos of LBJ leaning into and over fellow politicians and speaking to them in an animated fashion in what came to be known as the "Johnson treatment." If his size and booming voice weren't enough, he also didn't hesitate to reach into his extensive glossary of profanity in an effort to intimidate. Barry Goldwater, who lost to Johnson in the 1964 election, was quoted in a 1992 *New York Times* piece as saying that if Johnson could not persuade another person with his words, he would "lean over you and breathe in your mouth and deprive you of oxygen."

There is a series of 1957 photographs in the National Portrait Gallery of the Smithsonian Institution that show Johnson standing over Rhode Island senator Theodore Francis Green, a much smaller and older man, and gesticulating in an animated fashion. Green, who was 90 at that time, is trapped against a desk, leaning backward and, as one of Johnson's biographers, Godfrey Hodgson, pointed out, appears to be "physically terrified." Another famous photo shows LBJ towering over a smiling but clearly uneasy Supreme Court justice Abe Fortas. At Johnson's presidential library and museum in Austin, Texas, visitors can even have their photos taken with a likeness of Johnson looming above and giving them the "treatment."

Much has been made about the height of candidates playing a role in presidential elections. Although there is some dispute over the actual height of the candidates, Texas Tech political scientist Gregg R. Murray determined that the taller of the two major-party candidates won 58 percent of the time from the first election in 1789 through 2012. The taller candidate won the popular vote 67 percent of the time.

The trend is even more pronounced since the advent of television, when voters are able to see the two candidates side by side in a debate setting. In 19 presidential elections since 1948, the shorter man has won only five times, including Joe Biden in 2020. George W. Bush, who is generally listed at 5'11½', twice defeated taller guys, beating 6'1' Al Gore in 2020 and 6'4" John Kerry in 2004.

In earlier times, when most voters had no idea how big the candidates were, it was much different. From 1804 to 1852, the taller man won only twice. In 1852, Franklin Pierce overcame a seven-inch disadvantage to edge out Winfield Scott, who at 6'5" is the tallest man ever to run for president.

"The advantage of taller candidates is potentially explained by perceptions associated with height," Murray wrote. "Taller presidents are rated by experts as 'greater,' and having more leadership and communication skills. We conclude that height is an important characteristic in choosing and evaluating political leaders. Height

President Lyndon Baines Johnson towers over Supreme Court justice Abe Fortas in an effort to make his point. LBJ frequently used such tactics in what came to be known as the "Johnson treatment" (photo by Yoichi Okamoto. Courtesy Lyndon Baines Johnson Presidential Library).

is associated with some of the same perceptions and outcomes as is strength. For example, individuals with taller stature are perceived as better leaders and attain higher status within a wide variety of modern political and organizational contexts."

Murray, by the way, is the one who came up with that phrase "evolutionary psychology," which he said suggests that "human behavior is the result of not only people's environment, such as things they learn from their parents, but also long-term evolutionary forces, such as psychological mechanisms that evolved to solve our ancestors' problems regarding survival and reproduction."

The size of the candidates was an obvious issue in a few 20th century elections.

Thomas Dewey, who lost to both 6'2" Franklin Roosevelt in 1944 and 5'9" Harry Truman in 1948, was a small, dapper man with a stylish mustache but he was only 5'8". That led many pundits to say he resembled "the little man on the wedding cake."

When another 5'8" man, Michael Dukakis, ran against 6'2" George Bush in 1988, he was referred to as "the little Duke" and some newspapers billed the race as "the shrimp versus the wimp." It didn't help that Dukakis selected a vice presidential running mate, Lloyd Bentsen, who was six inches taller than he was. Photos of the two men together accentuated Dukakis' lack of stature.

Dukakis tried to make himself appear a little taller during his debate with Bush by having a three-inch platform hidden beneath the carpet where he stood at his lectern. But when he stepped down to shake Bush's hand at the end of the evening, the height difference was alarming. The pundits had a field day with that too. Johnny Carson said Bush should have opened the debate by telling Dukakis to "come down off that soapbox and look me in the tie!"

Four years later, when Bush ran against 6'2½" Bill Clinton, there was a viable third-party candidate in Texas millionaire Ross Perot. Although Perot disdained talk about his height and said he never spent any time thinking about it, plenty of other people did. One of his secretaries said he was 5'7" and others speculated he may be as short as 5'6", which would have tied him for the second shortest man ever to run for president.

Texas-based columnist Molly Ivins was among those who had fun at Perot's expense, calling him "a seriously short guy who sounds like a chihuahua." Political cartoons showed Perot talking to the knees of his opponents. Torie Clarke, Bush's 6-foot press secretary, said that if Perot was involved in any debates, she looked forward to walking over and patting him on the head.

Advisors told Perot to be careful never to be seen in public standing next to either Bush or Clinton, and he seldom was. Despite all the chatter about his height, he had one of the best showings ever by a third-party candidate, collecting 18.9 percent of the vote.

In addition to being very good at winning elections, taller-than-average men often have been regarded as having been great presidents. The two presidents who saw the United States through its most arduous times—Lincoln and FDR—were both 6'2" or taller. "In particular, during times of threat, we have a preference for physically formidable leaders," Gregg Murray said.

A Blessings-Murray poll in 1982 asked 846 noted historians to rate the first 39 U.S. presidents as either great, near great, above average, average, below average or failure. Middlebury College professor Paul W. Sommers determined that among the first 27 presidents, only one of those who was great or near great was less than 6 feet tall, that being Theodore Roosevelt. Only one president who was 6'0" or taller in that span, Chester Alan Arthur, received a grade lower than near great.

There is considerable deviation from the trend in recent times, however, and there have been four tall presidents since the research was conducted—George H.W. Bush, Bill Clinton, Barack Obama and Donald Trump—who almost certainly would come up well short of the great or near great label.

In modern times, there seemingly has been an increase in the number of exceedingly tall political leaders in other offices in the United States. Former FBI director James Comey, a focal point of controversy in the 2016 presidential election, is 6'8". James Thompson, who served as governor of Illinois from 1977 to 1991, frequently proclaimed himself the tallest governor ever at 6'6" although John White Geary, who was the governor of Pennsylvania and before that the territorial governor of Kansas, was about the same height. So were former Connecticut governor Lowell Weicker and current Massachusetts governor Charlie Baker. Former New York governor George Pataki was 6'5".

The tallest member of Congress ever was Maryland Democrat Tom McMillen, a former NBA player who is 6'11". Among the other very tall people to have served in the House of Representatives was 6'9" Harvey Munford of Nevada.

The tallest senator for many years was colorful Wyoming Republican Alan Simpson, but he was unseated in that role in 2017 when 6'8" Luther Strange, another ex-basketball player, was appointed to fill Alabama's vacant senate seat. Simpson was quoted on Rollcall.com at the time of Strange's appointment as saying he always felt his height was a great advantage in the Senate. It not only gave him a commanding presence but he joked that it also allowed him to look over the shoulders of fellow senators and see what was on their desk and have a clear view of what was going on.

"I could always sit near the back of the chamber and you could spy the guys whose jaws were getting tense, and you knew who was going to start firing bombs and you could go over and say, 'Just relax,'" Simpson recalled.

Needless to say, there are some who don't feel height is any sort of advantage at all in politics. Texas senator John Tower, who was 5'6", was famous for telling crowds, "My name is Tower and I don't."

"I don't think height makes any difference," former Rhode Island governor and senator John Pastore told the *New York News* in 1975. "After all, the bigger you are, the bigger fool you can make of yourself." Of course, Pastore may have been biased. He was 5'4".

We also have had some extremely tall economists who have helped shape the financial fortunes of the world. John Maynard Keynes, arguably the most influential economist of the 20th century, was 6'7" and one of those who followed in his wake, John Kenneth Galbraith, was 6'8½".

"I come from a family of tall men and I have always believed that the discrimination in favor of tallness is one of the most blatant and forgiven prejudices in our society," said Galbraith, a professor who also once served as the U.S. ambassador to India.

Galbraith told a story in a 1977 *Christian Science Monitor* article about a lengthy conversation he once had with General Charles de Gaulle, who served as president of France from 1958 to 1969. Galbraith spotted the 6'5" de Gaulle across a crowded room during a visit to Washington and the French statesman asked him his opinion of "our vast height."

Galbraith's response: "We tall men, being higher than anyone else, are much more visible and thus more closely watched. Therefore, it follows that our behavior is naturally superior. So the world instinctively and rightfully trusts tall men."

De Gaulle laughed and approved wholeheartedly with that assessment, but added: "The small men must be treated without mercy."

Probably the most noteworthy tall female government official in the United States was Janet Reno, who was 6'1" and who became the first female attorney general in American history.

Reno never made any mention of being ridiculed for her size as a child but she more than made up for it when she rose to national prominence. Talk show hosts such as Jay Leno and David Letterman had a field day with Reno, who wore little makeup, never married, dressed very conservatively and had a gruff, no-nonsense demeanor. Comedian Will Ferrell frequently lampooned her in sketches on *Saturday Night Live,* portraying her in several "Janet Reno's Dance Party" segments between 1997 and 2001.

Reno famously ignored all criticism. Her personal credo was "no spin," and the few times she spoke about her height, she said she thought *SNL* simply targeted her because she was so tall. Ferrell pretty much admitted that in interviews and Carl Stern, the former public affairs director for the justice department, also said, "It's because of her height; I don't read anything into it."

The consensus was that if Reno was a man, she never would have become an object of ridicule. "I thought it was just kind of a spoof on this 6-foot-1 big old girl," Reno said in a 1998 *Washington Post* story. "I can't figure out why anybody's that interested in me."

Tall leaders are not only limited to the United States. Uday Hussein, a prominent Iraq politician and the son of Saddam Hussein, is 6'8". Montenegro president Filip Vujanovic is 6'7", Serbia's Aleksandar Vucic is 6'6", Mexico's president Vicente Fox Quesada is 6'6", King Felipe VI of Spain is 6'5½" and both Osama Bin Laden and de Gaulle were 6'5".

Among women, Ursula Plassnik, the former foreign minister of Austria, and Salote Tupou III, who reigned as the queen of Tonga for 48 years, both were 6'3".

You can find exceptionally tall people in leadership positions all the way back to the middle ages and beyond. As esteemed economic historian Sir Roderick Floud wrote in 2011, "It is, in many primitive societies, part of the power of kingship that the rulers tower above the ruled.... Height is a salient characteristic, one of our primary means of identification, one of the features of the body which it is most difficult to disguise."

Of course, the exact heights of those latter-day rulers are subject more to legend than any sort of reliable reporting.

Charlemagne, who was the king of the Franks in the eighth and ninth centuries and the father of modern Europe (as well as being my 52nd great grandfather, by the way), has been depicted in legend to be 8 feet tall although the consensus of historians is that he was more like 6'4". That still made him more than a foot taller than the average male for his time.

According to a biography written by Eginhard, Charlemagne's friend and aide, the great man's "body was large and strong; his stature tall but not ungainly for the measure of his height was seven times the length of his own feet." A latter-day biography of Charlemagne written by Harold Lamb indicated he was more than 6 feet tall by the time he reached the age of 13. Researchers studying his remains in 1988 concluded that he was between 1.9 and 1.92 meters high, which means he was 6'3" or a little taller.

Charlemagne's father, ironically, was Pepin the Short. However, his descendants included Otto the Tall and Herman the Tall, each of whom served as the Earl of Brandenburg.

King Henry VIII of England also was believed to be anywhere from 6'1" to 6'4" and one of his predecessors, King Edward I, best known as Longshanks, probably was about 6'2". If you've seen the movie *Braveheart*, you know that Longshanks' long-time commoner nemesis William Wallace also was reported to be exceptionally tall, possibly as much as 6'7", even though Mel Gibson, who played Wallace in the film, is only 5'10".

Peter the Great, who was the tsar of Russia from 1682 to 1725, also was very tall. The directors of the Madame Tussaud wax museum in London take great pains to methodically research the height of historic figures when constructing their likenesses and they determined that Peter was 6'6¾".

Harold Sigurdsson Hardraada, king of Norway in the 11th century and often regarded to be the last of the Vikings, also towered over his subordinates. Some historical documents report him as being five ells. An ell is considered the same as a cubit—about 18 inches—which would make Harold well over 7'0".

Porus, the Hindu king whose army of 35,000 was defeated by Alexander the Great at Hydaspes River in 326 BC, sometimes is listed as 7'6". Alexander was believed to be about 5 feet tall, about average for Macedonians of that time.

Gaius Julius Verus Maximus, who lived from 173 AD to 238 AD, was almost certainly the biggest man ever to rule the Roman Empire. *Historia Augusta*, a collection of biographies of Roman emperors, reported him to be 8'6" and strong enough to pull an ox cart by himself. Some historians have reported that Maximus began from modest beginnings as an illiterate shepherd boy and likely never would have become emperor if not for his size. He only served as emperor for three years before being assassinated.

Among the other ancient rulers who have been described as being gigantic are fifth-century emperor Hanzei of Japan, who was 9 feet tall according to the Kojiki, and Eleazar, a high priest, son of Aaron and nephew of Moses, a biblical figure who is mentioned as being 10'6" in documents written by the Roman historian Josephus.

It's impossible to separate fact from fiction in most of those cases, especially when we're dealing with cubits, spans, ells and assorted other archaic measurements that may or may not be accurate and may or may not be inflated by mythology.

Suffice it to say all of those historical figures were extremely tall and their height undoubtedly contributed to them being placed in leadership roles and helping them be effective in those capacities. They always were the tallest one in the room so they were bound to end up leading something.

13

It Helps in the Business World, Too

Tom McMillen fondly recalls a moment from the 2012 Democratic convention. It was being held in a massive hall in Charlotte, North Carolina, and former president Bill Clinton was at the podium looking out over an ocean of people that covered an area of several hundred yards.

McMillen had been a three-term U.S. congressman from Maryland before going into the business world and he was standing far, far away at the back of the hall. But as Clinton scanned the horizon, his eye was drawn to a face he saw protruding above all the others.

"I'm like a football field away and he says, 'Hey, there's my good friend Tom McMillen out there,'" McMillen recalled. "I'm way, way away from him.... Being tall like that, sometimes you get that attention. It helps."

McMillen, the tallest congressman in U.S. history at 6'11", is one of those people whose life seemingly has been one long, continuous success story. He was only the second high school student ever to appear on the cover of *Sports Illustrated* and he was appointed to serve on the President's Council on Physical Fitness while still in high school, becoming the youngest presidential appointee ever. He had a landmark basketball career at the University of Maryland, played on the 1972 U.S. Olympic team, was the valedictorian of his senior class, became a Rhodes Scholar, spent 11 years in the NBA and was elected to Congress just as his playing days were ending. Since the end of his political career in 1993, he has been involved in a wide array of successful business ventures and he currently serves as the president and chief executive officer of the LEAD1 Association, which represents the athletic directors and programs of the Football Bowl Subdivision.

McMillen won't tell you that he couldn't have done a lot of those same things if he had been just 5'11" instead of 6'11", but he admits his height has been "a plus in a lot of ways."

"I think it's been more of a help than a hindrance," he said.

He admitted that wherever he goes and whatever he does, he can't help but be a commanding presence, a focal point of all activity.

"It's obvious when you go to a party, you're noticeable," he said. "I've been at conventions before where people said, 'Let's meet around Tom at 3 o'clock in the afternoon.' In a convention hall full of people, I'm a good beacon to meet at."

When you're tall, you naturally stand out in a crowd both literally and very often figuratively. As we've already pointed out, it helps in the political arena, but there is evidence that it might help even more in business.

It all goes back to that same evolutionary psychology we mentioned previously. People are conditioned from birth to look up to people who are significantly larger than themselves. We spend our formative years in the shadow of parents, teachers and other authority figures, who tower over us. It engenders an unconscious perception of superiority that most of us never lose.

There are all sorts of statistical studies that show that tall people, on average, make more money than their shorter counterparts and that they gravitate toward leadership positions. McMillen has seen the studies and he thinks there is some validity to some of the research. "But I think it's very individualistic," he said. "It depends on the individual."

In 2014, the London Business School, the Aalto University School of Business in Finland and the University of New South Wales in Australia joined together in a study that found the CEOs of what they defined as large companies were on average an inch and a half taller than average men. And they found that taller CEOs were paid about 4 percent more than normal-sized execs.

Author Malcolm Gladwell identified a predominance of taller men at the highest levels of business in his 2005 book *Blink: The Power of Thinking Without Thinking*. He found that 68 percent of all Fortune 500 CEOs in the United States were 6'0" or taller even though only 15 percent of the general population was that tall. He said that 30 percent of the CEOs topped 6'2".

There is a sizeable number of business leaders who tower above the crowd albeit not quite to the same extent that McMillen does. Billionaire Mark Cuban, whose international fame has expanded due to his appearance as a regular on *Shark Tank*, is either 6'2" or 6'3" depending on what source you consult. Steve Ballmer, the chief executive officer of Microsoft, is 6'5". (I don't know if there is a correlation here but both of those men own NBA teams.) Several prominent CEOs, including Tim Cook of Apple, John Watson of Chevron, Jeffrey Immelt of General Electric and Oracle Corporation co-founder Larry Ellison, all are either 6'3" or 6'4".

Then again, the trend may not be quite as pronounced as Gladwell's research indicated. If you look at a list of the 10 wealthiest men in the world in 2022, the average height is a very average 5'11". Only one of the top five—French mogul Bernard Arnault—is more than 6 feet tall and the only really tall guys on the list are Ballmer and Ellison, who come in eighth and ninth.

Still, there is no disputing that it's good to be tall. The same qualities that help in politics translate to business: a commanding presence, an ability to dominate the room and a proclivity for having your voice heard.

"I started observing business leaders in a social setting and I noticed that taller people were generally carrying most conversations," said John Warrillow, the founder of the Value Builder System and author of a few books on business. "If a short person was getting any attention at a cocktail party, it was often because the person was very loud or flamboyant. All things being equal, most eyes wander to the tall."

Warrillow said height impacts the perception of people in a subtle way. He pointed to Christine Lagarde, president of the European Central Bank, who is 5'11" but is closer to 6'2" when she's wearing heels. He said when Lagarde walks into a room full of fellow bankers, she "immediately commands more attention than if she were 5-foot-2."

"Height plays an important role in how we perceive the leadership potential of people," Warrillow added. "Evolution made us want to follow tall and physically strong leaders for their ability to protect us against danger. In other words, we're hard-wired to want to follow people who are physically commanding."

Business consultant Robert Tanguay, who is 5'7", sounded just a bit envious in writing about tall executives in 2017, noting that "it seems their elongated frames entitle them to authority. They are gods among humans, receiving wealth, admiration and top selection of mates."

As we've mentioned, the seeds of this mindset are planted early in life. When kids are taller than their peers in high school, they develop confidence and tend to be thrust into leadership roles. It carries over to adulthood.

"A slight advantage as a youth snowballs into massive inequities over time," Tanguay wrote. "We reward tall males for no other reason than their height."

Stephen S. Hall wrote in his 2006 book *Size Matters* that he felt teenage boys who are shorter in stature are less likely to be involved in sports and, as a result, they probably have less "exposure to success." He thought they were less active socially and possibly had less self-esteem, which could impact their ultimate success in whatever professions they pursued.

Hall was a shade under 5'6" and had no prayer of making the basketball team in high school. But he tried out for the wrestling team, and although he never was wildly successful at it, he thinks it bolstered his self-esteem. He said he became aware of the different lenses through which the world views us. "When the lens is size, the world clearly prefers tall to small, and not just on the basketball court," he wrote. "My hunch is that precisely around the time of puberty, short teenage boys become intensely aware that there are distinct social advantages to being tall, and clear social liabilities to being small, in ways they haven't noticed before."

Psychiatric social worker Ellen Perlman Simon said even little things that kids endure in school can quietly impact how they see themselves. How often in school are kids asked to line up according to height? After a while, the kids who are at or near the end of the line are going to feel inferior while the tall kids on the other end might very well feel better about themselves.

Warrillow makes another solid point about how height impacts people at the upper end of the business world. While many of the people who end up leading big companies seem to be tall, sometimes the scrappy entrepreneurs who start those companies lean toward the small side.

For every Ballmer and Ellison, there is a 5'7" Jeff Bezos or a 5'9" Mark Zuckerberg. Microsoft founder Bill Gates is a very average 5'10", but when he went looking for someone to run his company, he hired the 6'5" Ballmer.

"When you start a business, you're not leading anyone," Warrillow said in a 2014 article on Inc.com. "You're trying to refine a concept, and a premium is placed on ideas, intelligence, and tenacity. It doesn't matter how physically commanding you are, because there's nobody to command.... By contrast, the job of running a Fortune 500 company, many of which employ more than 100,000 people, is much more about communicating a vision, inspiring your senior people to lead their teams, rallying the troops, persuading regulators to side with you, and being the public face of your company to the media. In short, optics matter more than they do in a startup."

Height doesn't just play a role at the top of the flow chart. There are even more studies that demonstrate how tall people have advantages down through the rungs of the business ladder.

This has been the subject of research as far back as 1915 when New York University professor Enoch Burton Gowin wrote a book about it. He found that not only did executives tend to be taller than normal but that sales managers were taller than salespeople and bishops were taller than the clergy who reported to them.

A 1971 survey of University of Pittsburgh graduates found that those who were 6'2" or taller received starting salaries 12.4 percent higher than those under 6 feet. There have been dozens of these studies since then, all coming to very similar conclusions. It's probably best to sprinkle them with a few grains of salt since many, like the Pittsburgh one, have been done by scrutinizing college graduates. It's difficult to say if the same pay-scale parameters can be applied to workers at the local meat-packing plant or the guy you've enlisted to fix the leak in your kitchen sink.

A 2004 study conducted by Nicola Persico and Andrew Postlewaite of the University of Pennsylvania in conjunction with University of Michigan economist Dan Silverman probably carries more punch because it gets into many more factors and traces workers from childhood far into adulthood in both the United States and Great Britain.

It found that the compensatory bias involving workers on the basis of height was every bit as pronounced as it was for race or gender. The median wage of the tallest 25 percent of the subjects in the study was 13 percent higher than that of the shortest 25 percent. British men earned 2.7 percent more for every additional inch of height while U.S. workers earned 2.5 percent more. The study identified similar trends for women but only dealt with white, non–Hispanic workers due to a lack of data for minorities.

Interestingly, those conclusions for men were based on the height of subjects at age 16, not on the height they ultimately reached as adults. In other words, it didn't necessarily benefit those of us who were 5'11" as teenagers before ultimately getting to be 6'6¾". It seemingly all goes back to the confidence and self-esteem that was established in their formative years.

Another 2004 study, conducted by University of Florida psychologist Timothy Judge and Daniel Cable of the University of North Carolina, found that workers earned an average of $789 per year for every additional inch of height. They determined that a man who is 6'0" might earn $166,000 more over a 30-year career than someone who is 5'5". The study, published in the *Journal of Applied Psychology*, identified a direct correlation between height and self-esteem, leader emergence and performance in the workplace.

"The process of literally 'looking down on others' may cause one to be more confident," Judge said. "Similarly, having others 'looking up to us' may instill in tall people more self-confidence."

Judge also noted that the trend was especially noticeable in professions in which social interaction and customer perception were major factors.

However, people who work in sales positions have told us there is a fine line between influencing people and intimidating them. It's like so many of the other things we've talked about: It's good to be tall but maybe not too tall. Remember how we told you previously that some people are uncomfortable just standing next to a really tall person in line? You kind of wonder if that means we're not as likely to buy a television set from a 7'0" salesperson in an appliance store as we would if he was somewhere below the Vince Vaughn line. That sales clerk who is 6'2" or 6'3" is tall enough to be a commanding presence but not tall enough to scare the crap out of us.

A 2020 study done by a team of researchers at Renmin University of China looked at data from more than 3,500 Chinese adults to see if they could find a correlation between height and income, and they came up with similar findings. They estimated that each additional centimeter of height (about four-tenths of an inch) translated to a 1.3 percent increase in pay. The research team also tested the genetic and environmental background of the subjects and concluded that the same factors that made some of them taller also made them smarter and thereby better employees.

In 2012, Erik Lindqvist of the Stockholm School of Economics used government data including military enlistment statistics to analyze the connection between height and supervisory positions. He determined that if a person was four inches taller, they were 2.2 percent more likely to be a manager of some sort.

"A tall person might be more convincing as a leader, and thus able to convince others to follow his or her lead," Lindqvist said. "The perception of others is, after all, central to the effectiveness of a leader. Height can play a role in that perception, if only a minor one compared to other abilities."

He also stated that "about half of the height-leadership correlation is due to a positive correlation between height and cognitive and noncognitive ability."

That's more ammunition for the argument that tall people are smarter.

Joel Waldfogel, a professor of business and public policy at the Wharton School of the University of Pennsylvania, looked at the taller-is-smarter study of Anne Case and Christina Paxson in 2006 and reached comparable conclusions.

"If taller people are, on average, smarter, then we should see taller people working disproportionately in occupations that require intelligence," Waldfogel wrote. "Sure enough, in an analysis of U.S. data from the National Health Interview Survey, Case and Paxson find that tall people are more prevalent in occupations such as executive/manager, professional, and sales relative to occupations like laborer, farmer, or machine operator."

There is plenty of anecdotal evidence that it pays to be tall in the business world.

Atlanta area resident Rick LaRose said he noticed the benefits throughout a 43-year career in the financial industry. He said it helped in job interviews and meetings with co-workers.

"I think it just made me one step higher than other people," said LaRose, who is 6'6". "When you're taller, people look to you for leadership."

Many feel physical height may help as much in getting a job as it does in *doing* the job. Warrillow said he thought his 5'9" stature hurt him when he went to apply for a position in radio advertising.

"Did my height have anything to do with not getting the job? I don't know, but I'm pretty sure my physical appearance didn't help," Warrillow wrote. "I was young, short(ish), and did not fit the mold of a radio sales executive at the time. It was a field made up mostly of former high school jocks and tall, attractive women."

He finally went out and developed his own company so he didn't need to worry about getting beat out by taller people in the interview process.

If you think about it, job interviews are sort of like a jump ball on the basketball court. The taller person doesn't always get the tip, but it happens much more than half the time. They have a built-in advantage.

It's very difficult in a job interview to determine the intelligence or the work ethic of the candidate. Those are things you discern over the course of days, weeks, years. But it only takes a second to see how tall someone is, and if all else is equal, that can be a deciding factor. Kate Patterson, one of the leaders of a major executive search firm, said that most employers decide in the first five minutes of an interview whether or not they will consider the applicant for the job.

"It's about the observability," said Samuli Knüpfer, an assistant professor of finance at the London Business School. "You directly observe someone's height. It takes you a while to figure out cognitive and non-cognitive skills."

In one study, industrial psychologist Dr. David Kurtz asked 140 job recruiters to make a hypothetical choice between two candidates who were equally qualified in every way except height. One was listed as being 6'1", the other 5'5". Predictably, 72 percent chose the taller candidate and 1 percent chose the short one. The other 27 percent said they had no preference.

Thomas Samaras cited an experiment performed by educator Carl Bonuso, in which he mailed fake resumes to 585 high school district superintendents in the state of New York and asked them to rate the applicants' qualifications. The job candidates were almost identical except for gender, height and weight. More than 90 percent of the superintendents preferred the 6'0" candidates, and 84 percent liked the 5'9" candidates, but only 54 percent had any interest in the 5'6" candidates. Surprisingly, there was no evidence of gender discrimination. But the heights made a big difference.

"There's no doubt that we react to tall, imposing men and women with greater deference than to smaller ones," Samaras wrote.

One headhunter put it much more bluntly in an interview with the *New York News* in 1975: "I would never hire a short man. They always have a chip on their shoulders."

With all those things considered, it's not surprising that people who aren't tall sometimes feel, well, shortchanged. Saul Feldman, a 5'4" sociologist at Case Western Reserve University, coined a new term for this bias in 1972: heightism. He pointed out that while it was illegal to discriminate against people on the basis of age, sex or religion, heightism was perfectly acceptable. Only one state, Michigan, currently has a law against height discrimination although a few municipalities, mostly in northern California, have similar laws and a handful of states have statutes pertaining to discrimination on the basis of appearance.

There have been only a few instances of legal action regarding height. The Kohler Co. of Wisconsin was slapped with a discrimination suit in the 1990s because it only hired workers who were 5'4" or taller, feeling employees needed to be that big to handle the physical demands of the job. It actually was accused of sex discrimination because those limits excluded about half the female candidates as well as a small number of men. Kohler was forced to pay an $886,500 settlement and to hire 111 applicants for the jobs in question.

A few other ideas have been thrown out through the years as a way to alleviate the pay discrepancy between tall and short. Edwin Cohen, the U.S. assistant secretary of the treasury, publicly proposed in 1972 that anyone 5'6" or under should be required to pay only half the taxes of taller people. The suspicion was that the 5'5" Cohen had tongue firmly planted in cheek when he pitched the idea, knowing that all those tall folks who had been elected to high office would never permit such a thing to happen.

A few years later, a bookkeeper in Germany made a similar recommendation and he apparently wasn't kidding. Otto Engel, who was 3'11", proposed that any workers who were 4'10" or shorter in his country should get a special tax break.

"We want the government to recognize that little people are severely handicapped," he said in a meeting with 80 other members of the country's Organization of Little People. "That way we would pay less taxes and would be able to afford the conversions necessary in our homes and cars to make life easier."

Sure. And I would propose that we reduce taxes for everyone 6'6" or taller so that I can renovate that shorter-than-code doorway leading from the family room to the laundry room in my home. That way I can stop conking my noggin when I forget to duck.

14

Our Military Options Are Limited

For Grover Cleveland Doxsie, it was one of those unexpected strokes of good fortune.

Grover, who was my paternal grandfather, was a religious man who really didn't want to be involved in any sort of war. He was 24 years old when the United States became involved in World War I in 1917, and like everyone else in his age bracket, he dutifully went and registered for the draft. At the bottom of his draft card, though, where it asked if there was any reason he could not serve in the armed forces, he scribbled, "Yes. Religious belief—Nazarene."

To what I suspect must have been his absolute delight, Grover found he didn't even need to apply to be a conscientious objector. He was measured at 6'8" (he later was found to be 6'10"), which meant he was too tall to serve anyway. The Army at that time wouldn't take anyone over 6'6" because they didn't have uniforms to fit such a lengthy body. Grover failed miserably as a farmer, ended up being virtually homeless for a while in the middle of the Great Depression and never really prospered financially in any profession before passing away in 1964, but he succeeded in getting out of the military.

However, I suspect there have been millions of other men through the years who really wanted to join the service, who yearned to do their duty, who genuinely hungered to serve their country, but who were prohibited from doing so because they were just too darn tall.

The current limitations for service in the U.S. armed forces call for a male recruit to be at least 5 feet tall but no more than 6'8". The size range for female candidates is pretty similar. It goes from 4'10" up to 6'8", which obviously does not exclude very many women.

The same applies to most branches of the service with the Marine Corps being even a little more restrictive. Men need to be between 4'10" and 6'6" to qualify, women between 4'10" and 6'0". There also are more specific restrictions for pilots. I never had any great desire to fly a fighter jet or to be a Marine, but if I had, I would have been out of luck.

Of course, there have been a few people who got around this with the most notable case being David Robinson. As a junior in high school in 1982, Robinson was 5'9", just about the right size to have a long career in the Navy. He then went through an astonishing growth spurt and was 6'6" as a senior, which put him at the top of the height restriction for a Navy midshipman at that time. He enrolled in the U.S. Naval Academy at Annapolis with the intention of playing basketball there, but by the time he arrived on campus, he was 6'7". The superintendent of the academy granted him a waiver. After all, he was only an inch above the maximum.

But then Robinson hit another of those late growth spurts very much like the one I had in my first year of college. By the time it was time to graduate and serve his mandatory five-year stint in the Navy, he was 7'1". There was no way he was going to be able to go on active duty at that size, so he was allowed to serve two years of "restrictive" duty, primarily helping with promotional and recruiting efforts, and then serve four years in the Navy Reserve. He was able to begin playing pro basketball in 1989 and went on to have a 14-year Hall of Fame career with the San Antonio Spurs.

One of the reasons the military has for having height restrictions is that it isn't into producing custom-made uniforms. There are no big and tall shops on military bases. We're not sure what they did for uniforms with Robinson, but it's also pretty obvious that it would be very difficult for an extremely tall person to maneuver in a tank or submarine or almost any kind of ship for that matter. Airplanes also can be an issue. You don't see a lot of really tall pilots.

In fact, various segments of the military have special restrictions for men or women who want to operate a plane or helicopter.

The Air Force discarded its old height requirements in 2020 in an effort to find more candidates and increase the diversity of its pilots. Prior to that, an Air Force pilot candidate had to be between 5'4" and 6'6" with a sitting height of between 34 and 40 inches. That eliminated 44 percent of all women in the 20-to-29 age group, and although they occasionally granted waivers to candidates who did

David Robinson (No. 50) met the U.S. Navy's height requirements when he was first recruited to play at Annapolis, but he far exceeded them by the time he was done playing there (courtesy U.S. Naval Academy).

not fit into those parameters, many otherwise qualified people never even attempted to get into the Air Force because of those rules.

In 2020, the Air Force changed to an "anthropometric" screening process—we can't seem to get away from these 14-letter words—to measure the physical attributes of candidates rather than having a hard-and-fast height requirement. It also began redesigning flight equipment in 2019 to accommodate shorter pilots. One Air Force official described the changes as "a huge win, especially for women and minorities of smaller stature who previously may have assumed they weren't qualified to join our team." Of course, they did nothing to make it possible for taller people to become pilots.

Other branches of the service still have height requirements for pilots. In the Navy, pilots must be between 5'2" and 6'5" with a sitting height of between 31 and 40.9 inches and a sitting eye height of between 26 and 31.4 inches. The Marines use the same sitting height parameters but have no restrictions on standing height. For Army helicopters, candidates must be in the 5'4" to 6'6" range with a sitting height of 40.15 inches and an arm reach of 64.5 inches.

Obviously, with those restrictions for pilots, there also never has been a really tall astronaut in the space program. The launch vehicle for the Soyuz series of spacecraft, which has been in use since the 1960s, is only designed to handle someone 6'2½" or shorter although there have been a couple of astronauts as tall as 6'4". Jim Wetherbee was part of six space shuttle missions, serving as the commander on five of them, and James van Hoften also was 6'4".

Shorter hasn't always been viewed as being better as far as the military is concerned. In fact, throughout history it usually has been considered desirable to have big soldiers. The taller the better.

In ancient times, the Romans required soldiers to be at least 5'5" and Roman historians such as Tacitus and Seneca marveled at the size of the Germanic warriors who battled so ferociously against the Romans. Archaeological analysis of skeletons has determined that the Germanic soldiers were, on average, nearly 8 inches taller than the Romans.

Frederick William I, the king of Prussia in the 18th century, became obsessed with finding the tallest soldiers he could get. Frederick, who was only 5'5", had what has been described as "an almost pathological love for tall soldiers." His famous quote was "The most beautiful girl or woman in the world would be a matter of indifference to me, but tall soldiers—they are my weakness."

He formed an elite military corps called the Grenadier Guards, also known as the Potsdam Giants or the Lange Kerle (long fellows). Members of the unit were required to be more than 6'2" and their leader allegedly was more than 7'0". Frederick had recruiters who scoured Europe looking for tall men to be part of his force and other rulers sometimes sent him tall soldiers from their own armies. Frederick was even known to have men kidnapped and forced to be part of his unit, including a 7'1" Irishman named James Kirkland, and he even tried to breed taller men, forcibly pairing his giant soldiers with tall women. Frederick even attempted to stretch some of his soldiers by putting them on a rack but this practice was discontinued after a few of them died in the process.

The Grenadier Guards were outfitted in special, gaudy uniforms with 18-inch caps that made them appear even taller. Here is the irony of Frederick's army: It was all for show. During his reign, from 1713 to 1740, his supersized fighting force never once was deployed in a military action.

When Frederick died, the Grenadier Guards included 3,200 men but his son and successor, Frederick the Great, did not share his father's infatuation with tall soldiers. The giants began to be dispersed to other units and the unit was disbanded completely after being defeated by Napoleon in 1806.

Napoleon had developed his own oversized fighting force by that time although his famed Imperial Guard was not quite as tall in stature as Frederick's bunch. Soldiers in the Imperial Guard were required to be at least 5'6", which would have made them taller than average for that time. They also needed to be able to read and write, and they had to have fought in previous campaigns. They received better pay and special privileges that others in Napoleon's army did not.

By the end of Napoleon's reign, he had as many as 112,000 men in the Imperial Guard but they suffered heavy losses in the invasion of Russia in 1812 and failed miserably in a final advance on the British at the ill-fated Battle of Waterloo in 1815.

In the centuries since then, there doesn't appear to have been another effort to assemble an army comprised entirely of tall men.

However, there were some noteworthy oversized American soldiers in the 18th and 19th centuries.

A man named Peter Francisco was known as the "Hercules of the American Revolution" and distinguished himself several times during the fight for independence. At 6'6" and 260 pounds, he may not seem enormous by modern standards but consider that the average Revolutionary War soldier was only 5'4½". Francisco towered over everyone. He was wounded seriously in the battles at Brandywine and Monmouth, and after his three-year enlistment period ended, he joined a militia group and allegedly carried an 1,100-pound cannon to safety at the Battle of Camden in 1780. He then supposedly killed 11 British soldiers at the Battle of Guilford Courthouse and fought off nine of Tarleton's dreaded dragoons in another encounter in 1781.

During the American Civil War (1861–65), there were several very tall men who served in the military, including two very notable 7-footers who fought for the Confederacy.

Martin Van Buren Bates was reputed to be 7'11" when he left his job as a schoolteacher to enlist as a private in the 5th Kentucky Infantry. Bates, who also supposedly weighed 525 pounds, fought in several battles in the western theater of the war and rose to the rank of captain before being wounded and captured at the Battle of Cumberland Gap in 1863. He spent time in a prisoner of war camp at Camp Chase in Ohio before escaping.

Some other sources credit Henry Clay Thruston with being the tallest member of the Confederate army, at an estimated 7'6". Thruston became part of the Morgan County Rangers, a unit in the Missouri State Guard, a militia assembled by the Missouri legislature. He fought at the Battle of Pea Ridge in Arkansas in 1862, served under General Sterling Price in action at Elkhorn Tavern and later became part of the 4th Missouri Cavalry. (Yes, they apparently found a horse big enough for him.) He also saw action at Poison Spring and Jenkins Ferry in 1864.

Both Bates and Thruston found work following the war as sideshow attractions in circuses. Thruston was once billed by P.T. Barnum as the world's tallest man although he apparently was somewhat combative when anyone mentioned his size to him. There was a report of a shorter man once asking him that clever question "How's the weather up there?" Thruston responded with a torrent of spit and replied, "It's raining!"

The Union army also had at least one very tall soldier although David Van Buskirk was nowhere near as towering as Bates and Thruston. Van Buskirk, from Gosport, Indiana, was a mere 6'10½" and weighed 380 pounds. He served during the war with the 27th Indiana infantry and was promoted to second lieutenant in 1862 before being captured during a battle near Winchester, Virginia, in May of that year. He was imprisoned at the infamous Libby Prison in Richmond but later was allowed to move to a room elsewhere in town, where he was put on display for members of the public to pay to see the giant. Jefferson Davis, president of the Confederacy, reportedly was among those who paid to get a look at Van Buskirk, according to the Kenosha (Wisconsin) Public Museum. He later was paroled as part of a prisoner exchange, returned to the 27th Indiana, was promoted to captain and saw action at Gettysburg before being forced to resign his commission in 1864 because of problems with rheumatism.

It was in the years following the Civil War that the United States began to develop its first standards of height and weight for military recruits. Anthropometric data for Civil War draftees was collected by Colonel Jedediah H. Baxter, chief medical officer in the Office of the Provost Marshal General, and the first minimum and maximum standards were formulated.

The average U.S. soldier in the Civil War was about 5'7½" and a little more than 140 pounds, and those numbers changed very little by the time of World War I. However, government statistics indicate that by World War II, the average U.S. soldier was about 5'8½" and about 150 pounds.

Other countries also developed similar standards for their armies and navies but at least one country chose to bend its rules to accommodate smaller soldiers.

When World War I began in 1914, the minimum height to be a member of the army in Great Britain was 5'3". Following an initial deluge of recruits—many more than were needed—the minimum was changed to 5'6". As the war progressed and escalated, it was dropped to 5'4" and then 5'3", but shorter men who were eager to fight still were being turned away. One 5'2" miner from Durham was continually rejected in his efforts to enlist and angrily threatened to fight any man who told him he was too short.

The British government finally decided to develop special units for men who were between 5'0" and 5'3". Within days, two "Bantam" battalions were assembled including 3,000 "small, hard, plucky" men who previously had been rejected for service. By the end of the war, Great Britain had 29 such units, comprised of more than 30,000 men. They still generally were commanded by normal-sized officers, including Bernard Law Montgomery, who became an iconic field marshal in World War II, and those Bantam troops were instrumental in helping Great Britain to ultimately prevail over Germany.

As far as we can tell, Great Britain or the United States or any other country never developed any special units to give taller-than-average men a chance to serve, but perhaps they should.

Satoshi Kanazawa, who we previously mentioned for his research about the intelligence of tall people, determined in a 2007 study for *Human Reproduction* that tall soldiers are more likely to survive battle.

Kanazawa analyzed British army service records from World War I and found that soldiers who survived the war were, on average, 3.33 centimeters (more than an inch) taller than soldiers who were killed in action. As with so many similar phenomena, he was unable to give a viable explanation for why it happened and he predicted it was unlikely to continue in future wars.

15

There's Not Much Bigness in Show Business

By all accounts, Ted Cassidy was one of the most marvelously multi-talented men ever to grace the entertainment industry. He had a wonderful singing voice and could play the piano, the trombone and several other instruments. He was a classically trained actor who played Henry VIII during his early days in the theater and did riveting poetry readings. He was gifted enough athletically to have worked as a lifeguard and earned a college basketball scholarship. He was highly intelligent.

Friends said that given the chance, Cassidy could have done almost anything.

But the signature role of his two-decade acting career came when he played a ghoul named Lurch in the 1960s television series *The Addams Family.* Cassidy didn't really need to act very much as Lurch. He just stood there, all 6'9" and 280 pounds of him, looked as menacing as possible and uttered the line "You rang?" in a deep, guttural voice that sent chills down your spine.

Cassidy also was known for a memorable three-and-a-half-minute scene in *Butch Cassidy and the Sundance Kid* in which he threatened to supplant Butch (played by 5'10" Paul Newman) as the leader of the infamous Hole in the Wall Gang. Newman ends up whipping big Ted with the help of some dirty tricks in a scene that no doubt delighted David vs. Goliath rooters around the world.

Not surprisingly, Cassidy also played Goliath in a TV series depicting Bible stories. He also made a splendid Bigfoot in episodes of both *The Six Million Dollar Man* and *The Bionic Woman.*

But he could have been so much more. If only he wasn't so darn tall.

Cassidy admitted to having ambivalent feelings about his three years as Lurch. "It was nice to be working steadily and piling up some money in the bank," he once told reporter Mel Heimer, "but there really wasn't much to do except walk around and ... well, be Lurch."

He actually was prouder of some of the other aspects of his *Addams Family* days. He got to show his musical abilities on the occasions Lurch was shown playing the harpsichord during the series. And he also played Thing, the solitary hand that projected from a box and was part of the Addams clan. Cassidy figured it required more talent and imagination to play Thing than it did to be Lurch.

His less-than-stellar career is evidence of the same principle that applies to Hollywood as it does to personal attraction: It's good to be tall as long as you're not *too* tall.

If you're 6'1" or 6'2", you've got a chance to be viewed as a sex symbol or at least a legitimate thespian. If you're 6'9"? Forget it.

In the almost 100 years that the Academy of Arts and Motion Pictures has been handing out awards, the tallest man ever to win the best leading actor award is 6'4". That would be John Wayne, who won in 1969 for his role as the grizzled Rooster Cogburn in *True Grit*. There hasn't been a winner since then who was taller than 6'2".

The tallest person ever to win for best supporting actor is 6'5" Tim Robbins, who won in 2004 for *Mystic River*. The big parts almost never go to exceptionally big men.

Ted Cassidy's biggest claim to fame was playing the role of Lurch in the 1960s television series *The Addams Family*. He felt it was a waste of his talent. "There really wasn't much to do except walk around and, well, be Lurch," he said.

It all sort of makes sense. An actor who is 6'9" is going to fill up the screen and dominate every scene. Everyone else in the cast will appear comically undersized. That's OK in a scene or two but not for an entire film.

When someone is supersized, it's almost impossible for the camera to make them look normal-sized. On the other hand, it's relatively simple to make a small man look larger. In the classic film *Casablanca,* Humphrey Bogart frequently stood on boxes or sat on cushions to make him look as tall or taller than co-star Ingrid Bergman, who had a few inches on him. In *Top Gun,* 5'10" Kelly McGillis slouches noticeably at times and reportedly did several scenes in her stocking feet so she didn't tower over 5'7" Tom Cruise.

Hollywood lore is full of tales about 5'6" Alan Ladd standing on a crate to make him look taller for his screen roles. Ladd sometimes stipulated that no one else in any of his films could be taller than 5'8" and it was easy enough to make him look bigger than he was. But there was no way anyone was going to make Ted Cassidy look small.

If an actor is any taller than 6'4", as John Wayne and Rock Hudson were, he seems destined to be pigeon-holed into some sort of gimmick role, like Chewbacca in *Star Wars* or Karl the Giant in *Big Fish.* If you're a television actor, you get cast as Herman Munster in *The Munsters,* Hoss in *Bonanza,* Dauber in *Coach* or Gomer Pyle.

Or Lurch.

Cassidy never really got used to the attention that his height attracted. During his lifeguard days in Ormond Beach, Florida, people occasionally would ask to be photographed with him so they could show their friends back home that they found a gigantic lifeguard. Cassidy always politely refused.

He also bristled when people met him for the first time and assumed he was as slow and shallow as the character he portrayed on TV: "I can see it in their eyes that they think I'm dim-witted and sluggish. They look at me as if I were a circus giant, and talk to me in condescending tones. It makes me very antagonistic toward them right at the start."

Cassidy later came to terms with his stature and said he was proud of being so tall although he would have preferred to have been something more like 6'6".

Old friends who really knew him, including his old Stetson University basketball coach, Dick Morland, were a bit mortified to see him cast as Lurch. "If he could play a ghoul, his acting potential was unlimited," Morland said. "Ted was anything but lubberly and inarticulate, and if they'd ever let him really talk or sing, people would have seen his versatility. His adroitness in playing the harpsichord was the only thing that even slightly resembled his true capability."

When the *Orlando Sentinel* published a tribute to Cassidy at the time of his death at the age of 46 in 1979, the actor's fiancé pleaded: "Please, don't let him be remembered for his monster characters, he was so much more than that."

Cassidy was not alone in being typecast by the film and television industries because of his size and appearance. There have been tons who have met the same fate.

Peter Mayhew, who was even taller at 7'3", is listed with 28 different acting credits on TV and in film by the website IMDb.com, but in 15 of them he played Chewbacca, the monstrous Wookie in the *Star Wars* series.

Mayhew, who was born in Great Britain, suffered from gigantism, which caused assorted health problems. He underwent double knee replacement surgery in 2013 and after that he walked with a cane that was made to look like a light saber. He said his size was great because it allowed him to look down on normal-sized people and see their "defects" and "irregularities," but he admitted it came with all the same problems so many of us know.

"When I go to restaurants, I can never get my legs under a table," he said. "I bump my head in planes. People who sit behind me in the theater hate me. But I have given up apologizing to the world."

Richard Kiel, who was just an inch shorter than Mayhew at 7'2", had even more screen credits—79 of them—but they were all the same sort of parts. He played the villain Jaws in two James Bond movies, *The Spy Who Loved Me* and *Moonraker*. He also played Samson, a mammoth football player, in the 1974 version of *The Longest Yard*, where he was the victim in another of those David vs. Goliath type scenes. After a much smaller man strikes him in his face on the football field, Kiel wails, "He broke my fucking nose." It's funny but a bit demeaning.

Like Mayhew, Kiel suffered from a hormonal disorder called acromegaly, which caused gradual and abnormal growth in the bones throughout his body. But he had a great sense of humor about his appearance, especially when asked about his wife, Diane, who was 5'1".

"Somebody once asked Diane what attracted her to me," Kiel

told a United Press International reporter in 1978. "And she replied, 'We see eye to eye on so many things.'"

There have been a few really tall one-and-done actors. Nigerian-born 7-footer Bolaji Badejo had exactly one acting credit. He was in the 1979 film *Alien*. He played the Alien.

Matthew McGrory, who was 7'6", was best known as Karl the Giant in *Big Fish* and is listed in the *Guinness Book of World Records* as the tallest actor ever and also for having the largest shoe size not caused by elephantiasis: 29½. According to IMDb, McGrory weighed 15 pounds at birth and was five feet tall in kindergarten.

Those guys obviously fall into the gimmick category. But there also are a lot of very talented, very accomplished actors and actresses who have had much longer, more successful acting careers although some of them clearly were held back to some degree by their height.

James Arness, who was 6'6", starred as Marshal Matt Dillon on the TV series *Gunsmoke* for 21 years. Equally tall Ken Howard won Emmy awards for his work in both prime time and daytime series and served as the national president of the Screen Actors Guild.

Brad Garrett, who has been listed as either 6'8" or 6'9", was best known for playing the brother of the title character on the long-running sitcom *Everybody Loves Raymond*, but the comedian's attempts to move into more prominent and meaningful roles have not always been so successful. His IMDb page lists the four roles he is best known for and three of them are films in which he just provides the voice for animated characters: *Tangled, Christopher Robin* and *Ratatouille*.

Everybody loves Garrett. They just don't want to have to fit his gargantuan frame onto the screen with normal-sized performers. When he won the title role of portraying Jackie Gleason (who was only 5'10") in the 2002 movie *Gleason*, the filmmakers needed to go to great lengths to authenticate Garrett in the role. All of his co-stars wore 7-inch lifts and all of the furniture used in the film was custom-made in proportion to Garrett's size.

Although Garrett was tremendous in the film, it hasn't led to loads of other great roles. In recent years, he has been best known for portraying a disgruntled gangster in Jimmy John's commercials.

Another tall actor who has met repeated obstacles in his career is 6'7" James Cromwell. His father, John, was an accomplished actor and director but he advised his son not to go into acting because of his height. He suspected it would hold him back and he was right.

James' tall, angular frame and prominent nose led to him always being cast as a villain or as a comic figure of some sort, mostly in small, forgettable roles in sitcoms and TV dramas.

He had a recurring role as the tall and goofy Stretch Cunningham in *All in the Family.* He portrayed the hideous Jaglom Shrek in *Star Trek: The Next Generation.* He has been cast very frequently as a clergyman of some sort, including the recurring role of the Reverend Buryfield in *Mary Hartman, Mary Hartman.* In one of his most successful early ventures, he did the voice of Farmer Hoggett in *Babe.* As with so many of Garrett's screen credits, it's a role in which he could be heard but not seen.

Cromwell almost never was a leading man and that didn't bring him the fulfillment he sought. "I didn't have a career. I had this hodge-podge that made me very unhappy," he said in a 2001 interview with the Associated Press.

In fact, in that same interview, Cromwell reflected just how sheepish he was about his size. He told the reporter to put him down as being 6'6" although he admitted he actually is more like 6'7".

As he got into his 50s, 60s and 70s, Cromwell's talent helped him push into a few more prominent roles in film and television although he still has seldom been a leading man.

Peter Isacksen made an early splash as an actor at the age of 23 in the Don Rickles sitcom *CPO Sharkey,* but he was mostly a prop, a 6'7" target for the rapid-fire insults of the 5'6" Rickles. Isacksen never really built on that early success because there are so few parts for someone that tall. He told author Ralph Keyes that when people made comments about his height that he just tried to be nice and make them feel comfortable. "Sometimes I wish I were more vicious," he added.

Extreme size also has been an issue for some female actors. Probably the tallest actress of any great accomplishment is 6'3" Gwendoline Christie, who captured roles in several *Star Wars* films and two movies in the *Hunger Games* series before finding stardom as Brienne of Tarth in the popular HBO series *Game of Thrones.*

Christie has found success despite some horrifying personal experiences on the way up the acting ladder. She long ago grew tired of other tall women who approached her on the street and told her how nice it was to see a woman taller than themselves. "I've always felt like a giant," Christie said.

At the age of 14, doctors told her she was going to be much more than 6 feet tall and they actually presented her with a couple of options. They could give her hormones that would stunt her growth or they could perform an operation to make her shorter. Christie rejected both ideas and has been told repeatedly that she is just too tall to get anywhere in her chosen profession. One of her teachers in drama school put it very bluntly: "Life must be hard for you, because people will always think you're tall before they think you're beautiful."

Christie said in a 2020 interview with *Love Magazine* that she also has been admonished for the way in which she dresses and behaves as a tall woman: "The tall woman who is hunched, who is introverted, who often cannot be flamboyant in the way they dress. You see them wanting to shrink, to be invisible, to reduce themselves. If tall women don't do that, people find other ways to try and reduce them. I've fallen out with friends because of it previously. Up until a year ago, I would still entertain the notion that I was a freak, that I was really androgynous, that we should all make jokes about it. But actually I didn't regard myself as particularly androgynous, simply taller than the average woman. Because being tall is seen as some kind of blessing, people think it's OK to humiliate you and make jokes about you being of indeterminate gender, but I don't feel the need to reduce myself in that way anymore, and I don't think I need to allow other people to be reductive about me in that way."

You really need to admire her ebullience, her refusal to be the wallflower that the world expects her to be because of her size. Although Christie has had training as a Shakespearian actress, almost all of the roles she has played so far have depicted her as some sort of Amazonian superhero. The challenge will be to see if she can do something more mainstream in the future.

Another actress who frequently was discouraged from pursuing her dreams was 6'0" Allison Janney. She admitted she was very conscious of her size when she started out but she still was determined to make it in show business. When she was talking to the manager of an agency in New York one day, the agent finally told her: "What are you going to get cast as? Lesbians and aliens—that's the only thing I can think of."

"People say stupid things to actors when they're just starting out," Janney recalled in a 2011 interview with Postmedia News. "I think people like to be discouraging toward them."

It wasn't the only time she heard something like that. "I

remember someone saying to me, 'You're tall,' and I said that Christine Lahti and Sigourney Weaver and Kelly McGillis were all tall. And she said, 'They have something in common.' And I said, 'What?' And she said, 'They're drop-dead gorgeous.' I remember the tears coming up behind my eyes. I felt very discouraged that my height seemed to be something that people couldn't see as being cashable, or something. It was very challenging."

Fortunately, Janney was up to the challenge. She kept plugging away until people saw her talent and she has carved out an excellent career. She played leading roles in such TV series as *West Wing* and *Mom*. In fact, she has played a lot of moms, in such films as *The Help* and *Juno*. I'm especially partial to her poignant portrayal of the uncouth, unfiltered mother of figure skater Tonya Harding in *I, Tonya*. She did actually portray a lesbian once, playing Meryl Streep's lover in *The Hours*, although I don't think she ever has played an alien.

Another ultra-talented performer who seemingly may have been held back by her size was Susan Anton, a 5'11" sex symbol of the 1970s.

Anton said that before the age of 20 she thought there were two kinds of people in the world: the ones who said, "Hey, Stretch, how's the weather up there?" and those who said, "Hey, Shorty, how's the weather up there?"

She said she never really thought about being tall until someone asked her about it. "The fact is I am tall and there is nothing I can do about it," she said in a 1980 interview with *Orange Coast Magazine*. When she was younger, she wanted to just blend in and took to slouching to make it look as though she wasn't so tall. She said her mother often told her just to "be glad that all 5'11" of it works."

Her height didn't keep her from being named Miss California in 1969 and tying for runner-up in the Miss America pageant, and that led to a role as spokesperson for Muriel Cigars and a few movie roles. However, she never really made it that big despite also possessing a very versatile singing voice. She made light of her size in the first segment of a four-week NBC series in 1979 called *Presenting Susan Anton*, when she sang a duet with *Sesame Street* character Big Bird called "Being Tall."

In the end, she became more famous for dating shorter men, including 5'2" Dudley Moore and 5'10" Sylvester Stallone.

Award-winning actress Sigourney Weaver isn't quite as tall as

Janney and Anton, at 5'10½", but even at that height she may have been somewhat inhibited by her size. She grew up in a show business family—her father was the president of NBC and her mother was an actress—but she never thought she would be an actress because she grew to her full height by the age of 11. "I felt like a giant spider," Weaver said. "I never had the confidence to ever think I could act."

But in an odd way, she felt her height may have contributed to her acting acumen. She didn't fit in with the other kids, and as a self-professed "misfit," she thought she had exactly the sort of mind-set that might enhance someone's ability to act. She decided to attend drama school at Yale and was frequently told there to give it up. "They suggested I get out of the business," Weaver said in a 1979 NEA interview. "They often told me I was too tall ever to make it as an actress. I kept at it, I think, mostly out of spite."

Her persistence paid off when she was cast in *Alien*, opposite the imposing Bolaji Badejo, and her career blossomed from there. She has won three Tony awards and two Golden Globes and she has been nominated three times for Academy Awards.

Weaver said in that 1979 interview that she was not aware of ever having lost a role because of her size and thought that in a way it might have helped. "Certainly on stage being tall is good—it gives me a sense of power, and I have to act big to act my size." Asked again about it in a *New York Times* interview five years later, she revised her response, admitting that perhaps she had lost a job or two to tallness.

"I suppose there are some people, actors and directors, who think I'm too tall," she said. "I suppose I have lost some roles because of that, and all I can say to that is good riddance."

Geena Davis is another actress who has overcome the stigma of her stature. Davis is 6'1" and wears a size 12 shoe, and although she harbored ambitions of being an actress at a very early age, she had that same "misfit" feeling that Weaver experienced. She wasn't part of the cool group of kids and suffered from low self-esteem. She didn't view herself as being attractive but she still was determined to succeed. "I knew you had to take a hand in your own destiny, make things happen," she said in a 1996 *Parade* magazine article. "And that's what I decided to do."

After high school, she moved to New York, worked as a waitress and sales clerk, finally got a job as a model (she lied about her height, telling them she was 5'10") and then was cast in a minor role in *Tootsie* in 1982. That opened the door to bigger acting challenges. She won an Oscar for Best Actress in a Supporting Role in 1989 for *The Accidental Tourist* and was nominated for Best Actress in 1992 for *Thelma and Louise.*

Fortunately, there are signs that the times may be changing. We may begin to see a few taller actresses like Christie and not just in androgynous roles.

A prime example is Elizabeth Debicki, an up-and-coming actress who is 6'3" (or perhaps 6'2¾"). Debicki grew up in Australia, the daughter of two professional ballet dancers, but any thoughts of following in her parents' footsteps disappeared when she was taller than any of her teachers in middle school. She admitted she did a lot of the same slouching that other tall women have done to appear less tall, but her parents, as trained dancers, were sticklers for perfect posture. "They used to come up and grab my shoulders back," she said.

She eventually transitioned into contemporary dance and then acting, and she has found success in recent years. Her first big splash was in *The Great Gatsby* in 2013 and she played Princess Diana (who was fairly tall, at 5'10") in *The Crown.*

Her height was used as a plot element in the 2020 film *Tenet.* There is a scene in which she towers over a couple of her male co-stars and the film then goes quickly to a shot of what appears to be 6-inch stiletto heels to explain why she is so much taller. Insiders have said Debicki was not really wearing heels in the shot. She was just that much taller than the guys. There also is a scene in the film in which she is seated in the backseat of a car and stretches out a leg far enough to unlock one of the doors in the front seat with her toes.

Debicki suspects she may have lost out on a part or two in these early stages of her career because of her size, but like Weaver, she doesn't really care.

"My agent was never going to call me up and say, 'Look, they didn't want you because you're tall' because there's nothing I can do about that," she is quoted as saying on her IMDb page. "I'm sure it's happened. It's been a process in my life but I'm really proud of it. It's been a journey coming to terms with it."

The newest tall actress to make a splash in films is Ava Michelle, who benefited from the fact that Netflix opted to make a movie in 2019 called *Tall Girl.* Ava, then only 17, with a background as a dancer, fit perfectly into the role of an oversized, frequently persecuted high school student since she was 6'1½". Of course, the film occasionally makes it appear as though she is much taller than that, perhaps 6'6" or 6'7". They definitely give her the Alan Ladd elongation treatment.

Michelle didn't need to do any in-depth research to prepare for the role. She just needed to draw on her own experiences. She appeared as a dancer on the reality show *Dance Moms* but was cut from the dance team in Season 4 for being too tall. In a scene that will live forever in body-shaming infamy, obnoxiously insensitive coach Abby Lee Miller tells her, "Ava, you're too tall for us today. You're cut. Thank you, you can go." Ava, who was only 5'10" at that time, was crying as she departed.

She also was the target of extensive social media abuse even before that incident, which undoubtedly also prompted some tears.

"The things that people can say when they're behind a computer is just, it's insane," she said in an interview with Cheatsheet.com. "And being an 11-year-old and having people saying that I was

A 2019 Netflix film called *Tall Girl*, starring Ava Michelle, spotlighted the issues of tall teenagers. Michelle, who is 6'1½", was able to draw on her own experiences for the lead role. From left behind Michelle are Griffin Gluck, Sabrina Carpenter, Luke Eisner and Anjelika Washington.

anorexic and that my mom wasn't feeding me, it's really hard to understand the fact that they're not true."

Ava finally just stopped looking at social media. It still took a great deal of support and self-reflection for her to rise above the abuse. Landing the starring role in *Tall Girl* and the 2022 sequel, *Tall Girl 2*, certainly helped. She said the 2019 film, which includes all the questions about the weather and many of the other things with which we all deal, almost served as a form of therapy for her.

"I don't think I truly embraced or loved my height until I made this film, if I'm being honest with you," she told United Press International. "I think I told myself I did, but I was so self-deprecating all the time. I would make jokes about my height so that no one would first."

16

It's Possible to Be Too Tall

Every time I start to complain about being 6'6¾", I just need to think about Robert Pershing Wadlow. Or Don Koehler. Or Sandy Allen. Or Igor Vovkovinskiy. Or Sultan Kosen.

You think I have trouble getting comfortable in airplanes or finding clothes that fit? You think legroom or headroom in a car is a headache waiting to happen? You think people stare at or ask stupid questions of guys like me?

Those folks had it much, much worse. All of them were afflicted with gigantism, Marfan Syndrome, acromegaly, Klinefelter Syndrome, hypertrophy or some other physical malfunction that prompted their bodies to grow far beyond the normal bounds of biology.

Marfan Syndrome, first identified by a French pediatrician named Antoine Marfan in 1896, is a genetic condition caused by a mutation of the FBN1 gene. It limits a body's ability to produce proteins necessary in the development of connective tissues and can manifest itself not only in extreme height but also elongated fingers and toes, a narrow chest, impaired vision and problems with the heart, skeleton and blood vessels. It's hereditary with a person possibly having as much as a 50 percent chance of passing it along to their children.

Acromegaly is a rare condition in which the body produces too much human growth hormone. When diagnosed in people prior to puberty, it is more commonly referred to as gigantism. The condition frequently occurs because a non-cancerous tumor is pressing against the pituitary gland, a pea-sized gland situated beneath the brain. It can occasionally be caused by a tumor elsewhere in the body—pancreas, lungs or other parts of the brain—but that is especially rare.

Klinefelter Syndrome is the result of a genetic disorder. All male infants inherit an X chromosome from their mother and a Y chromosome from their father, but Klinefelter victims receive an additional X chromosome that can lead to a variety of issues, including extreme height and a lack of development in other parts of the body. If affects different people in different ways. There also is such a thing as XYY syndrome, in which males have an extra Y chromosome. It also prompts excessive growth but has different, wide-ranging symptoms that, according to experts, are "often subtle" and much more difficult to diagnose.

Fortunately, all of these conditions are rare. Marfan afflicts about one out of every 5,000 to 10,000 people. Acromegaly and gigantism impact only one in every 15,000 to 20,000. Klinefelter affects about 1 in 750.

The largest measured height ever for any human being—bear in mind no one took a tape measure to Goliath of Goth, Hanzei or Eleazar—is 8 feet, 11.1 inches. That's how tall Robert Wadlow was when he died in Alton, Illinois, in 1940 at the age of 22.

Wadlow's record likely never will be topped because modern medicine has found ways to at least partially limit the growth of people afflicted with gigantism and similar ailments. Wadlow's extreme growth was caused by hypertrophy, an enlargement of the pituitary gland that caused his body to be subjected to extreme amounts of human growth hormone. He still was continuing to grow at the time of his death, but as the *Guinness Book of World Records* pointed out, nothing like that would be allowed to happen today. "We can slow or halt excessive growth and deal with the complications of gigantism long before anyone gets close to Wadlow's superlative stature," Guinness has said. "As the world becomes ever more connected, it's unlikely that any child growing up with a pituitary issue more extreme than Robert Wadlow's will remain untreated by doctors."

There was no indication that Wadlow was any different than any other baby when he was born in Alton in 1918 as the oldest of five children of Harold and Addie Wadlow. He was of normal length and weighed 8 pounds, 6 ounces.

By the time he was a year old, he weighed 62 pounds. When he was 8, he already was 6'2". He was 6'6" at the age of 10 and the elementary school he attended had a special desk made for him that he carried from classroom to classroom. At 14, he was proclaimed the world's tallest Boy Scout at 7'4" and he continued to grow about two inches per year even after graduating from Alton High School and enrolling at Shurtleff College. He was measured periodically throughout his life by doctors at nearby Washington University in St. Louis, and they found him to be 8'11.1" on June 27, 1940, just 18 days before his death.

The people in his hometown accepted and adored Wadlow. He was of above-average intelligence—naturally, he was tall—and reportedly read about 300 books each year. He also had a winning personality. A lengthy profile that appeared in *American Weekly* magazine at the time of his death said he "was always good-natured about his vast size and willing to discuss laughingly the inconvenience and perils of living in a pygmy world. Probably this was because the kidding of the children he grew up with was tinged with awe and admiration."

Robert Wadlow of Alton, Illinois, shown with members of his family, was certified as the tallest man in the world at 8'11.1" (courtesy Alton Museum of History and Art).

But, as you can imagine, any time Wadlow ventured outside of Alton, he was the object of awestruck stares and insensitive comments. His size brought plenty of other problems. He had assorted medical issues associated with his height. He broke two bones in his foot during a routine fall when he was 14. When he was 17, he spent eight weeks in the hospital because of an infection in his foot and arthritis of the spine. Even the slightest little bruise or ailment took much longer to heal than with normal-sized people.

He also was continually outgrowing clothes and shoes, and it was extremely expensive to have apparel custom-made for him. You just couldn't walk into a store and find size 37AA shoes. His parents had a special 9½-foot bed and a massive, oversized chair made for him, and they hoped to someday have a home built with special high ceilings and doorways. But all of that required lots of money, more than Harold Wadlow could afford in his job as an engineer with Shell Oil.

Ultimately, it became necessary for the family to utilize Robert's size and accompanying notoriety for monetary purposes. It began with small things. His younger siblings once set up a lemonade stand with Robert sitting nearby. Naturally, people flocked to see the world's tallest man but Wadlow would only stand up if the gawking customer bought a lemonade. The kids made $100, an enormous amount of money in the early 1930s.

Wadlow became a celebrity both locally and nationally at a very early age. The hometown *Alton Evening Telegraph* published a story about his extreme height when he was only 10 years old. When he was 11, his massive shoes were put on display at Tom and Bob's shoe store in Alton. The shoes also were displayed at a national shoe convention in St. Louis in 1934 when he was still in high school and a mere 7'10", and the Associated Press did a story on him that was distributed all over the country.

For years, the Ringling Brothers Barnum & Bailey circus had made overtures to the Wadlows in an attempt to sign Robert as part of an act, but the family resisted, fearing that Robert would not do well in the transient lifestyle of the circus and that his dignity would be compromised in that sort of show.

In 1937, they finally relented and Robert signed to do a four-week run with Ringling Brothers at Madison Square Garden in New York City. There were special stipulations in the contract. Robert would only be with the circus for those four weeks and would not continue when the show went out on tour. Robert and Harold would be housed at the Astor Hotel so the 19-year-old would not be exposed to the normal circus life. And Robert would not be a sideshow act. He would appear in a 10-minute segment in the twice-daily shows and would be billed as "the world's tallest boy." Harold also had it put in writing that his son's role in the shows would be "dignified."

We don't know exactly what Wadlow did in the circus shows but it's hard to imagine it was too dignified. However, he stayed with the show for the full four weeks, playing to a total of about 800,000 spectators during that span.

The following year, Harold and the family loosened the reins a little bit more. Harold quit his regular job and they began touring the country on behalf of the Peters shoe company of St. Louis, which not only supplied Robert with custom-made Weatherbird shoes but also paid him a salary.

During an appearance in Rapid City, South Dakota, in 1939, the C.C. Anderson shoe store offered a free pair of shoes to the person who could come closest to guessing the number of beans that could be held in one of Wadlow's shoes, which was on display in the store in conjunction with his appearance there. In Hamburg, New York, the local shoe store had two 6'1" men see if they could reach high enough to pluck a $1 bill off the top of Wadlow's head. In Cedar Rapids, Iowa, Robert appeared for a few days at the Paramount Theater and did endorsement ads for the Hotel Roosevelt, Gabel's restaurant, Higbee's shoe store and the Rude Auto Company. (Those ads all appeared on the same page of the *Cedar Rapids Gazette* one day.) There were similar promotional events in Marshall, North Carolina; Laurel, Montana; Logan, Utah; Council Grove, Kansas; Salinas, California; Mountain Home, Arkansas; and innumerable other places.

Robert probably couldn't have squeezed himself into an airplane and many of the places they went may not have been accessible by train so he and his dad traveled around the country in a special car that had the front driver's side seat removed so Robert could drive it from the back seat. Sometimes other members of the family went with them. It has been estimated that Robert and family members traveled about 300,000 miles in the course of two or three years.

Wadlow was not always portrayed favorably in the final years of his life. A doctor named Charles Humberd wrote an article about him in 1937 in the *Journal of the American Medical Society* that depicted Robert as being ill-tempered and labeled him a "freak." The

Wadlows sued for libel and asked $100,000 in damages. They lost. A jury in St. Joseph's, Missouri, deliberated for less than an hour before deciding in Humberd's favor.

During the Wadlows' 1938 visit to Hamburg, a newspaper story noted that "Robert is apparently healthy, in spite of his tremendous height. He is very pale, however, and has difficulty in walking, using a 5 foot cane to assist him."

In addition to the cane, he was forced to wear braces on his legs in order to walk and to prevent further injury. In the end, that actually contributed to his death. While appearing at a Fourth of July event in Michigan, Robert developed a blister on his ankle due to the rubbing of a brace and that led to a serious infection. Because he had very little feeling in his legs and feet, the infection became very advanced before he even knew about it. He woke up one morning with a 106-degree temperature and never recovered in spite of blood transfusions and surgery to amputate one of his legs. He died in his sleep on July 15, 1940.

The reaction to his death reflected how popular Wadlow had become in Alton and elsewhere. His body was put on display at the Streeper Funeral Home and people flooded the streets, clogging traffic as they waited to pay their respects. The viewing of his body began at 4 p.m. on July 17 and continued through two nights before officials called a halt to it at 5 a.m. on July 19. It was estimated that 27,000 people filed through in that time although the *Guinness Book of World Records* has reported that it was 40,000. Alton's population at that time was around 30,000.

Wadlow's life is commemorated today with a life-size bronze statue at the dental school of Southern Illinois University Edwardsville, at the site of the former Shurtleff College, where Robert was a student. His special oversized chair is on display at the Franklin Masonic Temple in Alton. The ground above his gravesite in Oakwood Cemetery is raised so visitors can see how tall he was.

Wadlow was one of perhaps two dozen people who have been verified to be at least 8 feet in height by either Guinness or by some other reliable source.

There also have been a fair number of people who wildly exaggerated their height. For example, Zhan Shichai, who lived in China from 1841 to 1893, claimed to be 10'6". When he finally agreed to be measured by the folks from Guinness, he was found to be just a shade under 7'9".

Eddie Carmel, born in Israel in 1936 as Oded Ha-Carmeili, was an actor and entertainer who was sometimes known as the Jewish Giant or the Happy Giant. At various times, he claimed to be either 8'9" or 9'1", which would have made him even taller than Robert Wadlow, but he never was measured by anyone. The consensus is that he was closer to 7'3".

Jack Earle spent 14 years with Ringling Brothers Barnum & Bailey in the 1930s and 1940s being billed as "the world's tallest man" at 8'6½". When he died in 1952, he was found to be 7'7".

Ted Evans, who followed Earle as a Ringling Brothers performer, was billed as being 9'3" although Evans wrote an article for *Coronet* magazine in 1956 in which he professed to being 8'5". The folks at Guinness looked at photographs and other evidence and pegged him at 7'8½".

A Minnesota man named John Aasen billed himself as the world's tallest man in the 1920s, telling people he was 8'9". Just before his death in 1938, he was measured and found to be 7'1".

There have been a few people who legitimately stretched beyond the 8-foot mark. John Carroll of Buffalo, who lived from 1932 to 1969, was measured at about 8'0" but he had an extreme curvature of the spine known as kyphoscoliosis. Guinness officials calculated that had he been able to stand upright he would have been 8'7½".

John Rogan of Gallatin, Tennessee, who died in 1905, was 8'6" but was unable to stand because the joints in his knees and hips had been severely tightened by the adhesions that accompany acromegaly. Rogan was undoubtedly the lightest of the 8-footers at 225 pounds.

Leonid Stadnik, a former veterinarian and farmer from a remote area of the Ukraine, was certified by Guinness in 2007 as the tallest living man, at 8'5". Stadnik was of normal size until the age of 14 when a brain surgery apparently stimulated his pituitary gland. Guinness later stripped him of his tallest man title when the publicity-shy Stadnik refused to be measured, saying, "I have always wanted to be in the shadows. I tried not to stand out."

Don Koehler, who was born in Montana and grew up in Chicago was 8'2" and was considered to be the tallest man in the world from 1969 until his death in 1981.

Valno Myllrinne of Helsinki, Finland (1909–63), was a mere 7'3½" at the age of 21, then hit another mysterious growth spurt in his late 30s that added nearly another foot to his height, pushing him to 8'1". Gabriel Estavao Monjane, who was born in 1944 in Mozambique, and Zhao Liang, born in 1982 in Henan, China, also were 8'1".

Among those who likely were legitimate 8-footers who never were measured by Guinness were Fritz Winkelmeier, who lived in Austria in the 19th century and whose death certificate listed him as being 8'6"; Pornchai Saosri of Thailand, who claimed to be 8'10" and who carried a 2013 government-certified identification card that listed him as 8'5"; Vikas Uppal of India, who at times was listed anywhere from 8'1" to 8'9"; Ajaz Ahmed, a farmer from Pakistan who claimed to be 8'4"; and Edouard Beaupre, a Saskatchewan native whose 1904 Canadian death certificate stated that he was 8'3".

There has been only one woman who was certified as taller than 8'0". Zeng Jinlian, who was born in China in 1964 and did not live to see her 18th birthday, was 8'1". Jinlian did not have any other family members taller than 5'5".

Jane Bunford, born in 1895 in Birmingham, England, came very close to reaching the 8-foot level. She began growing at an abnormal rate following a head injury at the age of 11 and within two years was 6'6". When she died in 1922, she was measured at 7'7" although she had a severe curvature of the spine and it was estimated she may actually have been as tall as 7'11". Her skeleton is on display in the anatomical museum at the medical school of Birmingham University.

As you can tell, almost none of these extremely tall people lived to a ripe old age and many of them had tormented, desperately unhappy existences while they were alive.

Although he made his living off his height, Ted Evans admitted in his aforementioned *Coronet* magazine piece that "I've learned to hate every inch. I dream only of the day when I can afford to quit being a freak on exhibition."

Leonid Stadnik referred to his height as "God's punishment" and told Reuters in a 2004 interview that "for my entire life I wanted to be shorter. I was bowing down, stooping."

Perhaps that's why the very tall people who have risen above their circumstances and maintained an upbeat attitude, at least outwardly, often have come to be revered and adored by the general public.

That certainly was true of Robert Wadlow. It was the same way with 8'2" Don Koehler, who had a twin sister who was 5'9". They once won an award as the world's most unidentical twins.

Koehler worked for more than 20 years as a salesman for the Big Joe Manufacturing Company, a job that afforded him the opportunity to meet new people who never, ever forgot the towering man with the engaging personality. Koehler said he liked to let his height do the talking on the job. He would walk into a business, hand the secretary his business card and just stand back and watch. "When she calls her boss to say the salesman from Big Joe is here, she almost always adds, 'And boy, is he big!'" Koehler told the *Chicago Tribune* in 1973. "I get to see the boss—and the next time I come, he remembers me."

Like Wadlow, Koehler needed to have his car altered to be able to drive it. He said hotels treated him royally when he was on the road. They always were happy to push two beds together to accommodate him and they often sewed together sheets especially for him. He just had to be a little careful when he ventured outside his hotel room.

"I have to be careful walking down the hallways late at night," he said. "Often I run into some conventioneers returning from a night on the town, and when they see me they all sober up in a hurry."

Koehler, who tried playing basketball once but quickly gave it up after getting injured, lived in a normal-sized apartment with 8-foot ceilings and normal furniture. He said he developed a sixth sense to avoid bumping his head. "The only time I bump my head is when I have a bad cold," he said. "My radar gets blocked up."

Koehler said he attributed his positive attitude to the influence of his parents, who encouraged him not to feel sorry for himself, and to the friendship of people in Chicago's Paramount Tall Club, who opened him up socially and influenced him to be proud of his stature. He also credited the company he worked for all those years.

"They didn't try to exploit me the way other tall people have been, and because of this job I've never had to appear in circuses or sideshows," Koehler said, noting that the tall people who subjected themselves to being objects of curiosity generally ended up as miserable recluses.

Another person who served as an inspiration to ensuing generations of giants was Sandy Allen, who grew up in Shelbyville, Indiana, and ended up being 7'7" and weighing more than 400 pounds. Allen's growth, as with so many others, was the result of a tumor on her pituitary gland, which was not discovered until she was 22. She ended up having it removed in 1977, preventing her from possibly becoming the tallest woman who ever lived.

She worked as a secretary in Indianapolis, appeared in a few films and ended up appearing for a short time with Ringling Brothers, as so many of these really tall people did. The circus billed her as "the world's tallest woman," and at least in this case, it was an accurate label. Allen did actually hold that title from 1992 to 2008.

She also wrote a book titled *Cast a Giant Shadow* that undoubtedly helped many other people come to grips with their extreme size.

Allen was teased and bullied as a kid and was exposed to all the same sort of stares and questions as other tall people but she ultimately came to embrace the scrutiny. She felt it helped her accept her size and become more confident. Her close friend, Rita Rose, said that when Allen was recognized by Guinness as the tallest woman in the world, it "brought her out of her shell. She got to the point where she could joke about it."

"If I could choose to be 5-foot-8 tomorrow, I don't think that I would do it," Allen said in a 1978 *Philadelphia Inquirer* story. "I have accepted myself, and I think I like myself fine just the way I am."

Like Koehler, Allen lived into her early 50s and never married. She loved to tell people she was an old-fashioned girl who would not date a man shorter than her.

In more modern times, other very tall people have adopted the same upbeat approach as Wadlow, Koehler and Allen.

Sultan Kosen, a farmer from Turkey, was found in 2011 to be 8'2.8" by Guinness officials, who proclaimed him to be the world's tallest living man. He also held the title of having the largest hands although his measurement of 11.22 inches from his wrist to the top of his middle finger is far short of Robert Wadlow's 12.75 inches.

He is another person who was the victim of a tumor pressing on his pituitary gland. He had multiple surgeries to remove it only to have the tumor grow back. Surgeons at the University of Virginia finally used something called "gamma-knife radio surgery" to remove portions of the tumor in 2010 and that appeared to have finally halted his growth.

As with Sandy Allen, Kosen was brought out of a somewhat sheltered existence by his Guinness recognition. "Before being crowned with the title, I lived my life almost like in a box," he said.

After that, he was given a free apartment in Ankara by the Turkish government, appeared in a television documentary, visited several countries and was gifted a free dental makeover by a dentist in

San Clemente, California, according to a 2010 story in the *Orange County Register.*

"Some people are fascinated and some people are scared," Kosen said of the way strangers react to his size. "Don't be afraid of me just because I'm tall."

Around the time that Kosen was labeled the tallest man in the world by Guinness, Igor Oleksandrovych Vovkovinskiy of Rochester, Minnesota, was anointed the tallest man in the United States.

Vovkovinskiy was born in the Ukraine in 1982, and by the age of 6, he already was 6'0" and weighed 200 pounds. He eventually reached a height of 7'8.3".

He was diagnosed at a very early age as having a tennis ball-sized tumor that was pressing on his pituitary gland at the base of his brain and releasing extreme amounts of HGH. However, because of the proximity of the tumor to his brain, doctors in the Ukraine determined that surgery was far too risky. Vovkovinskiy's mother, Svetlana, wrote to medical experts around the world and finally found a receptive ear at the Mayo Clinic, which agreed to take on the task (and the expense) of treating Igor. That prompted the family's move to Rochester in 1989.

The Mayo doctors told Igor that he was on pace to be even taller than Wadlow and probably would become the world's first verified 9-footer. They prescribed two drugs—bromocriptine and somatostatin—to shrink the tumor and that was followed by a seemingly endless string of surgeries, the first of which, in early 1990, involved going through Igor's gums above his upper teeth and trying to remove as much of the tumor as possible with a long instrument.

That did not completely stop Igor's extreme growth—he was 6'6" and 300 pounds as a 10-year-old fifth-grader—but it at least slowed it down. He underwent an estimated 16 surgeries between 2006 and 2012 but continued to endure excruciating pain in his extremities and vital organs.

"Sometimes I have pain that is so severe I have a picture in my brain of a truck that keeps running over my leg," Igor said in an interview with *Rochester Magazine*. "Sometimes for three or four hours at a time. It's hard to breathe. I see black spots. My heart starts hurting."

In spite of all that, he maintained a lighthearted approach to his size and the fact that it fascinated everyone with whom he came into contact. He admitted that all the attention and questions bothered him when he was young but he came to embrace it. "I finally realized it was better to give people what they want, for all of us," he said.

By the time he was a teenager he was carrying around cards that said he would tell people his shoe size (which was 26, by the way) if they'd give him a dollar. He wore a t-shirt that said, "Life is short, I'm not." When people asked if he played basketball, he would ask if they played miniature golf.

As a 7'5" high school student, he did actually try to play junior varsity basketball, but he was very prone to injuries. He suffered a stress fracture in his foot and broke an elbow once when he fell down, bringing an abrupt end to his hoops career.

In 2010, Igor was verified as the largest living American by Guinness.

As with Wadlow and others, he became a major local celebrity and even attracted some national attention. He appeared on *The Dr. Oz Show*, played a small role in the 2011 film *Hall Pass*, wrote letters to the editor of the local newspaper, helped raise money for Ukrainian troops in its 2014 war with Russia, and supported Barack Obama for president. In a 2009 rally at the Target Center in Minneapolis, he wore a t-shirt that read "World's Biggest Obama Supporter" and was singled out by the future president.

He had trouble finding shoes that fit him and allowed him to walk without giving him mind-boggling pain so he made a public plea in 2012, saying he needed $16,000 to get the specially made size 26 10E shoes he required. He received donations amounting more than double what he needed and Reebok then announced it would provide the shoes free of charge.

Through all of the suffering that his size and the repeated surgeries brought, he always seemed to have an upbeat approach. He admitted that "sometimes the pain is so bad I can't do anything useful," but he said he tried to focus on the positive things. "I think that even for the simple things in life, people should be more grateful," he said. "Especially because you live in America. Really count your blessings. Really appreciate all of the little things you have."

All of the treatments and surgeries took their toll and Igor's heart finally gave out. He died in August 2021 at the age of 38.

The public funeral proceedings weren't as extensive as they had been for Wadlow 81 years earlier but there were outpourings of sentiment in the mainstream media and on social media, many of those coming from people who had only brief but buoyant encounters with Igor.

One person wrote: "He made my daughter feel like she'd just met a superhero."

"My five-year-old daughter got to meet Igor," another person added, "and she talked about it for a month straight."

The *Rochester Post-Bulletin* published an editorial in which it noted that "never, to our knowledge, did he display impatience with his condition or discomfort with the public recognition he frequently received."

"Our hearts are broken by the loss of this substantial man," the editorial added. "Godspeed, Igor, and may the gates of heaven be extra-high to receive you."

17

We Can Do Just About Anything

We've already explained how tall people make great basketball and volleyball players. They also make good political candidates and frequently prosper in the business world.

But the truth is, tall people can do just about anything if they set their minds to it. They can be chefs, chiropractors, ministers, journalists, firemen, policemen, barbers, attorneys, zookeepers, salesmen and rock stars.

Here are some noteworthy examples. We're not guaranteeing that all of these people are absolutely, unequivocally the tallest in the world at their chosen professions. Our research and global reach isn't quite as extensive as that of the *Guinness Book of World Records.* There may be someone taller doing the same thing as these folks. But not many.

Tallest lawyer: Clifford Thompson was once thought to be the tallest person in the world, at 8'7", although Guinness officials thought he was about 7'5" based on photographic evidence. Even if that's the case, he almost certainly is the tallest person ever to tower over a jury. Born in North Dakota, Thompson grew up on a farm near Scandinavia, Wisconsin, and worked as a sideshow giant for eight years with two different circuses. He then sold beer for a while before deciding to attend Marquette University's law school. He graduated in 1944, practiced law in the town of Iola, Wisconsin, for a while, then later moved to Los Angeles and ultimately Portland, Oregon. That's where he died in 1955, just a week before his 51st birthday.

Tallest chiropractor: As someone who is 7'2", almost no one knows as much about how much tall people suffer from back ailments as Torsten Stein. He has had spinal issues since he was 14 years old and never was able to find relief through conventional medical treatments. A visit to a chiropractor while attending a New Jersey Nets rookie camp—yes, he was a basketball player—opened his eyes and he decided to become a chiropractor himself, setting up practice in the Phoenix area.

Tallest orthopedic surgeon: Daniel Ivankovich of Chicago is 6'10", wears a size 17 shoe and has a heart to match. In addition to being a gifted surgeon and a talented blues musician, the former Northwestern University basketball player also is the co-founder of OnePatient Global Health Initiative, a nonprofit foundation whose mission is to treat patients "who have musculoskeletal health disorders, regardless of their ability to pay."

Tallest female sports psychologist: Dr. Nicole Forrester, who is an assistant professor in the RTA School of Media at Ryerson University in Toronto, is 6'3½". She competed in the high jump in the 2008 Olympics and won a gold medal at the 2010 Commonwealth Games.

Tallest firefighter: 6'11" Brandon Berridge became a member of the fire department in Tullahoma, Oklahoma, in 2016 and was

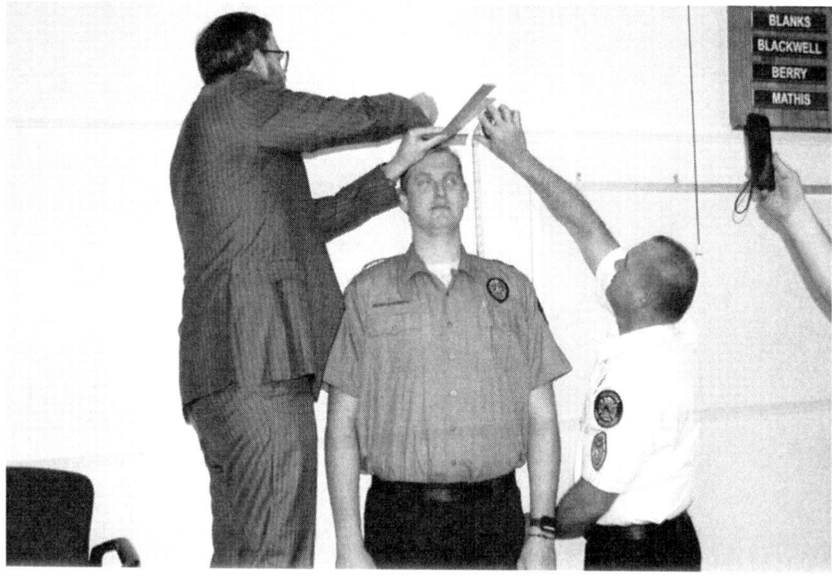

Brandon Berridge of Tullahoma, Oklahoma, is measured by officials to confirm that he is 6'11", and the tallest firefighter in the world, according to the *Guinness Book of World Records* (courtesy *Tullahoma News*).

certified as the world's tallest firefighter by Guinness in 2020. Berridge, whose wife is 4'11", obviously has a job in which it is sometimes necessary to crawl into tight spaces but he's a handy guy to have around when it's time to inspect or install smoke alarms. "This world is not necessarily made for taller people, but there are certain aspects where we can shine," Berridge said. "Find what you enjoy and do it. Greet challenges and conquer them. Height can be an advantage."

Tallest law enforcement officer: You might remember George Bell, who we mentioned as a 7'8" basketball player at Morris Brown College. He also played basketball with the Harlem Globetrotters and Harlem Wizards before becoming a Norfolk County (Virginia) sheriff's deputy. Bell, certified by Guinness in 2007 as the tallest man in the United States, gradually came to appreciate his size. "I have no choice but to like it," he told the Associated Press. "I'm used to a small man's world. I've been dealing with a small man's world since I was a kid."

Tallest chef: Chicago's Jeff Goldfarb is 7'0" and actually has trademarked the phrase "World's Tallest Chef." He knew at a very early age that he wanted to cook, following in the footsteps of his father, and never had much interest in sports. "Much to the chagrin of the high school basketball coaches I chose to work at KFC instead of playing ball," he says in the bio on his website. Goldfarb, whose extreme growth was caused by gigantism, underwent surgery in 2012 for the removal of a tumor from his pituitary gland. He has worked at various types of food preparation facilities all over the United States, but he admitted that at times it's not easy working in a kitchen made for normal-sized people. "Sixteen-hour days do not do wonders for one's back or one's feet when you're 7 feet tall," he said in a 2012 interview. "The kitchen environment was not made for a tall person, a tall chef."

Tallest female television chef: Despite being 6'2", Julia Child never viewed her height as any sort of impediment in life. "Being tall is an advantage especially in business," she said. "People will always remember you. And if you're in a crowd, you'll always have some clean air to breathe." Child never set out to be a chef. She majored in history in college, joined the Office of Strategic Services (OSS) in 1942, and met and married fellow OSS employee Paul Child. Her love of food blossomed while living in Paris following World War II. She ended up graduating from the famed Cordon Bleu school and co-authored the best-selling *Mastering the Art of French Cooking*. That led to her becoming arguably the most popular (and most lampooned) TV chef ever.

Tallest female news anchor: Laurie Dhue, who is 6'3", worked for CNN and MSNBC before becoming an anchor for Fox News from 2000 to 2008. More recently, she was employed by TheBlaze.com.

Tallest male news anchor: David Gregory, who worked in various capacities for NBC including being the host of *Meet the Press,* is 6'5". More recently, Gregory has done work for CNN. President George H.W. Bush, who liked to give everyone a nickname, referred to Gregory as "Stretch."

Tallest meteorologist: "Too Tall" Tom Szymanski, who works for KFGO radio in Fargo, North Dakota, may be the best qualified person to really tell us how the weather is up there. He claims to be the tallest weather person in the world, at 6'10½". He even has the Twitter handle @tallweatherguy. Not surprisingly, Szymanski played basketball at Western Michigan and East Carolina in the late 1970s.

Tallest barber: Stan Piotrowski, proprietor of Stan's Barber Shop of Newtown, Pennsylvania, was 6'8". Piotrowski, who passed away in 2020, had special raised counters in his shop and all the barber chairs were on 4-inch platforms to bring the clients up to his level.

Tallest priest: Gregory L. Parkes, who is 6'8", has served as the bishop of the St. Petersburg, Florida, diocese since 2017 and feels size is a plus in his line of work. "As far as the gift that it is, I suppose people remember you first of all and you tend to draw attention to yourself, so I try to use that in a very good way and very positive way to serve God's people," Parkes said in a 2012 Catholic News Agency piece. During a meeting with Pope Francis in 2019, the pontiff took note of Parkes' size and posed one of the standard questions: "Did you play basketball?"

Tallest pastor: Keith Tower, the lead pastor of HighPoint Church in Ocoee, Florida, near Orlando, is 7'0". And yes, he very definitely did play basketball. Tower starred at Notre Dame and spent four seasons in the NBA before deciding to found his church along with former Orlando Magic teammate Andrew DeClercq.

Tallest astronaut: Former pro football star and *Good Morning America* host Michael Strahan, who is 6'5", broke a record by going into space as part of an independently-funded Blue Origin flight on December 11, 2021. People temporarily grow in space as their vertebrae decompress from a lack of gravity but Strahan was only up there for 10 minutes so that probably didn't make him much taller. Previously, there had been two NASA astronauts who were 6'4". Jim Wetherbee was part of six space shuttle missions between 1990 and 2002 and James "Ox" van Hoften was on space shuttle flights in 1984 and 1985.

Tallest first lady: Eleanor Roosevelt was 6'0" (actually she may have been more like 5'11½"), giving her a slight edge on 5'11" Michelle Obama and 5'11" Melania Trump. Roosevelt sometimes seemed even taller to people because she stood so erect, the product of arduous exercises prescribed by her grandmother to give her near-perfect posture. She was never one to slouch to make herself seem shorter. "Eleanor Roosevelt's stately height and broad shoulders are always a surprise to those seeing her for the first time," *Miami Daily News* women's editor Grace Wing wrote in 1953.

Tallest celebrity zookeeper: Remember Jim Fowler from the old *Wild Kingdom* television series? He was 6'6". Fowler lettered in football, baseball and track and field at Earlham College in Richmond, Indiana, is in the school's athletic hall of fame and once rejected a $30,000 offer to play for the Philadelphia Athletics. He did not play basketball, however.

Tallest fashion editor: The *New York Times* called Andre Leon Talley "an unmistakable figure everywhere he went" and not only because he was one of the few Black men at the highest level of the world of high fashion. He also was 6'6". Talley, who worked for *Women's Wear Daily* and *Vogue* and was a judge on *America's Next Top Model*, passed away early in 2022.

Tallest traveling salesman: We've already told you about 8'2" Don Koehler and his time as a salesman for Big Joe's Manufacturing Company, but he wasn't the only supersized guy who pounded the pavement trying to peddle something. Jack Earle, who was 7'7", acted in silent films in the 1920s and spent 14 years with the Ringling Brothers Barnum & Bailey circus before finding happiness as a salesman for the Roma Wine Company. Earle also was a gifted artist who painted, did sculptures and wrote poetry.

Tallest real estate agent: Travis Canby didn't have a glorious basketball career at Kansas State, collecting only 48 points in 75 games, but he has scored big success as the 6'10" proprietor of Canby & Co. Real Estate, a division of the Aaron Kirkman Group in the Los Angeles area. Canby also can be seen performing poetic hip-hop in dive bars and hosting an edgy weekly podcast with his fiancé, Judith Lovingfoss.

Tallest female high school teacher: Jamie Long teaches the Fundamentals of Technology and Computer Repair at Skiatook High School in northeast Oklahoma and also serves as the school's head volleyball coach and assistant girls basketball coach. The 6'5" former basketball player at Oral Roberts has her own website: Talltechteacher.com.

Tallest female elementary school teacher: Molly Steede is a second-grade teacher at Raleigh Academy in Duluth, Minnesota, and at 6'6", actually is the shortest sibling in what has been declared the tallest family in the world. (More on that later.)

Tallest rock star: This one is open to debate. The tallest might be 6'7" Krist Novoselic, who came to fame as the bass player for Nirvana and who later became a political activist, once contemplating a run for lieutenant governor of the state of Washington. Peter Steele (born Petrus Thomas Ratajczyk), who was the lead vocalist and bass player for Type O Negative and who previously performed with Fallout and Carnivore, has been listed anywhere from 6'5" to 6'8". Others who are either 6'5" or 6'6" are Joey Ramone of the Ramones, Buckethead (real name Brian Patrick Carroll), Oliver Riedel of Rammstein and Mick Fleetwood of Fleetwood Mac.

Tallest singer/songwriter/record producer: 6'8" Montell Jordan made it big with the 1995 No. 1 hit "This Is How We Do It" before going into other areas of the music industry. He even made reference to his size in his hit song, saying, "And all they said was 6'8" he stood." Jordan said in 2010 that God had told him to leave the music industry and he became the worship leader at Victory World Church in Norcross, Georgia.

Tallest country singer: There are a ton of really tall guys in this category and many of them seem even taller because of the hats that they wear. The tallest one, however, appears to be Matt Stell, who had a big hit in 2019 with "Prayed for You" and who is 6'7". (Yes, he played basketball, attending Drury University on a hoops scholarship.) Trace Adkins, Charles Kelly, Eric Paslay, Darryl Worley and Brett Young all are 6'6" and there are plenty of other tall ones, including 6'4" Blake Shelton, who has lamented the difficulty of finding fashionable clothing that actually fits. "If you see me on red carpets and I've got a look of disgust on my face, it's because I'm uncomfortable with whatever I have to be wearing," Shelton said.

Tallest classical composer: Sergei Rachmaninov, one of Russia's best-known romantic style composers and pianists of the early 20th century, was 6'6" and had massive hands. He could span 12 piano keys with one hand and, as a result, some of his compositions are a major challenge for people with stubbier fingers. An inordinate number of the other great composers were notoriously short. Beethoven, Mozart, Schubert, Haydn, Grieg and Ravel all were 5'4" and under.

Tallest authors: We've already mentioned Michael Crichton, who was 6'9", and Thomas Wolfe, who was variously listed as either 6'6" or 6'8". Roald Dahl, who wrote such popular children's books as *Charlie and the Chocolate Factory,* also was 6'6" and shared some idiosyncrasies with Wolfe. Both men disdained the use of a typewriter or even a ballpoint pen, scratching out their stories longhand in pencil. Wolfe was so uncomfortable sitting at the desks of the 1920s and 1930s that he wrote almost everything from a standing position, using the top of his refrigerator as a desk.

Tallest comedian: Brad Garrett is the tallest one we know of at 6'8½", but Lewis Spears, who we've quoted often in these pages, and British comic Greg Davies both are close behind at 6'8". Davies frequently jokes about his height onstage, including a story about a little old lady who, upon being startled by his size, asked, "Would you like a job at my house changing light bulbs?" In another tale, Davies was offended when a cab driver asked him, "OK, Big Bird, where to? Sesame Street?"

Tallest female comedian: Kim Blacklock, who began doing a standup act in the 1990s as Kim Atoa (her Samoan family surname), is 6'7" and claims to be the "world's tallest female comic." She likes to tell about when she was a kid and was acting up on the playground one day, enough that some of the other moms approached her mother and asked, "Why can't Kimmie play as nicely as the other 6-year-olds?" Mom had an explanation: "She's 2."

Tallest professional poker player: Phil Gordon is 6'9" and obviously has that natural intelligence that comes with being tall. He graduated from Georgia Tech at the age of 20 and worked on artificial intelligence projects for the military before making millions playing cards. He also hosted *Celebrity Poker Showdown* on Bravo.

Tallest ballet dancer: Fabrice Calmels was born in France in 1980 and grew up wanting to be a pilot. Since he grew to be 6'6½", that wouldn't have been a good choice, and as a teenager, he pirouetted to what seemed an equally implausible goal. After years of tagging along with his sister to ballet classes while his parents were at work, Calmels pursued his dancing dreams and achieved them as the lead performer for the Joffrey Ballet in Chicago. "I looked at my body like an engine," Calmels said in an interview with danceinforma.com. "I had to tune it to make it work appropriately. So, I figured out all my weak spots and worked really hard to be able to compete with people half my size."

Tallest temperance activist: Carrie Nation, who was arrested 32 times in the early 1900s for smashing barrooms with a hatchet in protest of the alcohol industry, was inordinately tall. Daniel Okrent in his 2011 book *Last Call* depicted Nation as being "6 feet tall, with the biceps of a stevedore, the face of a prison warden, and the persistence of a toothache."

Tallest motivational speaker: Anthony Robbins, who has written six best-selling books and is perhaps the best-known life and business strategist in the world, is an anomaly. He is a tall person with a drive to succeed that comes from not being tall enough. Robbins was only 5'7" when he was 16, then grew 12 inches after that because of a tumor on his brain that greatly increased his level of human growth hormone. He attributes his determination to achieve success and help others to his travails as an undersized teenager.

Tallest politician: At least four former college or pro basketball players who are 6'10" or taller have been elected to political office. The tallest is 7'0" former Ohio State and NBA stalwart Brad Sellers, who serves as the mayor of Warrensville Heights, Ohio, a suburb of Cleveland. Tom McMillen (6'11") served in the U.S. House of Representatives, Jon Godfread (6'10") is the insurance commissioner for the state of North Dakota and Robert Cornegy, Jr. (6'10"), is a city councilman in New York City. Godfread, who played collegiately at Northern Iowa and professionally in Germany, actually was certified as the tallest politician in the world in 2019 by the *Guinness Book of World Records*.

Tallest professional boxer: There have been at least three fighters who have been reported to be 7'4". Gogea Mitu of Romania (born Dumitru Stefanescu), known as the Giant of Marsani, fought two bouts in Bucharest in 1935 and won both of them with first-round knockouts. John Rankin claimed a four-round unanimous decision in his only fight, in New Orleans in 1967. Irish-born Jim Cully, billed as the Tipperary Giant, went 3–3 as a heavyweight between 1942 and 1948 although the website boxrec.com lists him as being a mere 7'2".

Tallest pro boxing champion: Nikolay Valuev of Russia, an imposing sight at 7'0" and 330 pounds, won the World Boxing Association heavyweight title with a 12-round decision over John Ruiz in 2005. Valuev held the title until losing to 6'1" Ruslan Chagaev in 2007, then regained the championship the following year by again defeating Ruiz. He retired with a record of 50–2 after losing to David Haye in 2009.

Tallest UFC fighter: Netherlands-born Stefan Struve is 7'0" (some say 6'11") and is aptly nicknamed Skyscraper. With arms longer than any of his opponents, he has carved out a reputation for forcing opponents into submission with devastating chokeholds. "His enormous limbs are ideal for wrapping around opponents," UFC blogger Siri Karri wrote.

Tallest kickboxer: At 7'2" and 365 pounds, South Korea native Hong Man Choi has taken part in kickboxing, pro wrestling and mixed martial arts at various times in his life. Hong Man was known to change his hair color with every match and during his wrestling days he was known as the Techno Goliath because he danced to techno music following every victory. He once did a milk commercial on TV in South Korea in which he stood and flexed his biceps while a girl hung off one of his arms.

Tallest female professional wrestler: 6'8" Lindsay Kay Hayward, better known to her wrestling fans as Isis the Amazon or Aloisia, was a star on the wrestling scene from 2008 to 2011 and also did some acting. In fact, she was certified by Guinness in 2013 as the "tallest actress in a leading role." As with so many oversized people, Hayward was teased mercilessly as a teenager but she has risen above that. "Anything that makes you unique is something that you should be using as your strength and something that you should be celebrating!" she told *Life & Style* magazine in 2017.

Tallest bodybuilder: Olivier Richters of the Netherlands is just a sliver under 7'2" and was certified by Guinness in 2021 as the world's tallest bodybuilder. Richters also has carved out a decent acting career, appearing in such films as *Black Widow* and *The King's Man*, in which he played the role of Huge Machine Shack Guard.

Tallest Australian rules football player: While American football has had one 7-footer (Richard Sligh) play at its highest level, the Australian game got its first one in 2022 when 7'0" former University of Hawaii basketball player Mate Colina joined the Richmond Tigers of the AFL. Colina, who played football as a kid growing up in Melbourne, is a ruckman, a position that involves something akin to a jump ball in basketball. He replaced 6'11" Aaron Sandilands as the tallest AFL player ever.

Tallest baseball umpire: Jordan Baker, who is 6'7", made his debut in the major leagues in the middle of the 2012 season. Some have questioned if he is able to get low enough to provide a good strike zone or to get a good view on close tag plays because of his stature. But he probably caused more controversy in 2013 for his habit of throwing wads of gum onto the outfield grass between innings. It was estimated he did it as many as 20 times in one game.

Tallest fashion and bikini model: Alexis Skye was officially given this title by Guinness in 2008. In addition to modeling, the 6'5" Skye has had at least one acting role. She played Too Tall Maggie in an episode of *My Name Is Earl.*

Tallest game show host: Richard Osman, host of several different British game shows including *Pointless,* is 6'7".

Tallest magician: Penn Jillette, the larger half of the iconic duo of Penn and Teller, is 6'6". Teller is only 5'9". Jillette had a special 7,932-square foot house built for himself in Las Vegas that was tailored for tall people. The house, which he called "The Slammer," had higher-than-normal kitchen counters, extra-high windows and expanded steps to accommodate his size 14 feet.

Tallest serial killer: Edmund Kemper sometimes was listed as being 7'0" but the consensus is that he was only 6'9". In either case, he created big problems by killing at least 10 people, including his grandparents and his mother. Kemper had an IQ of 136 but endured a troubled childhood. At the age of 10, he killed a neighbor's dog and beheaded his family's cat. He shot and killed both his grandparents when he was 15, was subsequently declared insane, and after showing signs of progress during five years in a mental institution, he was released. He spent the next several years preying on female hitchhikers in northern California, frequently raping, mutilating and possibly even devouring his victims. He finally killed his mother in 1973 but then contacted police and confessed to eight murders. No connection ever has been drawn between his size and his murderous ways.

Tallest career criminal: Jude "Tiny" Medcalf of Newton Abbot, Great Britain, once found an unexpected advantage to being 7'2". He was freed by a judge because he was simply too massive to reside in prison. Correction officials were unable to find uniforms big enough or beds long enough for him so he was released. But he never has managed to stay out of jail for very long. Over the course of a few years, he was convicted of more than two dozen offenses, including theft, impersonating a police officer, sending malicious communications, burglary, criminal damage, stealing lights off emergency vehicles, firing BB guns at people and assorted other things. Medcalf suffers from Klinefelter Syndrome, a growth disorder that has given him an enormous frame but which allegedly has impaired his ability to learn.

Tallest family: The Trapp family of Esko, Minnesota (population 1,869), was certified as the tallest in the world by Guinness in 2022, with an average height of 6'8". Scott Trapp is 6'8", his wife Kristine is 6'3½" and they have three children—Savanna (6'8½"), Adam (7'3") and Molly (6'6"). That 6'8" average doesn't even include Molly's husband, Dalton Steede, who is 6'9". Needless to say, Scott took the precaution of removing all of the ceiling fans from the family's home. "If you've ever hit your head on a spinning ceiling fan, it's not the most fun thing to do," Adam Trapp said.

Tallest set of male identical twins: Michael and James Lanier, who grew up in Troy, Michigan, really weren't exactly identical since Michael was 7'7" and James only 7'6". Both of them played college basketball, Michael at Hardin-Simmons and UCLA and James at the University of Denver. Michael went on to become a senior designer for General Motors' power train division before dying at the age of 48 in 2018.

Tallest set of female twins: Claire and Ann Recht, who we previously mentioned as playing volleyball at American University, both were 6'7".

Tallest married couple: Martin Van Buren Bates, believed by some to be the tallest soldier to serve in the Civil War at 7'9", was not turned off by the fact that his wife, Anna Haining Swan, was taller than he was at 7'11". The couple was married June 17, 1871, and spent much of their adult lives touring with various circuses. They conceived two children together, both of whom were very large but did not live very long. An 18-pound girl died at birth and a 23-pound, 8-ounce boy—believed by some to be the largest baby ever—survived for only 11 hours.

18

All in All, I'd Rather Be Tall

In the spring of 2022, as I was ruminating about something that I've tried hard not to refer to as a "deformity," I posted an impromptu poll on the Facebook page for members of Tall Clubs International.

I really wanted to know how fellow tall people felt about their size so I asked: "If you could choose to be any height, which would you choose?" There were three multiple choice options:

A. To be taller than I am now.
B. To be shorter than I am now.
C. To be exactly the height I am now.

I knew A was going to be the loser. No way any of us were going to go for that one, right? I really expected B to be the landslide victor. Most tall people, like myself, seem to be connoisseurs of fine whine so we'd all choose to be a more normal height.

It did turn out to be a landslide, but the winner was C. About 58 percent of the respondents said they would like to be exactly the height that they are. Only 29 percent said they would want to be shorter and a mere 10 percent actually yearned to be taller.

All in all, most liked being tall.

It was illuminating and inspiring at the same time. My fellow tall folks were saying that the secret to happiness in life is to accept and embrace what you are and who you are and to accentuate the positives.

There is an element of incongruity to that because TCI, an organization with more than 5,000 members worldwide that has survived for more than 80 years, began from a place of negativity. In 1938, a woman writing under the name Kae Krysler penned a freelance article for the *Los Angeles Times'* Sunday magazine about the travails of being tall.

Krysler—real name Kae Sumner Einfeldt—was a 6'3" artist at Walt Disney studios, who in a delicious twist of irony, did extensive work on the animated film *Snow White and the Seven Dwarfs*. The purpose of her op-ed piece was to point out to people who bore a resemblance to Doc, Dopey and Sneezy that being an oversized woman wasn't nearly as glorious as they envisioned it was.

"Few realize that altitude can be as much a disadvantage as it may be an advantage," she wrote. "Most of the advantage and enjoyment is a matter of attitude. When you find the humorous side to the situation—either large or small, then you're hitting the high road to happiness."

Kae, who was not quite 22 years old at the time, laid out a lot of the same complaints we've been telling you about in the previous pages. The difficulty in buying clothes and shoes. The bane of low-hanging chandeliers. The agony of trying to sit comfortably in a theater, especially when others are trying to navigate past your tangle of pretzelized legs to get to their seats. The impossibility of trying not to stand out in a crowd. The ignominy of dancing cheek-to-chin with a man who is six inches shorter.

She had still more complaints. She hoped to become an airline stewardess but had to eliminate that goal when she got to be too tall. She loved to go horseback riding but never was able to keep her extra-long legs in the stirrups.

Kae's article did not fall on deaf ears. She tossed out the idea of tall folks gathering together to deliberate and commiserate. "We could form a longfellows club," she said. Six weeks later, she and eight other ultra-tall people gathered together socially at Kae's home and the California Tip Toppers Club was born. It was the beginning of the worldwide organization now known as Tall Clubs International.

TCI members now gather in regional chapters to do all sorts of positive things. They crown beauty queens and raise money for Marfan research and mostly just socialize with people their own size. They hold a national convention in which it isn't necessary to build small ramps for its members at the hotel check-in desk. Although their organization is not about replacing Tinder, eHarmony or Hinge, it occasionally has had that impact. Kae Sumner herself met a man named George Einfeldt at one of her meetings and she married him in 1948.

Mostly, it's just a way to help one another deal with all the negatives of extreme height while emphasizing the positives. It provides a refuge for kindred spirits, a place to get away from the stares and comments and questions. One person said the other club members have become "family."

"It changed my life," said Rick LaRose of suburban Atlanta, who has been a member of TCI for 43 years even though there no longer is a chapter of the club in his area. "I'll be in it the rest of my life.... When everybody else is tall, you feel like there are other people out there just like me who are tall."

The exact same feeling came to Donna Stocker when she attended her first TCI convention in Las Vegas in 2012. Stocker, who is 6'1" and was named Miss Tall International in 2021, said in a 2022 newspaper story that it was "like walking into a room of relatives. For the first time in my life, I felt like I belonged somewhere," she added.

Sue Morrison, TCI's current national president until 2022, never even knew that tall clubs existed until 1983 when she applied for a nursing position at Fairview Hospital in Minneapolis. The head nurse told her about the local Voyageurs Tall Club, a TCI affiliate. She went to a meeting, then attended a TCI weekend in Chicago and was hooked. Instead of being the giantess who stood out in the crowd, she blended in as one of about 350 very tall people at the event. "I had never felt so comfortable in a group of people in my life," she said.

Over the course of nearly four decades with the organization, Morrison also has come to view its members as family. When she got married—to a man three inches shorter than she was—two of her three bridesmaids were TCI members. She said almost all of her closest friends are people she met through tall clubs.

The success and longevity of TCI is further evidence that there clearly is an obsession around the globe with the concept of height. The world sometimes seems to be filled with two kinds of people: those who are tall and those who wish they were.

Not that all that attention always is bad. TCI member Gordon Darby found that out when he and his wife visited China a few years ago. They were not besieged with all the stares, comments and questions about the weather, even though at 6'11", Gordon towered over everyone with whom they came into contact. Maybe it was because of the language barrier. Perhaps people were saying, "Nàbiān tiānqì zěnmeyàng?" (How's the weather up there?) to Gordon and he just didn't understand.

Mostly, people there were curious but in a respectful, restrained way. Most of them wanted to just have photos taken with someone so tall and it turned into a thoroughly enjoyable experience.

Author Don Doxsie found the people of Kenya were fascinated by his size during a visit to Africa in 2000 (author's collection).

"I had photos with groups of school children, teens, adults and seniors," Darby said. "Pretty funny to think of being in their photo albums.... China will forever be one of the most memorable experiences."

I ran into a similar experience a few decades ago on a visit to Kenya. Somewhere in Kapsait, buried deep in the Cherangani Hills, there are distance runners with snapshots of a towering, bearded mzungu wearing a *Quad-City Times* Bix 7 shirt.

It was a reminder that being tall can actually be sort of fun, if only as a way to make new friends.

As our friend Thomas Samaras has pointed out, the obsession with height is a global thing and it has become very common for people to exaggerate their heights. A lot of guys who are 5'10" or 5'11" readily round things up and pass themselves off as being 6'0". I myself have gone through most of my life saying I'm 6'7" rather than sounding like a nerd and saying I am precisely 6'6¾". In fact, I've neglected to mention until now that the ravages of time have caused me to shrink by about half an inch. I'm actually now about 6'6¼".

As a sportswriter, I've interviewed plenty of basketball players who were listed in the game program as 6'10" or 6'11", but appeared to be almost exactly my height. Inflation doesn't just happen in the economy. There is a lot of it on basketball rosters.

This obsession with height in sports also is evidenced by the fact that almost every roster in a team sport, especially basketball, lists each athlete's height and weight.

"The preoccupation with being tall is a sad fact that creates much unnecessary misery in our lives and spares almost no one since we all tend to get shorter with age," Samaras wrote.

Samaras actually proposed in his 1994 book that we "introduce a program of education in our schools and communication media where we provide a more favorable view of smaller stature. This would require adding material in school textbooks on the pros and cons of tall and short human stature. Television and movies could also portray the benefits of smaller size, and non-fiction books could work the message into their subjects."

In other words, he proposed a wholesale propaganda campaign to promote the idea that short is beautiful.

"Our society's adulation of height has caused millions of children and adults incredible pain and suffering," Samaras added. "It will continue to produce pain in parents and short children of unborn future generations. Therefore, a change in attitude towards shorter stature will produce a much healthier society."

He also suggested that short people could benefit from a change of attitude, that they have no need to feel inferior and that they should appreciate what they have. This is the place where he makes a ton of sense: "Let's change our attitudes so that personal worth becomes entirely independent of height."

In a telephone interview with me, Samaras said: "Part of the reason I'm passionate about this is because of the prejudice that shorter people have to live with.... Kids at school get teased when they're small, that really bothers me."

I pointed out that tall kids get teased and bullied, too. Tall people also sometimes are subjected to "incredible pain and suffering." He agreed.

"We should be judging them on who they are as people, not by whether they're tall or skinny or short," he said.

Can we give Samaras a standing ovation for that assessment? He is echoing the same nugget of common sense that so many others have stated: We're never going to eliminate the body shaming that goes on any more than we're going get rid of all the other bigotries that distort and diminish our world. We just need to ignore the bullies and shame the shamers, recognize them as the superficial Cretans that they are and understand our own value as human beings.

John Hollinden, a 7'6½" former basketball player with an equally lofty view of life, told the Associated Press in an interview that being tall is "a silly thing to worry about" and said anyone who spends much time fretting about their body size or shape is wasting their time. "They worry about being tall and they worry about being short, about being skinny and about being fat. Shoot, why can't people just be happy the way they are?"

It's a message echoed by many. Helen Pappas, founder of Talltique.com, finally came to grips with her 6'4" frame and learned to appreciate it.

"Being tall brings laughter to my life every day," she wrote in a blog on her site. "Laughter at all of the ridiculous comments at which I simply smile or roll my eyes. Laughter at the misconceptions that 'average' people have of tall women. Laughter (and some knee pain) at trying to squeeze into the back seats of cars, airplanes, and other forms of transportation. Laughter at my legs being too long to fit under many tables. Laughter at the ridiculous notion that growing up I wished I were 'average.' To every tall teen out there: You are different. You are tall. You may not feel you fit in now, but in time you will come to know that as a gift."

Alicia Jay, the 6'6" blogger on TallSWAG.com, said that people who accept their height are destined to get the last laugh.

"I at least get the giggles every day because I know that the people who question our beautiful tall quality are ashamed that they don't have it," she added. "I know that when I wear my 5-inch heels that the reaction should empower me because there is no way that the people staring could do it themselves. I know that tall is beautiful every day, all day, 365 days a year.... Love everything that God has given you and celebrate it with the world!"

Robert Cornegy, Jr., the 6'10" New York city councilman, said he felt his success in politics as well as basketball was a message to people that they could do anything they wanted, that they need not be limited in any way no matter what size they were.

"You don't need to be relegated to a particular segment of society based on how you look," he told *USA Today* in 2019.

In one of the final scenes of *Tall Girl*, main character Jodi Kramer stands up in front of her tormenters at the Homecoming dance and tells them to continue to ask her about the weather and to make other wisecracks. "I can take it," she says, "because the weather up here is pretty great."

Of course, it's simple to say we should thumb our nose at the abuse, inquisitions and expectations. It's not as easy to do it. It's incumbent on parents to help their children navigate adolescence and puberty as a tall person and not to make the kids feel inadequate because of their height. Parents—and friends and teachers—need to do whatever they can to be positive and bolster self-esteem.

Dr. John Coleman of Brighton, England, said in a 1994 *London Independent* article that parents need to identify the things their children are good at and support everything they do. "We know that one of the most powerful factors that affects a teenager's self-esteem is his or her parents' interest."

Dr. David Weeks, another British psychologist, added: "It is the parents' responsibility to maximize their children's gifts.... Show them that their shape is only a small part of their overall personality."

Bottom line: Embrace your height, whether it be 5'5", 6'5" or 7'5", as a part of who you are. Don't waste time agonizing over something that you really can't control. If you think about it, you can change the style and color of your hair, you can gain or lose weight, you can get tattoos or grow facial hair, do all sorts of things to alter your appearance. But you're stuck with your height. As a 1988 *American Scholar* article pointed out, "Your height is the one card you cannot toss in and exchange for another." So, play the hand you have. There are positives connected to every level of stature. Believe that there is a reason God chose to make you the size that He did.

It would seem fewer people are doing that these days. A *Psychology Today* poll of 62,000 people in 1972 found that only 13 percent of them were dissatisfied with their height. A half-century later, I guarantee you that number is much higher, probably even higher than our little Facebook poll would indicate.

Nevertheless, when it came time for me to vote in my own poll, I said I would choose to still be 6'6¼".

I know what you're saying. I've spent a few hundred pages complaining about this, about all the drawbacks, all the pitfalls, talking about cramming into airplane seats and searching (often in vain) for fashionable clothing that actually fits and groaning about all the bumps on the head, pointing out what a pain in the ass (and the head and the back) that it is to be tall.

And now I'm saying it's what I'd prefer?

I certainly considered casting my vote for being shorter. Not a lot shorter. Maybe just a little. It might have been nice to be just 6'1" or 6'2", down in that sweet spot of sexual attraction, down below the Vince Vaughn line. I could wear normal clothes, drive normal cars, relax in modes of public transportation, not bang my head on things.

Come to think of it, it also might not have been all bad to be four or five inches taller. I might have been able to do more in basketball, maybe gotten my college education paid for.

But I've kind of gotten used to being 6'6¼". I think of all the people who have approached me with the dumb questions and obvious statements. Once we got beyond the initial rudeness and curiosity, many of them turned out to be pretty cool people and very good friends. My size was an inadvertent and fortuitous conversation piece.

So, I voted for C.

All in all, I'd rather be tall.

Bibliography

Books

Chamberlain, Wilt, and David Shaw, *Wilt*, 1976, Warner Books.
Cohen, Arianne, *The Tall Book*, 2009, Bloomsbury.
Crichton, Michael, *Travels*, 2014, Vintage.
Davenport, Gwen, *The Tall Girls' Handbook*, 1959, Doubleday.
Drummer, Frederick, *Very Special People*, 1973, Amjon Publishers.
Floud, Roderick, Kenneth Wachter, and Annabel Gregory, *Height, Health and History: Nutritional Status in the United Kingdom, 1750–1980*, 2011, Cambridge University Press.
Gladwell, Malcolm, *Blink: The Power of Thinking Without Thinking*, Back Bay Books, 2005.
Grimsley, Will (supervising editor), *The Sports Immortals*, 1972, Prentice-Hall, Inc.
Hall, Stephen S., *Size Matters*, 2006, Houghton Mifflin Company.
Hodgson, Geoffrey, *JFK and LBJ: The Last Two Great Presidents*, 2015, Yale University Press.
Keyes, Ralph, *The Height of Your Life*, 1980, Little, Brown.
Kleinke, Chris L., *First Impressions*, 1975, Prentice-Hall, Inc.
Lamb, Harold, *Charlemagne: The Legend and the Man*, 1954, Doubleday.
Lorant, Stefan, *The Life of Abraham Lincoln*, 1963, Mentor Books.
M, *The Sensuous Man*, 1971, Lyle Stuart, Inc.
Oates, Stephen B., *With Malice Toward None*, 1977, Generic Publishing.
Paterson, Donald G., *Physique and Intellect*, 1923 (republished in 2011 by Nabu Press).
Samaras, Thomas T., *The Truth About Your Height: Exploring the Myths and Realities of Human Size and Its Effects on Performance, Health, Pollution and Survival*, 1994, Tecolote Publications.
Scheinfeld, Amram, *The New You and Heredity*, 1961, Lippincott.
Toffler, Alvin, *Future Shock*, 1970, Bantam Books.
Understanding Human Behavior, 1974, Columbia House.
Wallechinsky, David, Irving Wallace, and Amy Wallace, *The Book of Lists*, 1977, William Morrow & Company.
Wooden, John, and Jack Tobin, *They Call Me Coach*, 2003, McGraw-Hill.

Articles

Alter, Charlotte, "Donald Trump may not be as tall as he says he is," *Time*, Dec. 23, 2016.
Alton Evening Telegraph, "Robert Wadlow to get new pair of shoes—cost $30," Oct. 8, 1928.
Alton Evening Telegraph, "Throngs line street to visit Wadlow bier," July 18, 1940.
Alton Evening Telegraph, "27,000 persons visit bier of Robert Wadlow," July 19, 1940.

Alton Evening Telegraph, "Wadlow signs contract with Ringling circus," March 26, 1937.
American Weekly, "Heartaches of Robert Wadlow, boy giant, over at least," August 11, 1940.
Anderson, Dave, "'Dinosaurs' hold Stanley Cup key," *New York Times*, May 13, 1979.
Anderson, Stefan, "Manute Bol lied about his age, may have been 50 years old when he played in the NBA: report," *New York Daily News*, Nov. 21, 2017.
Anderson, Sylvia, "Don't slouch, it's stand tall week," *St. Joseph (Mo.) News-Press*, April 15, 2012.
Ansdell, Charles, "A tall order: What physical characteristics do we seek in business leaders?" *secnewgate.co.uk*, Sept. 22, 2020.
apRoberts, Alison, "Small minded: Short people say the perceived advantages of being tall are the height of folly," *Sacramento Bee*, Dec. 16, 2006.
Aristides, "Short subject," *American Scholar*, Autumn 1988.
Arndt, Bettina, "Height pays," *Indianapolis Star*, April, 19, 1987.
Associated Press, "America doesn't stand as tall as it used to, study finds," July 16, 2007.
Associated Press, "Gentle giant has problems in small world," Nov. 7, 1979.
Associated Press, "He'd tax short people only half as much," April 29, 1972.
Associated Press, "Kohler settles sex-discrimination suit," Sept. 24, 1999.
Associated Press, "Size No. 35 shoes and wearer hold session spotlight," Jan. 9, 1934.
Associated Press, "Snapshots: Kristen Johnson," June 16, 1996.
Associated Press, "Tall women have easier labor," Oct. 28, 1988.
Associated Press, "Tallest woman in the world taught children to accept differences," August 14, 2008.
Associated Press, "Ukrainian is world's tallest man, Guinness World Records says," August 8, 2007.
Associated Press, "World's tallest twin dies at age 48," April 28, 2018.
Baker, Russell, "The sorrows of the long people," *New York Times*, Jan. 31, 1978.
Ball, Aimee Lee, "Short people and tall ones: The height report," *Redbook*, May 1978.
Balson, Diane, "Let's hear it for short men," *Glamour*, April 1979.
Barisic, Sonja, "Va. Deputy named tallest U.S. man," *Associated Press*, Nov. 8, 2007.
Barreiro, Dan, "Mikan helped lay the foundation for today's NBA," *Minneapolis Star Tribune*, Dec. 22, 1999.
Baylor, Mariah, "The tall girls' guide to professional and personal perfection," *baucemag.com*, Jan. 30, 2018.
Beck, Jason, "Greiner gearing up to be Tigers' backstop," *mlb.com*, Jan. 30, 2019.
Bismarck Tribune, "ND official is world's tallest male politician," Nov. 13, 2019.
Bissi, William, "Problems of a T-A-L-L boy," *Chicago Tribune*, Jan. 20, 1952.
Bombeck, Erma, "At wit's end," *Field Enterprises*, April 5, 1979.
Borden, Mark, "Shortchanged," *New Yorker*, Oct. 2, 2006.
Borreli, Lizette, "How tall are you? A man's height may predict chances of premature hair loss," *medicaldaily.com*, March 13, 2017.
Bozzi, Vincent, "Tall, dark first date," *Psychology Today*, July 8, 1989.
Brada, Tom, "Leg-lengthening: The people having surgery to be a bit taller," *BBC News*, Dec. 5, 2020.
Brown, Dan, "Johnson recalls moment that changed it all," *Sacramento Bee*, July 25, 2015.
Brown, Valerie S., "The height report: The tall & short of it," *Teen*, August 1988.
Bryant, Bill and Jay Stockman, "Two tall tales," *The Sporting News*, Feb. 16, 1980.
Butterbrodt, Laura, "Northern Minnesota family named tallest in the world by Guinness World Records," *Forum News Service*, Feb. 23, 2022.
Byrne, Bridget, "James Cromwell rediscovered," *Associated Press*, Sept. 24, 2001.
Cambage, Liz, "DNP—mental health," *Theplayerstribune.com*, August 11, 2019.
Canavan, Tom, "Muresan returns with all 7-foot-7 for Nets," *Associated Press*, Oct. 23, 1999.
Caputo, Sunni, "Ted Cassidy: Big man with big talent, heart," *Orlando Sentinel*, Jan. 30, 1979.

Carpenter, Glen, "The height of discrimination: One's size," *United Press International*, Nov. 7, 1971.
Catholic News Agency, "Pope meets United States' newest and tallest bishop," May 13, 2012.
Cedrone, Lou, "Weaver liked working with those wild, crazy 'Ghostbusters' guys," *Baltimore Evening Sun*, June 20, 1984.
Chamberlain, Charles, "Never short of tall tales," *Associated Press*, Jan. 23, 1976.
Changing Times, "Who says you gotta be tall?," July 1954.
Christensen, Joe, "Giant Dutch pitcher makes an impression in Twins camp," *Minneapolis Star Tribune*, March 2006.
Chukhman, Zinovy, "Dallas chiropractor discusses back pain among tall people," *Dallaschiropractor.com*, August 20, 2018.
Chung, Jeff, "7-foot-2 Korean star coming here to battle," *Honolulu Advertiser*, April 15, 2007.
Cook, Everett, "Quite a beach path," *Los Angeles Times*, Sept. 20, 2014.
Corr, John, "At 7 feet 7, she looks up to life," *Philadelphia Inquirer*, Jan. 6, 1978.
Cowley, Geoffrey and Mary Hager, "Do short, healthy kids need hormone shots?," *Newsweek*, July 13, 1992.
Cramer, Maria, "James R. Thompson, longest-serving governor of Illinois, dies at 84," *New York Times*, August 15, 2020.
Crenson, Matt, "Industrialized nations outgrow U.S.," *Associated Press*, July 16, 2007.
Crossley, Lance, "Men more intelligent than women: prof," *CanWest News Service*, Sept. 8, 2006.
Daniels, Mary, "Tall women lands on short end of jokes," *Chicago Tribune*, Feb. 25, 1976.
DeAcetis, Joseph, "Son of a Tailor leads a new revolution in precision engineering and sustainability," *Forbes*, August 6, 2021.
De Castella, Tom, "Bantams: The army units for those under 5ft 3in," *BBC News*, Feb. 9, 2015.
Deford, Frank. "A gentle Goliath," *Sports Illustrated*, Oct. 25, 1999.
Devi, V. Gomala, "When Is National Kick Tall Person Day 2021?," *latestnews.com*, Oct. 21, 2021.
Dittman, M., "Standing tall pays off, study finds," *American Psychological Association*, July/August 2004.
Doheny, Kathleen, "Short or heavy women most likely to have difficult labors," *Los Angeles Times*, May 31, 1988.
Donnelly, Antoinette, "A famous tall woman gives hints to others," *New York Daily News*, July 13, 1960.
Donohue, Meg, "Why tall people make more money," *CNN.com*, Feb. 2, 2007.
Dougherty, Jack, "The tragic death of 7-foot-7 NBA legend Manute Bol," *Sportscasting.com*, June 30, 2020.
Dowd, Maureen, "Where they stand," *New York Times*, June 21, 1992.
Doxsie, Don, "Fitting in: How does The Mark measure up in comfort, seat and leg room?," *Quad-City Times*, May 27, 1993.
Doxsie, Don, "So you want to be tall? Well, try this on for size ...," *Quad-City Times*, Feb. 20, 2000.
Doxsie, Don, "Tall expectations: At 7-foot-2, West senior Eric McPherson suffers through growing pains on the basketball court," *Quad-City Times*, Feb. 20, 2000.
Dunham, Wayne, "Giant may be last of his kind," *Chicago Tribune*, Dec. 9, 1973.
Dunn, Marcia, "Strahan flies in space with Blue Origin," *Associated Press*, Dec. 12, 2021.
Eastman, Janet, "Susan," *Orange Coast Magazine*, July 1980.
Eberhart, Lori, "Lincoln's forgotten duel," *lib.niu.edu*.
Ebony, "Problems and pleasures of the tall woman," March 1979.
The Economist, "Short guys finish last," Dec. 23, 1995.
Edelson, Sharon, "Long Tall Sally grows," *Women's Wear Daily*, April 20, 2012.
Edmonson, Daisy, "The surprising truth about children's height," *Parents*, September 1987.

Edmonton (Alberta) Journal, "Science for what purpose?," Sept. 10, 2006.
Eichenlaub, John E., "What to do about your size," *Today's Health*, July 1954.
Ell, Kellie, "Long Tall Sally closing forever," *Women's Wear Daily*, June 16, 2020.
Ell, Kellie, "Tall order: Tackling fashion's vertical challenges," *Women's Wear Daily*, Dec. 19, 2019.
Elliott, Christopher, "Do you have the right to recline your airline airplane seat? No, and here's why," *USA Today*, Nov. 8, 2019.
Enserink, Martin, "Did natural selection make the Dutch the tallest people on the planet?," *science.org*, April 7, 2015.
ESPN Magazine, "Big man confidential," Nov. 28, 2016.
ESPN Magazine, "A view from the top," Nov. 28, 2016.
Evans, Ted, "The torment of a giant," *Coronet*, September 1956.
Everstine, Brian W., "Air Force removes height requirement for pilot applicants," *airforce.mag*, May 22, 2020.
Fackelmann, Kathy, "Heart risk: The long and short of it," *Science News*, Nov. 23, 1991.
Feintzeig, Rachel, "Want to be CEO? Stand tall," *Wall Street Journal*, June 9, 2014.
Ferriman, Annabel, "Tall tales and short stories," *London Independent*, May 22, 1994.
Fleming, Olivia, "Gabby Reece gets candid with her daughter about body image," *Harpers Bazaar*, Sept. 9, 2016.
Forbes, "Presidential timber tends to be tall," May 19, 2004.
Fort Worth Star-Telegram, "Lesser height doesn't shortchange kids," Sept. 26, 2004.
Fortune, "Keeping up: Legs," April 23, 1990.
Foss, Brad, "Inventor out to protect the knees of tall fliers," *Associated Press*, Oct. 24, 2003.
Framke, Caroline, "Janet Reno's long and storied career was plagued by sexist 'jokes,'" *Vox*, Nov. 7, 2016.
French, Laura, "Tenn. man, dubbed 'Shorty,' named world's tallest firefighter by Guinness World Records," *firerescue1.com*, Oct. 26, 2020.
Friedman, Vanessa and Jacob Bernstein, "André Leon Talley, editor and fashion industry force, dies at 73," *New York Times*, Jan. 19, 2022.
Friend, Tim, "Clotbusting drugs benefit big men most," *USA Today*, March 20, 1995.
Fries, Joe, "Did you know there's a club for tall people?," *Kelown (B.C.) Daily Courier*, July 2, 2022.
Galton, Lawrence, "Are we growing into giants?," *Popular Science*, December 1959.
Gilbertson, Dawn, "Spirit Airlines adds comfier seats, even in the middle," *USA Today*, Sept. 9, 2019.
Gilly, Steve, and Rod Mullins, "The Kentucky River Giants: Martin Van Buren Bates claimed 7'11"," *blueridgecountry.com*, Oct. 28, 2020.
Gilmore, Eric, "From lanky to legendary," *Contra Costa (Calif.) Times*, Sept. 9, 2001.
Golf Today, "The tallest professional golfers," April 8, 2018.
Gorney, Cynthia, "Dating dilemma: She's tall, he's short," *Seventeen*, August 1979.
Greenblatt, Dr. Robert B., "Girls too tall, boys too short," *McCall's*, July 1959.
Griner, Brittney, "Phoenix Mercury center Brittney Griner opens up and bares all," *ESPN Magazine*, July 6, 2015.
Gropnik, Adam, "A point of view: Why short men makes better husbands," *BBC News*, Oct. 5, 2014.
Grossman, Ron, "Looking back at the 'Alton Giant,'" *Chicago Tribune*, April 12, 2021.
Habib, Hal, "A tall order," *Palm Beach (Fla.) Post*, March 21, 2010.
Haines, Angela, "Controlling height," *New York Times Magazine*, April 4, 1976.
Haines, Max, "Giant with a license to kill," *Nanaimo (B.C.) Daily News*, Oct. 28, 1979.
Haines, Max, "Stalker of the innocent," *Nanaimo (B.C.) Daily News*, Nov. 4, 1979.
Hale, Debra, "Study finds link between height, intelligence in children," *Associated Press*, Oct. 22, 1986.
Hamblin, James, "The virtue of being short," *Chicago Tribune*, April 20, 2015.
Hanna, Laurie, "Britain's tallest criminal, once released from prison for being too big, is back behind bars for repeat offenses," *New York Daily News*, Oct. 24, 2015.

Harbison, Georgia, "A chance to be taller," *Time*, Jan. 8, 1990.

Harwell, Drew, "It's no wonder fliers are fighting over legroom. Just look at these numbers," *Washington Post*, August 27, 2014.

Haskell, Molly, "Sex symbols: Have they changed or have we?," *Ladies Home Journal*, January 1979.

Hawthorne, Fran, "Fact of fiction?: It's no tall tale, height matters," *Scientific American*, Nov. 14, 2008.

Heimer, Mel, "'Lurch' moves on; 'Injun Joe' soon," *King Features Syndicate*, August 15, 1967.

Herkt, David, "Jane Smiley: 'I have run my love life like a guy,'" *stuff.co.nz*, April 27, 2016.

Hiassen, Carl, "Days of 'friendly skies' become a distant memory," *Miami Herald*, Sept. 11, 2014.

Holt, Jim, "Measure for measure: The strange science of Francis Galton," *New Yorker*, Jan. 24, 2005.

Housekaboodle.com, "Celebrity real estate: Penn Jillette 'The Slammer' house is 2.1 million," June 28, 2013.

Huckshorn, Kristin, "Taking Perot's measure," *Knight Ridder*, May 22, 1992.

Hummer, Steve, "A stacked deck," *Atlanta Constitution*, Sept. 21, 2005.

Ibisworld.com, "Plus-size men's clothing stores industry in the U.S.—market research report," March 9, 2021.

Indianapolis News, "Shorts cuts," Dec. 24, 1977.

Iovine, Julie, "Do short men make betters lovers?," *Mademoiselle*, November 1987,

Jarrett, Keith, "Nation's tallest player has foot partially amputated," *Asheville (N.C.) Citizen-Times*, Oct. 18, 2008.

Jiang, Allison and Clara McMahon, "21 of the best places to buy clothes for tall people who just want to look stylish," *Buzzfeed.com*, March 16, 2022.

Johnson, Allan, "Judy Gold uses her 6-foot-3 stature to tell some tall tales," *Chicago Tribune*, Feb. 21, 1992.

Johnson, Niel A., "History of the Army weight standards," *Military Medicine*, August 1997.

Jyfmuseums.org, "Peter Francisco—Hercules of the American Revolution," Oct. 13, 2015.

Kaltenbach, Chris, "Isaiah 'Ike' Dixon, state delegate from Baltimore," *Baltimore Sun*, May 5, 2013.

Kanazawa, Satoshi, "Why are taller people more intelligent than shorter people?," *Psychology Today*, Jan. 25, 2009.

Karri, Siri, "Stefan Struve: A skyscraper with code violations," *Thebodylockmma.com*, March 3, 2018.

Katzowitz, Josh, "Height's handy on the court," *Cincinnati Post*, July 21, 2005.

Khan, Razib, "Why are taller people more intelligent?," *Discover Magazine*, April 11, 2013.

King, Jason, "Big challenges and spicy 'Lights,'" *yahoo.com*, Jan. 21, 2008.

Kingston, Peter, "Tall people are richer and live longer, research show," *The Guardian*, Oct. 27, 1997.

Kleiner, Dick, "Sigourney Weaver's acting lessons," *NEA*, August 5, 1979.

Knighton, Andrew, "Napoleon's Imperial Guard—elite soldiers who served the emperor," *warhistoryonline.com*, Dec. 28, 2016.

Kramer, Carol, "Short, dark and handsome," *New York Daily News*, June 1, 1975.

Krysler, Kae, "Six-foot-three (What will it be?)" *Los Angeles Times Magazine*, March 28, 1938.

Lai, Dr. Chao-Qiang, "How much of human height is genetic and how much is due to nutrition?," *Scientific American*, Dec. 11, 2006.

Lange, Steve, "America's tallest man, and a heavy weight," *Rochester Magazine*, Oct. 4, 2021.

Lardine, Bob, "TV's 'biggest' star,'" *New York Daily News*, August 1, 1965.

Levine, Brittany, "Tallest man: 'Don't be afraid of me because I'm tall,'" *Orange County (Calif.) Register*, August 26, 2010.
Lindqvist, Erik, "Potential leaders: Height helps but so does being smart," *Ideas For Leaders*, February 2015.
Lippe, Jeryl, "'My Giant Life' star Lindsay Kay Hayward is one badass lady who also happens to be 6'9"," *Lifeandstylemag.com*, Oct. 6, 2017.
Livingston, Bill, "Goliath syndrome traps Kareem," *Knight Ridder*, May 26, 1983.
Lock, Isaac, "How Game of Thrones star Gwendoline Christie proved she's not just a 'tall funny girl'," *Love Magazine*, April 3, 2020.
London Independent, "Theory of 'Napoleon complex' is debunked," March 29, 2007.
Long, Sonny, "Does height matter?" *Victoria (Texas) Advocate*, Jan. 11, 2010.
Looney, Douglas, "The tall and the short of it," *Sports Illustrated*, May 4, 1981.
Louv, Richard, "Short people live longer," *Chula Vista (Calif.) Star-News*, Oct. 12, 1978.
Loveday, Steven, "The best cars for tall people," *U.S. News & World Report*, Dec. 13, 2021.
Lowrance, Dee, "Glamazons," *Arizona Republic*, Nov. 14, 1943.
Lynwander, Linda, "Club rule: No short people allowed," *New York Times*, April 28, 1991.
Macias, Amanda and AFP, "Scientists measured 15,000 penises and determined the average size," *Businessinsider.com*, March 3, 2015.
MacMillan, Amanda, "5 ways being tall affects your health," *Time*, Sept. 8, 2017.
Mahany, Barbara, "Bigger than life," *Northwestern Magazine*, Winter 2011.
Maksian, George, "A big break as Sharkey's 'lumbox,'" *New York News*, July 3, 1977.
Mano, D. Keith, "Coming up short," *Esquire*, April 11, 1978.
Marinov, Dr. Dimitar, "Does HGH make adults taller?" *besthghdoctor.com*.
Maron, Dina Fine, "Are you a magnet for mosquitoes?," *Scientific American*, June 20, 2017.
Martin, Deanna, "Tallest woman in the world taught children to accept differences," *Associated Press*, August 14, 2008.
Martinez, Jose, "MTA will retool more express buses for leg room after complaints," *thecity.nyc*, March 2, 2022.
Mathews, Jay, "The height report: Short is beautiful," *Washington Post*, March 7, 1995.
Max, Arthur, "The Dutch are the world's tallest people," *Associated Press*, Sept. 16, 2006.
Mayerowitz, Scott, "The safety risk of shrinking airline seats questioned by DOT," Associated Press, April 15, 2015.
Mazziotta, Julie, "Strong's Gabrielle Reece had to work for her healthy body image," *People*, May 24, 2016.
McAuliffe, Kathleen, "A shot in the arm for short kids?," *U.S. News & World Report*, Dec. 1, 1986.
McCrary, Lacy, "Cheers for the big-heads," *Akron (Ohio) Beacon Journal*, Nov. 16, 1969.
McDonald, Samantha, "Long Tall Sally isn't going out of business anymore—This is why," *yahoo.com*, August 20, 2020.
McGee, Bill, "'Airline creep' may be on rise at Amtrak," *USA Today*, Nov. 12, 2018.
Meddings, Alexander, "Here is what happened when a king tried to create an army of giants—yes, giants," *Historycollection.com*, November 13, 2017.
Melnichuk, Anna, "Being 8 feet 4 is a giant problem," *Associated Press*, April 21, 2004.
Mewis, Joe, "Peter Crouch 'sick of fans joking about his height' so has come up with an ingenuous solution," The Mirror, Dec. 9, 2017.
Miller, Tracy, "Are tall people smarter than short people?," *New York Daily News*, March 4, 2014.
Mimaroglu, Alp, "How Tony Robbins overcame his 5 biggest setbacks," *Entrepreneur*, June 20, 2017.
Montreal Daily Star, "Tall children more intelligent than short ones," Feb. 2, 1932.
Montville, Leigh. "Giant: The Bullets' Georghe Muresan is developing a game to match his colossal size," *Sports Illustrated*, Oct. 2, 1995.

Moriello, John, "Olympic star Flo Hyman's tragic death saved lives," *sportscasting.com*, June 19, 2020.
Moskowitz, Dan, "The 10 richest people in the world," *Investopedia.com*, April 2, 2022.
Mundy, Liza, "Why Janet Reno fascinates, confounds and even terrifies America?," *Washington Post*, Jan. 25, 1998.
Murray, Gregg R., "It's weird, candidate height matters in elections," *Psychology Today*, Oct. 30, 2012.
Murse, Tom, "Why height and physical stature play a role in American politics," *thoughtco.com*, Oct. 24, 2019.
Naftulin, Julia, "Men are paying $76,000 for a limb-extending surgery that involves breaking leg bones and inserting nails and screws," *insider.com*, Jan. 9, 2020.
Nelson, Mariah Burton, "Tall," *Ms.*, April 1987.
Newsweek, "The height report: Men and heart attacks," Nov. 25, 1991.
Newsweek, "Leveling off," June 21, 1976.
Nightingale, Dave, "Who are these Eagles anyway?," *Chicago Tribune*, Dec. 23, 1979.
Norment, Lynn, "What kind of men have sex appeal?," *Ebony*, March 1979.
Oelbaum, Jed, "For men who will try anything to get taller, there's a world of grifts and gimmicks," *gizmodo.com*, May 2, 2019.
Oestreicher, Martha Pywen, "Does it really matter how tall you are?," *Cincinnati Post*, May 13, 1980.
Osborne, Hannah, "Netherlands: Tallest people on earth getting taller due to natural selection," *International Business Times*, April 8, 2015.
Ostrower, Jon, "American Airlines is cutting more legroom in economy class," *cnn.com*, May 3, 2017.
Palmer, Brian, "I wish I was a little bit shorter," *slate.com*, July 30, 2013.
Palmieri, Jean E., "Destination XL exceeds $500 million in sales in fiscal 2021," *Women's Wear Daily*, March 17, 2022.
Paoletti, Gabe, "Meet Ekaterina Lisina, the woman with the longest legs in the world," *allthatsinteresting.com*, Sept. 14, 2017.
Pappas, Helen, "Growing up tall," *talltique.com*, April 1, 2014.
Pathe, Simone, "Alan Simpson is no longer the tallest senator, and he's OK with that," *rollcall.com*, Feb. 9. 2017.
Patterson, Ada, "The original Gibson Girl tells why being 'divinely tall' so very often hampers love and living," *Seattle Times*, June 23, 1918.
Pereira, Michelle, "Does a person's body size impact their organ size?" *scienceabc.com*, Jan. 22, 2022.
Piastowski, Nick, "Who's the tallest player in PGA Tour history? He's playing this week," *golf.com*, April 29, 2021.
Pinsker, Joe, "The financial perks of being tall," *The Atlantic*, May 18, 2015.
Pluto, Terry, "Cavs' Daugherty fights to overcome Goliath Syndrome," *Knight Ridder*, Oct. 31, 1990.
Pompei, Dan, "There's a ceiling on NFL height," *The Sporting News*, 2005.
Popenoe, Dr. Paul, "Tall girl needn't ever feel like freak," *Paterson (N.J.) Morning Call*, Aug. 31, 1964.
Popova, Maria, "Maya Angelou on identity & the meaning of life," *dailygood.org*, July 22, 2014.
Porter, Tom, "Shorter people likely to have lower IQs, claim scientists," *International Business Times*, March 2, 2014.
Portman, Jamie, "Making it over a Hollywood hurdle," *Postmedia News*, August 11, 2011.
Prevention Magazine, "Zinc: A key element for growth," December 1987.
Prewitt, Alex, "The legend of Z: Zdeno Chara remains obsessed in his pursuit of outsized excellence," *Sports Illustrated*, April 3, 2018.
Price, S.I, "Standing tall," *sportsillustrated.cnn.com*, Sept. 16, 1998.
Prime, Mary, "Woman to woman," *United Press International*, April 19, 1959.
Putnam, Bob, "Towering advantage," *Tampa Bay Times*, June 1, 2007.

Quebecor Media, "MLB ump's gum-tossing ritual comes under fire," June 7, 2013.
Radbourne, Lucas, "Being 6'8" since I was 16 has not been easy," *The Women's Game*, April 20, 2020.
Rader, Dotson, "I created my own life," *Parade*, Sept. 15, 1996.
Rapaport, Dan, "British Open 2021: This Challenge Tour giant (6-foot-9!) makes Bryson look tiny—and his story is incredible," golfdigest*.com*, July 14, 2021.
Reinstein, Mara, "Sigourney Weaver reminisces on her career, Alien, Avatar and the new Ghostbusters," *Parade*, June 7, 2019.
Riley, Nan, "Contest was 'big payoff' for queen Bess Myerson," *Miami News*, March 7, 1958.
Rochester Post-Bulletin, "As a neighbor and friend, Igor's shoes will be hard to fill," August 31, 2021.
Russon, Mary-Ann, "Humans have grown 4 inches in 100 years since World War I," *International Business Times*, May 1, 2014.
Sager, Mike, "Julia Child: What I've learned," *Esquire*, August 15, 2014.
St. Louis Post-Dispatch, "Robert Wadlow loses his suit against doctor," March 11, 1939.
St. Louis Post-Dispatch, "Science examines your brain power," Feb. 16, 1931.
Samaras, Thomas T., "Height and longevity—A changing viewpoint," *World Journal on Pharmacy and Pharmaceutical Sciences*, September 2020.
Samaras, Thomas T., "Short is beautiful," *The Futurist*, August 1978.
Santos, Isaura, "Study suggests that height might be associated with increased risk of dementia," *Alzheimers News Today*, Nov. 4, 2014.
Schrad, Mark Lawrence, "Hatchet Nation," *Slate.com*, Sept. 7, 2021.
Schrager, Allison, "There are real advantages to being tall, and it can't just be explained by personality," *Quartz*, Oct. 3, 2019.
Schulze, Matthias, "Short, tall stature associated with risk for type 2 diabetes," *Healio.com*, Sept. 10, 2019.
Science News, "Panel clears testing of Lincoln's DNA," May 25, 1991.
Scott, Vernon, "Richard Kiel: Movies' biggest man," *United Press International*, Jan. 20, 1978.
Scott, Walter, "Personality Parade," *Parade*, Dec. 1, 2022.
Scott, Walter, "Personality Parade," *Parade*, Sept. 12, 1993.
Shearer, Lloyd, "Are the tall smarter?," *Parade*, April 26, 1987.
Shields, Aaron, "The top 10 tallest jockeys of all time," *casino.org*, May 12, 2021.
Shrock, Cliff, "At 75, Carol Mann's legacy is more than a 'tall tale,'" *Golf Digest*, Feb. 4, 2016.
Simon, Jeff, "Jude Law's portrayal of Thomas Wolfe in 'Genius' is juicily ridiculous," *Buffalo News*, June 16, 2016.
Skinner, Cornelia Otis, "I was known as the tall girl," *Reader's Digest*, April 1957.
Smith, Harrison, "Jim Fowler, intrepid host of 'Wild Kingdom' nature series, dies at 89," *Washington Post*, May 9, 2019.
Smith, Lydia, "Scientists use 'The X Files' to reveal why women are shorter than men," *International Business Times*, Feb. 7, 2014.
Smith, Mark, "Letter from The Netherlands: Tall people being given short shrift," *The Guardian*, Nov. 15, 2011.
Smith, Stewart, "U.S. military enlistment height and weights standards," *thebalancecareers.com*, June 6, 2019.
Smithers, Dominic, "World's tallest female pornstar prefers shorter men," *ladbible.com*, Jan. 19, 2022.
Sommers, Paul W., "Is presidential greatness related to height?," *tandfonline.com*, 2018.
Spector, Joseph, "NYC councilman distinguished as the world's tallest politician," *USA Today*, March 28, 2019.
Steinberg, Dan, "Record-setting twins bring raw skills to AU volleyball team," *Washington Post*, August 26, 2006.

Stevens Point (Wis.) Journal, "Cliff Thompson, Scandinavian giant, dies," Oct. 13, 1955.
Stewart, D.L., "Nothing slight about Mr. Sligh," *Dayton (Ohio) Journal Herald*, July 11, 1968.
Still, Thomas W., "2 stations drop 'Short People' record," *Wisconsin State Journal*, Dec. 17, 1977.
Takata, Daniel, "The tallest male Olympic swimming medalists," *swimswam.com*, Sept. 23, 2021.
Tanguay, Robert, "How height affects men and leadership opportunities—The high shelf," *Roberttanguay.medium.com*, Oct 27, 2017.
Tc.columbia.edu, "No shrinking violet," Jan. 23, 2007.
Terhune, Albert Payson, "Trouble of a big guy," *American Magazine*, June 1926.
Thomas, Eva, "These are the 7 best stores for tall women," *whowhatwear.com*, Dec. 25, 2021.
Tinubu, Abeni, "Ava Michelle's height got her cut from 'Dance Moms'; How tall was she?," *Cheatsheet.com*, March 12, 2022.
Tiven, Lucy, "This is what actually determines penis size," *attn.com*, Feb. 15, 2016.
Topel, Fred, "'Tall Girl 2' reflects Ava Michelle's height struggles," *United Press International*, Feb. 10, 2022.
Tran, Cindy, "Height of fashion! Woman who stands at 190cm launches her own clothing business for tall women after struggling for most of her life to find stylish outfits that fit," *London Daily Mail*, Jan. 21, 2018.
Travers, Mark, "Your height has a big impact on your salary," *Forbes*, April 16, 2020.
Triplett, Gene, "Kelly McGillis stood tall in 'Top Gun,'" *The Oklahoman*, Feb. 8, 2013.
Tsai, Stephen, "Colina's footy deal helps promote UH basketball," *Honolulu Advertiser*, Sept. 16, 2020.
Unger, Arthur, "John Kenneth Galbraith explores the 'age of uncertainty,'" *Christian Science Monitor*, June 5, 1977.
United Press International, "German asks tax break for short people," Oct. 1, 1974.
U.S. News & World Report, "Why youths are getting bigger," June 3, 1955.
Vandershaf, Sarah, "The prejudice of height," *Psychology Today*, March 1987.
Vosmer, Barbara, "Tallest man visits Hamburg," *The Sun and the Erie County Independent*, July 6, 1939.
Waldfogel, Joel, "Tall on intelligence," *Toronto National Post*, Sept. 14, 2006.
Warrillow, John, "Why shorter people make better entrepreneurs," *Inc.com*, Sept. 24, 2014.
Weaver, Nicole, "How tall is 'The Voice' coach Blake Shelton?" *Cheatsheet.com*, March 1, 2021.
Webmd.com, "How your height affects your health," Nov. 16, 2021.
Welkos, Robert W., "Is Crichton close to a blockbuster guarantee?," *Los Angeles Times*, Jan. 9, 2000.
Wendler, Ronda, "Link to 'tallness' disorder discovered by Milewicz," *uth.tmc.edu*, January 1996.
Wilbon, Michael, "Robinson too tall to go to sea, likely will go to NBA," *Washington Post*, Jan. 10, 1987.
Wilusz, Luke, "'World's Tallest Chef' needs brain surgery," *Homewood-Flossmoor (Ill.) Patch*, Oct. 26, 2012.
Wing, Grace, "Can you tell a Communist?," *Miami News*, March 13, 1953.
Wolf, Stephanie, "For world's tallest dancer, Fabrice Calmels, height is only a number," *Danceinforma.com*, Jan. 5, 2016.
Woods, Michael, "Short people face long wait for air bag decision," *Toledo Blade*, Dec. 3, 1997.
Wulf, Steve, "A truly tall tale," *Sports Illustrated*, March 6, 1989.
Zhang, Benjamin, "Here's how much legroom you get on America's airlines," *businessinsider.com*, Sept. 3, 2016.
Zhang, Shanshan, "Orthopedic surgeon discusses making a difference in local communities," *Daily Northwestern*, Feb. 26, 2016.

Studies and Reports

Bardsley, Martha Zeger, Karen Kowal, Carly Levy, Ania Gosek, Natalie Ayari, Nicole Tartaglia, Najiba Lahlou, Breanna Winder, Shannon Grimes and Judith L. Ross, "47, XYY Syndrome: Clinical Phenotype and Timing of Ascertainment," *National Institute of Health*, October 2013.

Beeri, Michal, Michael Davidson, Jeremy M. Silverman, Shlomo Noy, James Schmeidler and Uri Goldbourt, "Relationships between body height and dementia," *American Journal of Geriatric Psychiatry*, February 2005.

Case, Anne, and Christina Paxson, "Statue and Status: Height, Ability, and Labor Market Outcomes," *Journal of Political Economy*, June 2008.

Coeuret-Pellicer, Mireille, Alexis Descatha, Annette Leclerc and Marie Zins, "Are tall people at higher risk of low back pain surgery? A discussion on the results of a multipurpose cohort," *National Library of Medicine*, January 2010.

He, Qimei, Brian J. Morris, John S. Grove, Helen Petrovitch, Webster Ross, Kamal H. Masaki, Beatriz Rodriguez, Randi Chen, Timothy A. Donlon, D. Craig Willcox and Bradley J. Willcox, "Shorter men live longer: Association of height with longevity and FOXO3 genotype in American men of Japanese ancestry," *Public Library of Science*, May 7, 2014.

Humphreys, Lloyd G., Timothy C. Davey and Randolph Park, "Longitudinal Correlation Analysis of Standing Height and Intelligence," *Researchgate.net*, January 1986.

Judge, Timothy A., and Daniel M. Cable, "The effect of physical height on workplace success and income: preliminary test of a theoretical model," *National Library of Medicine*, June 2004.

Kanazawa, Satoshi, "Big and tall soldiers are more likely to survive battle: a possible explanation for the 'returning soldier effect' on the secondary sex ratio," *Human Reproduction*, November 2007.

Lemez, Srdjan, Nick Wattie and Joseph Baker, "Do 'big guys' really die younger? An examination of height and lifespan in former professional basketball players," *Public Library of Science*, Oct. 2, 2017.

Lindqvist, Erik, "Height and leadership," *The Review of Economics and Statistics*, Nov. 1, 2012.

Petot, Grace J., Ursula Vega, Fatoumata Traore, Thomas Fritsch, Sara M. Debanne, Robert P. Friedland and Alan J. Lerner, "Height and Alzheimer's disease: Findings from a case-control study," *National Library of Medicine*, June 2007.

Samaras, Thomas T., "How height is related to our health and longevity: A review," *National Library of Medicine*, 2012.

Samaras, Thomas T., "Shorter height is related to lower cardiovascular disease risk—a narrative review," *National Library of Medicine*, 2012.

Samaras, Thomas T., "Should we be concerned over increasing body height and weight?," *National Library of Medicine*, 2008.

Samaras, T.T., and H. Elrick, "Height, body size and longevity," *National Library of Medicine*, 1999.

Samaras, T.T., and L.H. Storms, "Impact of height and weight on life span," *National Library of Medicine*, 1992.

Thomsett, Michael J., "Referrals for tall stature in children: a 25-year personal experience," *National Library of Medicine*, January-February 2009.

U.S. Department of Health and Human Services, "Anthropometric Reference Data For Children and Adults: United States, 2011–14," August 2016.

Websites

Alloyapparel.com
Allthetallthings.com
Americantall.com
Awritersden.wordpress.com
Baseball-reference.com
Boxrec.com

Canbyandco.com
Classicfm.com
Encyclopediaofarkansas.net
Facebook.com—Tall Clubs International
Founders.archive.gov
Gooddeedseats.com
Greyhound.com
Growtallernow.com
Guinnessworldrecords.com
Highleytall.com
Highpointorlando.com
Humanbodysize.com
IMDb.com
Kingsize.com
LBJLibrary.net
Mediumtallclothing.com
Museums.kenosha.org
Navaslab.com
Nicoleforrester.com
Playboy.com
Quora.com
Rarediseases.org
Reddit.com
Riversandroutes.com
Roadsideamerica.com
Roman-empire.com
Ruedriis.com
Seatguru.com
Simplytall.com
Songfacts.com
Sportschew.com
Tall.org
Tallsome.com
Tallswag.com
Talltechteacher.com
Tallwomen.org
Thetallestman.com
Thetallsociety.com
Thetallstreetjournal.com
Theturekclinic.com
2tall.com
Wordpress.com
Worldstallestchef.com
Worldstallestchiropractor.com
Worldwar1centennial.org

Videos

"Are Taller People Really Better Off?," VICE News, *youtube.com*, 2020.
"Greg Davies Live at the Apollo," *youtube.com*, 2012.
"Greg Davies on the Troubles of Being Tall," *youtube.com*, 2009.
"In Search of Giants, Parts 1 and 2," TLC (producer Jonathan Dent), *youtube.com*, 1999.
"Tall Boy Reviews Tall Girl," Lewis Spears, youtube.com, 2021.
"10 Things I HATE About Being Tall," Lewis Spears, *youtube.com*, 2019.
"Top 10 Things About Being Freakishly Tall," Lewis Spears, *youtube.com*, 2019.
"We Are the World's Tallest Family!," Guinness World Records,, *youtube.com*, 2022.

Index